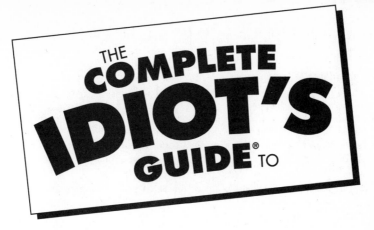

THE **COMPLETE IDIOT'S GUIDE** ® TO

Meditation

Second Edition

by Joan Budilovsky and Eve Adamson

ALPHA

A member of Penguin Group (USA) Inc.

For Bud

Copyright © 2003 by Amaranth

International Standard Book Number: 0-02-864441-7
Library of Congress Catalog Card Number: 2002115289

07   9 8

Interpretation of the printing code: The rightmost number of the first series of numbers is the year of the book's printing; the rightmost number of the second series of numbers is the number of the book's printing. For example, a printing code of 02-1 shows that the first printing occurred in 2002.

Printed in the United States of America

Publisher: *Marie Butler-Knight*
Product Manager: *Phil Kitchel*
Managing Editor: *Jennifer Chisholm*
Senior Acquisitions Editor: *Renee Wilmeth*
Book Producer: *Lee Ann Chearney/Amaranth*
Development/Senior Production/Copy Editor: *Christy Wagner*
Cartoonist: *Chris Eliopoulos*
Cover/Book Designer: *Trina Wurst*
Indexer: *Julie Bess*
Layout/Proofreading: *Angela Calvert, Megan Douglass, Nancy Wagner*
Illustrator: *Wendy Frost*
Photographer: *Saeid Lahouti*

Contents at a Glance

Contents

Foreword

I found this book to be full of information, humor, and wisdom. It is an excellent resource and guide—and definitely not for idiots! An idiot is silly, ignorant, and unschooled, according to my dictionary, and this gem would never be noticed or read by one. The material presented here is put together in a way that makes it simple to understand and useful to beginners or accomplished meditators. If you are interested in living and have the inspiration, the information is here in *The Complete Idiot's Guide to Meditation, Second Edition*.

Do not be frightened by the word *meditation*. It has been a part of the process of self-transformation for thousands of years. To quote from one Hindu Mahatma, "Action, wisdom, devotion, and meditation are the keys to self-transformation." They are all combined here for you to take advantage of.

Meditation can give you the benefits of not living constantly with a sense of time and urgency. You will be able to get in touch with your sense of the eternal. And as a benefit, if you never know what time it is, you avoid aging. That's a wonderful side effect among many that studies have shown are good for the state of health of meditators.

You will be more aware of your authentic nature, have more energy and freedom, and find yourself happier and more loving. These things happen not because you meditate upon these desires and thoughts, but as the side effects of what this guidebook will teach you about meditation. Joan and Eve present the information in a style I enjoyed reading. Their childlike sense of humor is woven through the vast and informative contents, making it easy and joyful, at times, to read.

Carl Jung said analysis is like having surgery without anesthesia. Well, my sense is that meditation and analysis can give you the same result, but meditation is a painless way to self-exploration and discovery. It also costs less and can be done on your schedule.

People often discuss concentration as the key factor that meditation focuses on and teaches. I feel that the word *concentration* can be misleading because meditation doesn't limit one but creates a greater awareness of life and creation. So read, meditate, and enhance your awareness of your life and become more mindful of the life around you.

Meditation for me is also a connection to our Creator's wisdom. Prayer and meditation are forms of the same thing, and that is why the names and labels we place on our actions can be confusing to some. When we meditate and use it as a ladder to reach a level of creativity, we are becoming co-creators and are becoming aware of the wisdom of the source of creation.

My final word of advice is to tell you to read this book, learn from it, and meditate. I guarantee that the revelation that ensues will lead to your transformation. Now don't be an idiot and ignore my advice.

Bernie Siegel, M.D.

Bernard S. Siegel, M.D., a New Haven surgeon, is the author of the best-selling *Love, Medicine and Miracles*, *Prescriptions for Living*, and other books.

Introduction

Where are you right now? "Sitting here reading this book," you might answer, rolling your eyes. Well, of course you are, but that's not what we mean.

We mean, where is your mind right now? As you skim the pages of this book, are you thinking about where you have to go next, or where you've just been? Are you mentally reviewing your endless "to-do" list, or planning how many errands you can squeeze in on the way home from the bookstore, or thinking about how much work you can get done before the end of the day? Or maybe you aren't really anywhere because stress has closed down the brain train, and you feel a little bit like you're stuck on a malfunctioning subway, getting nowhere fast.

And while we're at it, how does your body feel right now? Are you relaxed, fidgeting, bored, tired, tensed up? How does your body feel, right now, in this moment? Is your physical self sending your mental self a subtly, or not-so-subtly, opinionated message? If your body could talk to you just this minute, what would it be saying? "Slow down and listen to me," perhaps? "Pay attention!"

Stress is an insidious force many of us are subject to on a daily basis. Along with it come mindlessness, unhappiness, dissatisfaction, physical discomfort, and sometimes even illness. Are you "settling" for a life less than you once imagined?

You can do more than merely get through the day. You don't have to compromise your dreams. You can be the best possible you, and you can live the life you always wanted to live. How? By getting back in touch with who you are, what you want, and where you are going. By paying attention to your mind-body.

Meditation in its many manifestations is the key. It's easy to spend your life on hold, waiting to be done with this task or this job or this stage of your life. Meditation can teach you to live in the now, to know yourself—body, mind, and soul—better and to find the life you need. It can dissolve the stress and the insecurities that hold you back, clearing the path for a journey in which each step is the destination. Meditation teaches you to be alive *right now* because this is your life. With a little retraining and a few simple techniques, you can harness the awesome power of your own mind-body. Meditate and get back in touch with you. Learn to wake up. Learn to *live*. Don't miss another moment.

How to Use This Book

This book is divided into six parts, each designed to help you make meditation a part of your daily life—indeed, a part of *you*. As you read this book, you'll find that meditation is not just about your mind or just about your body; it's about your *mind-body*. And you'll discover (no doubt to your amazement!) that meditation not only relaxes and centers you, but also gives you a confidence and renewed energy that will enhance your productivity and help you make the most of each and every moment. Meditation *boosts* energy!

Part 1, "Feeling Great? Meditate!" tells you what meditation is and why you'll benefit from it. Meditation is not only a great stress reducer, but it's also mind-body fitness and healing power, too. People around the globe and throughout history in every major cultural tradition have benefited from a regular practice of meditation. You can, too! You'll start by performing a mind-body scan meditation to see what your mind and body are telling you today and then you'll get to see how some of the great meditative traditions use meditation.

Part 2, "The Physical and Beyond: Meditation Mind-Body-Spirit Union," tells you what's happening in your brain during meditation. Meditation boosts mind power! We'll show you what neurophysiologists are saying about *your* brain on meditation. You'll also learn about the many energy systems various cultures have used to describe the human life force, as well as the three bodies (physical, astral, and causal), and the five sheaths of existence that belong to *you*. We'll show you how sleep is related to meditation, and how to use the chakras—psychospiritual energy centers in the body—to channel and release the life force energy through meditation.

Part 3, "Get Ready to Meditate," introduces the concept of mindfulness and teaches you how to use mindfulness meditation techniques to combat stress. We'll tell you how to set up a meditation space at home, how to fit meditation into your schedule, even what to wear to make meditation more comfortable. We'll give you sound advice for choosing the best meditation class (if a group effort is more your style), and we'll offer tips and strategies for beginning your daily meditation practice, with a whole chapter on breathing techniques and exercises that will show you why breathing is essential to meditation.

Part 4, "Ommmmmm: How to Meditate," gives you seated meditation positions—from easy pose to lotus, as well as chair meditations. A chapter on walking meditations and other movement meditations takes you on sacred walks, through some basic yoga poses, and even into a Sufi-inspired whirling meditation. Learn, too, how to use yoga's ultimate relaxation pose, shavasana. Also, find out how to use mantras—words spoken, sung, or chanted during meditation—to enhance your meditation practice—seated, walking, or moving!

Part 5, "More Ways to Meditate," gives you even more alternatives. Mandalas, beautiful circular art forms, are wonderful subjects for meditation; find out how to create your own personal mandala. Use guided imagery and creative visualization techniques. Discover how sports, automatic writing, and automatic drawing can help you reach a meditative state of peak performance called "flow." Learn how to adapt the world's great traditions, from ancient Mexico to medieval Europe, Africa to the Middle East, the Far East to Native America to create your own personalized meditative exercises.

Part 6, "Meditation for Your Life," gives you invaluable information on how to use meditation to benefit your health and well-being, including how to address medical problems and conditions from back pain to heart disease and more. Find out what the best foods are to enhance meditation and how diet impacts your mind-body's health. Learn special meditative techniques for women (from fertility to pregnancy to breast-feeding to menopause), men, children, and seniors, too. Finally, consider the ways in which you are a part of a global community by exploring the world's most sacred places, meditating on your role as a sentient being on Mother Earth, and helping heal the earth and all its inhabitants through meditation.

Meditation Wisdom

Throughout this book, we'll be adding four types of extra information in boxes to help you attain enlightenment:

Mindful Minute

These boxes are full of fun anecdotes and trivia about meditation that will enhance your understanding of the many forms and types of meditation practiced by people across the globe and throughout history.

From A to Om

These boxes will give you definitions for meditation-related terms. Considering their meaning can be a great subject for your meditation sessions!

Bliss Byte

These special boxes will offer you tips and advice for living your meditation.

Relax

These cautionary boxes contain information about how to avoid potential problems and overcome misconceptions about meditating.

Acknowledgments

Thank you to our parents: Joan's, who through ways both quiet and genteel raised her to accept yet question everything, and by doing this, led her toward a meditative path; and Eve's, who feel much more comfortable with prayer than with meditation but who make a valiant effort to relate to the universalist point of view.

Thank you to Joan's brother, John, fondly known as "Bud," for his courageous and fun-loving spirit. Bud physically died while completing the first edition of this book, though his spirit continues on. We lovingly dedicate this book to him. Thank you to Josephine, Bud's and Lourdes' daughter, for her ever growing love and beauty. Thank you to Joan's twin sister Jane, for her courage and kind ways, and to Rebecca, and Richard for their evolving and continuing insights. Thank you to Kathie Huddleston (Yoyoga webmaster) who is constantly offering the helpful reminder, "Yoga, Joan, yoga." Thank you to Chuck, Rudi, Jack, and Katrina, for their helpful reminders to "Breathe, Joan, breathe." Thank you to Fr. Frank Stroud, of the Demello Spirituality Center, for increasing Joan's awareness. Thank you to Joseph DeRosier, executive editor of *Suburban LIFE* newspapers for his support and creative foresight. A deep gratitude to Joan's many students who are teachers and her many teachers who are students—who encourage a beginner's mind no matter how many years they have studied. Thank you to Joan's foster children who may only briefly hold the key to her home, but will forever hold the key to her heart.

Thanks to Eve's two kiddos, Angus and Emmett, whose boisterous boy-child spirits continue to make meditation a necessity four years after the first edition of this book, and special thanks to Jim, for inadvertent lessons in attachment and nonattachment and the complex play between the two.

Thank you to Lee Ann Chearney at Amaranth for her continual positive encouragement and editorial expertise, to Katie Lahiff, for her sensitive and thorough tech review, and to the incredible staff at Alpha Books. Thanks, as always, to our talented illustrator Wendy Frost and wonderful photographer Ann Censotti. Also thanks to photographer Saeid Lahouti. We continue to skip gratefully along the orange-and-blue-book road with you.

And thank you to everyone who has ever aggravated, irritated, ignored, or pushed us to the brink of reason. Because of you, we have become better meditators, breathers, truth-seekers, and practitioners of patience.

Through our meditations, we send out love, blessings, and joyful energy to all of you.

Special Thanks to the Technical Reviewer

The Complete Idiot's Guide to Meditation, Second Edition, was reviewed by an expert who not only checked the accuracy of what you'll learn in this book but also provided valuable insight to help ensure that this book tells you everything you need to know about meditation and its effects on the mind, body, and soul. Our special thanks are extended to Kathleen Lahiff, also known as Swami Nadananda, Mahaswami.

Swami Nadananda, Mahaswami has been a lifelong student of spiritual, mystical, and religious practices of all traditions. She is a disciple of Goswami Kriyananda, who carries the flame of the lineage of Babaji and Paramahamsa Yogananda. Goswami Kriyananda, founder of the Temple of Kriya in Chicago, ordained her into swamihood in 1994 and elevated her to Mahaswami in 1997. Swami Nadananda, Mahaswami remains affiliated with the Temple of Kriya where she leads music meditations, teaches in the Seminary and Hatha Yoga teacher training programs, and performs ordinations.

A professional musician and music instructor, Swami Nadananda, Mahaswami has been especially drawn to the musical aspects of the various spiritual traditions: mantra, chants, prayers set to music, the effects of sound on the spiritual-psycho-physical being. She has directed and performed on several recordings of mantra and spiritual songs and currently has in production a recording of prayers, chants, and mantra from around the world.

Trademarks

All terms mentioned in this book that are known to be or are suspected of being trademarks or service marks have been appropriately capitalized. Alpha Books and Penguin Group (USA) Inc. cannot attest to the accuracy of this information. Use of a term in this book should not be regarded as affecting the validity of any trademark or service mark.

Part 1

Feeling Great? Meditate!

Meditation is power. Sure, it may not look like much, just sitting there on the floor or in a chair, not doing anything and—seemingly—not getting anything done. But in reality, you are getting much done and much accomplished when you meditate. In this first part, we'll introduce you to the power of meditation: mind power, fitness power, stress-busting power, and the power that comes from learning to love and accept who you are right now.

Like physical exercise for the body, meditation is mental exercise for the mind and spirit. Creating a buffer zone between you and the stresses of life, meditation is an oasis of tranquility. For thousands of years, people all over the world—from yogis in ancient India to Zen monks in Japanese monasteries to nuns cloistered in medieval Europe—have enjoyed the power of meditation. You can enjoy the power of meditation, too, as it changes you, making you healthier, calmer, more immune to stress, and filled to the brim with joy.

Flexing Your Mind Muscle

In This Chapter

- What's so great about meditation?
- How do you stop thinking? (And why would you want to?)
- How meditation can be considered a workout
- The healing power of meditation
- Meditation and your self-image
- Living mindfully

Ommm … Ommm … Ommm … Oh, hello! Don't mind us, we were just finishing up our daily workout. "Workout?" you might ask, incredulously. "But you were just sitting there on the floor with your eyes closed!" You bet it was a workout, and not an easy one, either, but well worth the effort! Meditation puts you in tune with the universe. *Om* is a Sanskrit word meant to give voice to the sound of the universe's vibration. It is often used in meditation to help center and clear the mind so the mind-body can become more conscious. Om is thought to be the basis of all sounds—and of all manifest creation!

"But what kind of a complete idiot works out by sitting down and chanting to get in tune with the universe? That's not going to tone your muscles!" you might protest. Actually, we think we're pretty smart to take advantage of the amazing power of meditation—the ultimate workout for the mind-body, the "mind-muscle," and the whole self.

You see, fitness, health, self-concept, well-being, confidence, happiness, and contentment all originate in the mind-body, that "whole you" that's more than just your body or just your mind. But your whole self won't, and can't, feel truly balanced or effective if your workout only works out the body half of the mind-body. Enter meditation, the key to mental maintenance, mind-body integration, and, ultimately, personal joy.

The mind-body *is* the whole self. The term carries with it the connotation that mind and body are inextricably linked, and what affects, benefits, changes, or hurts one does the same for the other.

What Is Meditation?

But what is meditation, anyway? Meditation means many different things to many different people, so what meditation means for you, or has the potential to mean, depends largely on who you are, what you learn, who your teacher is, and on what tradition you base your practice. Many cultures consider meditation an integral part of life, but what form that meditation takes varies widely. In this book, we'll try to give you a broad base of meditation knowledge so you can find the method and technique that works for you. For example, many people consider prayer and meditation to be the same—regardless of what religion they practice and to whom or what they pray. As you read this book, you'll come to a definition of meditation that works best for your own interests and inclinations. Some of the schools of thought we'll talk about include the following:

- Breath meditation

- Mantra or sound meditation

- Mandala/visual meditation

- Movement meditation, including tai chi, QiGong, and Hatha Yoga

- Classic Zen Buddhist meditation

- Classic yoga meditation

- Meditation from other cultures, including Chinese, African, Muslim, Native American, and Jewish meditation

- New Age meditation

- Prayer

- Mindfulness meditation

- Medical meditation, as used in stress-reduction clinics and for other medical problems

- Guided imagery

- Creative visualization

- Creativity meditation, or art as meditation (writing, drawing, sculpting, etc.)

We're sure you'll find at least one—and probably several—types of meditation that will appeal to you and that you'll love to incorporate into your daily life.

To Think or Not To Think?

As different as meditation traditions and systems may be, most have a few things in common. One of those things is learning how *not* to think—how to slow down and relax the incessant mental process. All meditation techniques use a focusing of attention to one-pointedness so the thoughts are no longer scattered and undirected, but instead centered on one thing: a sound, a visual object, or a thought.

Now, slowing down your thoughts, almost "nonthinking," is a tricky notion. It doesn't mean nonconsciousness. In fact, concentrated thought (letting go of the thousand details that pass nonstop through our frenzied brains) is a key to superconsciousness. No one will deny that thinking is helpful, even necessary for survival, but our overdeveloped human brain really took that "thinking" ball and ran with it. These days, we've become so adept at thought that we can think up just about anything, from the theory of relativity to the recipe for chocolate génoise—sometimes at the same time!

The problem is that even when we want to relax for a while, we just keep thinking.

Especially when we get stressed, worried, nervous, or upset, our thoughts can seem completely

> **Bliss Byte**
>
> It isn't easy to stop thinking, but focusing on a sound or visual image can help keep superfluous thoughts away. Repeat a mantra (a word or series of words chosen for their vibrational centering qualities; see Chapter 16) or gaze at a candle flame or a mandala (a symmetrical, usually circular design meant to center the mind by drawing the eyes toward a visual center; see Chapter 17).

random and unproductive instead of focused and steady. Meditation uses particular tools and techniques to help boost concentration and focus thoughts.

If you've ever been plagued with insomnia, lying in bed wide awake at 4 A.M., wondering what you'll wear for the meeting tomorrow or if you remembered to pay the electric bill or whether your daughter's new boyfriend has orange or blue hair, you understand the value of being able to turn off the thought faucet.

Your thoughts clutter pure consciousness and the awareness of your own mind. Learning when thinking is helpful and knowing when to give it a rest builds your mind power, just like lifting weights and then resting for a day builds your muscles—the actual increase in muscle fiber happens during those days of rest, when your body repairs itself.

The same thing applies to meditation. Your brain works hard at thinking all day long. Give it a little break each day, and it will grow stronger, more effective, more efficient, and more aware.

> **Bliss Byte**
>
> Meditation can make you feel better when you aren't at your best, but if you are feeling depressed, angry, or negative, physical exercise is sometimes a better quick fix. Meditation is best practiced when you are feeling positive. Otherwise, start with a brisk walk, run, aerobics class, or yoga workout. Remember our saying: "Feeling down? Move around. Feeling great? Meditate!" However, a meditation practice begun and sustained through good times will come to your aid when times are rough.

Variations on meditation take the slowing down of your thoughts and the quieting of your mind further. Once you've mastered clearing your mind, you can then introduce concepts, thoughts, problems, or needs into your meditation. Answers to problems might suddenly become clear. Changes you would like to make might become manifest if you periodically visualize them as already having occurred. Thoughts, answers, insights, and meaning might offer themselves to you in an environment where, at last, they can be heard because they are no longer drowned out by your brain trying to remember that last item on the grocery list or that client's first name.

To Have It All, Let It All Go

Another benefit of meditation is the way it can adjust your thinking. When you live for a little while each day in a space filled with nothing but pure, uncluttered awareness, you begin to see things in perspective. The little things that were ruling your life—what those rich neighbors think of your not-so-upscale used car, or whether the boss noticed that run in your pantyhose during your big meeting—suddenly look little. The important things—whatever they are for you (love? happiness? *nirvana?*)—regain a significance they might have lost in the clutter of everyday living.

How does meditation accomplish this reprioritizing? By teaching your mind to let go of attachments. Nothing is really ours as we pass through this world. We find people to love but not to own. And as far as "stuff" is concerned, well … it's all just stuff, right? Meditation can help make this more clear. Of course, everyone's priorities are different, and meditation, too, is a highly personal and individualized experience. But in general, it will help you see that letting go of the concept of ownership, greed, and desire for the material aspects of life will actually result in ultimate happiness. You'll suddenly feel as if you "have" it all.

From A to Om

Nirvana is the Buddhist term for the state of absolute bliss attained upon recognition that the self is an illusion and non-existent.

Bliss Byte

Even though many schools of meditation suggest that the material world is an illusion, that doesn't mean you'll have to sell your house, give away the bulk of your wardrobe, and hand over your money to anyone. In fact, material comfort can actually reduce stress, making meditation even more effective. The trick is not to be too attached to anything that could be lost at any moment.

Meditation Is a Great Stressbuster

It isn't easy to get through the day without hearing something about stress in the modern world. Television shows, magazine articles, and books tell us we are a stressed-out society. They tell us what causes our stress, they tell us why stress is bad, and they give us all kinds of suggestions about what we should be doing to relieve our stress. In fact, the barrage of stress-talk out there is pretty darned stressful!

But it's true, we are a stressed-out society. Stress helps define the character of the modern world, and it can even be helpful when you need to get a job done fast or when you need to handle an emergency. In fact, stress is incredibly beneficial in times of crisis. The problem is, long-term stress is dangerous and damaging to your health.

The stress/illness link is a hard one to pinpoint because stress causes such a wide variety of symptoms and has different manifestations in different people, but stress is most directly associated with the *adrenal glands*. These glands secrete hormones in reaction to situations or conditions, whether physical or psychological, that cause tension or strain to the body and/or the mind.

> **From A to Om** _____
>
> The **adrenal glands,** located at the top of each kidney, produce special hormones such as **adrenaline** (also called epinephrine) and corticosteroids, including **cortisol** (also called hydrocortisone), in response to stress. These hormones prepare the body to react to a crisis, causing changes such as deepening breathing, speeding up heart rate, raising blood pressure, flooding muscles with oxygenated blood, and preparing for anti-inflammatory and healing action.

One of the best known of these hormones is *adrenaline*, which heightens our senses and reflexes, preparing us for action to handle the stress. Another is *cortisol*, a hormone that has been shown in many studies to be elevated in times of stress and decreased by relaxation activities like meditation and massage. Some of the physical symptoms of stress caused by the secretion of stress hormones are the following:

- Elevated blood pressure
- Muscle contraction
- The movement of blood toward the muscles and nervous system and away from the digestive organs
- Fluid retention in the kidneys
- Increased levels of chemicals responsible for coagulating blood
- The breakdown of certain proteins to form glucose, which acts as an anti-inflammatory

These conditions are useful in emergencies. For example, muscles prepare for defensive or offensive action. Fluid is retained in the kidneys, and the blood becomes ready to coagulate quickly in case of bleeding. The body readies itself to fight inflammation and infection. But bodies aren't meant to function under these conditions for long periods of time. Eventually, your body will break down.

Of course, stress is inevitable in our culture, and the best way to handle it is to avoid what stress you can, but also to prepare your mind and body to handle the unavoidable and necessary stress. A healthy diet will help and so will exercise. But in this particular world at this particular time, most of us don't have to face wild animals, hunt and dig for our own food, and deal with the physical drama of a nomadic existence. Our stresses are mainly mental. How many times a day do you clench your fists, your face, or your mind and think, "What am I going to do about *this?*"

That's why meditation is so crucial for handling stress, right now, today, in your life. Needless to say, any practice that puts your life in perspective, makes your priorities clear, and stems the incessant chatter in your brain will relieve stress. But meditation relieves stress in other ways, too. Meditation has measurable physical effects, and the relaxed state it induces in the body seems to affect the body's health directly.

Mindful Minute

Anyone who maintains an aquarium knows that caring for fish involves paying attention to what's called fish stress. Small details such as water, tank size, and temperature all contribute to the health of the fish. If even one thing is off too much, or everything is off a little, the fish are said to be "stressed" and will die. People should take care of themselves the same way. Incidentally, studies show that people who keep fish in aquariums have lowered stress levels, particularly when looking at their aquariums.

Many studies have demonstrated the beneficial effects of meditation (some studies included other stress-relief techniques and/or lifestyle changes such as yoga practice and massage), which include the following:

♦ Fewer doctor visits

♦ Lower cholesterol levels

♦ Lower blood pressure levels

♦ Less heart disease

♦ Reversal of arteriosclerosis (hardened arteries)

♦ Reduced *angina* (chest pain)

♦ Lower levels of stress hormones in the blood

♦ Altered brain wave patterns reflective of a calmer state

♦ Fewer accidents and less absenteeism at work

From A to Om

Angina is chest pain or discomfort due to some degree of obstruction in the coronary arteries and might be caused by any condition in which the heart has to work harder, such as physical or emotional stress, strain, or exertion.

- Less depression

- Increased confidence, awareness, and general health

And that's just the beginning! Believe it or not, meditation can actually increase your fitness level.

Meditation Promotes Mind-Body Fitness

We can hardly talk about mental fitness without bringing physical fitness into the conversation. Really, fitness applies to your whole self—physical and mental—so anything that helps one aspect will help the other.

For example, meditation helps you have a calmer, more tranquil mind that can better handle stress. It also reduces stress in your body, so your body is able to maintain a healthy state more effectively. A healthy body feels good, and feeling good makes you feel even better about yourself and your life. When you feel good, you want to maintain the feeling. When you feel good about yourself, you want to take care of yourself.

Exercise is one of the best ways to take care of yourself and can help increase and maintain that feeling of health and well-being. Exercise has also been shown to improve the mental state, from a general mood lift to lessening the symptoms of severe depression. A positive mental state is ideal for meditation, and meditation can make the most of a positive mental state. See how it's all connected?

Mind-body fitness is the ultimate fitness goal and the only true complete approach. Meditation, then, should be as integral to your fitness program as your daily run in the park, your weightlifting sessions, your *yoga* class, or your regular *massage*.

From A to Om

Hatha Yoga is a form of exercise that emphasizes physical postures or positions, called **asanas,** for increased health and awareness. **Hatha Yoga** is the most studied form of yoga in the United States. (See Chapter 3 for more on yoga.) **Massage** is a form of health-enhancing touch that relaxes while boosting the immune system. For more on yoga or massage, see *The Complete Idiot's Guide to Yoga Illustrated, Third Edition* (Alpha Books, 2003), and *The Complete Idiot's Guide to Massage* (Alpha Books, 1998) by the authors of this book.

Meditation Is Healing Power

But meditation is more than stress relief, fitness ally, and preventive medicine. Meditation can help when injury or illness is already in the picture. Studies have shown that meditation and similar relaxation techniques can reverse certain aspects of heart disease. Meditation is also used with sometimes-dramatic effectiveness in pain clinics, helping patients deal with pain more effectively, and in some cases, reduce or eliminate pain.

While some forms of meditation may be more effective than others for particular health problems, the overall benefits are undeniable. The mind is a powerful ally in healing the body, and meditation keeps the mind primed.

Mindful Minute

The words *meditation*, *medicine*, and *medication* all share the same Latin root, *medicus*, meaning "to cure," and originally, "to measure." Jon Kabat-Zinn, Ph.D., the founder and director of the Stress Reduction Clinic at the University of Massachusetts Medical Center, once explained (in an interview with Bill Moyers) that both medicine and meditation have to do with measure. Both work to restore "right inward measure, when everything is balanced and physiologically homeostatic."

Meditation also keeps the mind-body balanced. It's easy to become imbalanced when life gets busy—we neglect our health maintenance routines, become increasingly stressed, and suddenly lose perspective. Have you ever exploded over something clearly not worth a major episode, such as a misplaced pen or a coffee spill? Maybe a headache puts you out of commission for the rest of the day because it becomes the proverbial straw that broke the camel's back. "Forget it!" you might cry, throwing up your hands. "I'm going home to bed!" Stress throws us out of balance because it alters our body systems away from their normal operating conditions, or *homeostasis*.

To compensate, we often take medications, which may further imbalance our homeostasis (although in some cases, of course, medication can help restore an imbalance). For some conditions, including general stress and many chronic health problems, meditation is a better and more effective way to restore homeostasis than aspirin, antacids, or caffeine pills.

From A to Om

Homeostasis means "balance," whether of the internal systems of the body or entire ecosystems. It refers to a condition in which all systems are working together effectively to maintain a balanced, healthy, operational environment.

Meditation "reminds" your body of how it is supposed to be by clearing out the distractions and stressors lingering in your busy brain. Meditation can help the body to get back on track and reclaim its healing power. And when you finally start to heal, you'll start feeling really, really good.

Love Thy Mind, Love Thy Body, Love Thyself

One of meditation's most important benefits may be the effect it has on your self-concept. Sure, you like yourself. You're okay. But you probably have a long list of your own glaring imperfections, even if most or all of them are things no one would notice but you. Most people are fairly self-critical, and self-examination is good. You can learn from your mistakes if you study yourself and use what you observe to continually evolve. But self-flagellation isn't good. If you can't give yourself a break, why should anyone else?

Meditation takes away all that petty, nit-picky self-loathing. As Ruth Brillhart writes, "The best thing to do behind a friend's back is to pat it." Depending on your philosophy, meditation helps you love yourself by showing you who you really are inside, by teaching you that you are simply one individual expression of nature, or by empowering you to know and control your own mind-body (and not become so attached to your concept of it).

Here is an exercise in learning to be more detached from your fluctuating emotions. Instead of saying "I am depressed," say "There is depression in my life." Your life is much bigger than one depressing word, after all!

Mindful Minute

Personal happiness may be one of the most important factors in determining health. One study conducted by psychiatrist George Vaillant followed 200 Harvard graduates for 30 years, correlating annual health surveys with psychological tests. Those who were "extremely satisfied with their lives" experienced one-tenth the rate of serious illness and death compared to those in the "thoroughly dissatisfied" group, even when alcohol and tobacco use, obesity, and ancestral longevity were factored out. "Be happy" may indeed be an important prescription for health.

Moving toward any of these ideas will help you learn to love your mind, love your body, and meet your mind-body (perhaps for the first time). Most important, meditation can teach you to love yourself—your whole self.

So even if you've always thought meditation sounded a little weird, you are probably willing to admit the benefits sound compelling. What have you got to lose? Twenty minutes? Chances are it will eventually become the best 20 minutes of your day.

Living Your Meditation

Maybe you've decided you can probably squeeze 20 minutes of meditation into your schedule. But guess what? Those 20 minutes are only a start. No, we're not going to suggest you quit your job and spend your entire day sitting in the lotus position chanting "Om." What we will suggest is that even when you aren't sitting in meditation, you can be *living* your meditation.

Living your meditation doesn't mean being zoned out or out of touch with reality. On the contrary, it means going through your days sharply focused, centered, and living in the now. Your daily meditation sessions will help to clear, calm, and focus your mind. The result? The rest of your life will become clearer, calmer, and more focused.

Practicing mindfulness throughout your day is the key to prolonging and making the most of the effects of your meditation sessions. Mindfulness is like proactive meditation, and it can dramatically improve your life.

Many people go through their lives on automatic pilot. They are so absorbed in routines and obligations that they never really notice where they are, how they feel, or what they are doing. Especially during times of stress, it is difficult to notice what's going on. How well do you actually remember your wedding, the birth of your child, or that big speech you gave? You may have been too distracted with the details, in too much pain, or too nervous to actually *experience* your experience.

Mindfulness changes all that. Mindfulness means going through life awake and aware. To live mindfully simply means to pay attention—to your body, to your mind, to your surroundings, to the people in your life, to the tasks you undertake, to the beauty of the world, to every detail of existence—not to control it, shape it, force it, or be worried by it. Simply to experience it. To live mindfully means to *live*, with a capital "L."

Bliss Byte

For the incredibly stressed, it may seem impossible to stop your mind from racing. One way to start is with a daily 10-minute mindfulness walk. The only rule: Notice. How do your body, your breathing, and the air feel? Notice the sights, sounds, and smells around you. If your mind strays, guide it back to your immediate surroundings. Live completely in the "now" for 10 minutes. Eventually, you'll be able to extend mindfulness to other areas of your life.

Of course, living mindfully isn't easy. If it were, we'd all be doing it! It's a lot easier to drive your car on cruise control than to operate a stick shift. It's easier to take the elevator than to climb the stairs. And it's easier to cruise through life without noticing. But not noticing has a physical, mental, emotional, and spiritual price.

The Price of Mindless Living

Maybe you used to live mindlessly and then something went wrong. Pain, accidents, illness, and personal tragedy have a way of jolting us awake. Whether we are suddenly plagued with a migraine headache, the flu, arthritis, or frequent accidents, we might feel betrayed. "Hey, what's this? Why has my body betrayed me?"

We certainly won't pretend to explain the source or cause of pain, illness, accidents, and personal tragedy. If they occur, one way to deal with them is to consider them a wake-up call to your mind-body: "Hello in there? You are important. You deserve the very best in life. You are the very best of life! Wake up! Learn. Listen, listen, listen." As Swedish statesman and former secretary general of the United Nations (1953–1961) Dag Hammarskjöld once wrote, "The more faithfully you listen to the voice within you, the better you will hear what is sounding outside."

> **CAUTION**
> **Relax**
>
> Some doctors estimate that 50 to 80 percent of physical illness is stress related. The result of long-term stress varies between individuals, but might include chronic indigestion, headaches, back pain, lowered immunity, fatigue, ulcers, atherosclerosis, and even the onset of rheumatoid arthritis.

Don't clobber yourself or retreat to a state of self-pity. Use this valuable wake-up call to ask yourself "What is this experience saying to me? How can I best take care of my mind-body? What do I need to change?"

> **Mindful Minute**
>
> According to the *Yoga Sutras*, a collection of aphorisms by an Indian sage written thousands of years before the birth of Christ, concentration precedes meditation on the path to enlightenment (see Chapter 3 for more information on yoga). Most meditation techniques are actually concentration techniques. Concentration is the process of continually bringing the attention back to focus on whatever the object of focus is—and meditation occurs when one becomes absorbed in this process.

Even small symptoms might be sending you a message. Are you tired all the time? Do you get colds a lot? Do you often feel so stressed you want to scream, even though you aren't sure why? Or maybe you know why you are stressed, but you don't have the time or the energy to do anything about it. After all, you can't tell off your demanding boss, you aren't about to trade in your three kids, you don't have time or money for marriage counseling, you'll always be out of shape because you hate to exercise, and it's all you can do to get through the end of the day with a clean kitchen and an almost-balanced checkbook. Right?

We're happy to tell you you're wrong. We're not going to advocate that you go and tell off your boss, but we do know that there are ways to deal with stress that avoid turning negative experiences into chronic, unhealthy physical and emotional stress for you. Life is movement, and things will *always* be happening. Meditation can help balance the waves of life's ups and downs, but it will not necessarily stop the waves from coming. Meditation helps us navigate good times and challenging times as we learn to survive and thrive amidst them.

So for all of us who regularly meditate and still do indeed have to live in an imperfect world where negative stress might arise from time to time, the process of meditation teaches us how to live so the stresses we encounter will be easier to handle. You don't have to miss out on your life. You can regain control and attain serenity of mind. You can wake up, and you can certainly enjoy yourself again. All it takes is a little mental maintenance to unlock a happier, healthier, calmer, better you. And meditation is the key.

The Least You Need to Know

- Meditation is fitness for the whole self, toning the mind and relaxing the body.

- Thinking can clutter awareness. Meditation teaches the temporary suspension of thought by showing us how to become absorbed in one-pointed focus.

- Long-term stress is dangerous to your health, and medical studies prove meditation relieves emotional and physical stress.

- Meditation can help in healing and in managing pain, from the chronic pain of arthritis to minor discomforts.

- Meditation can improve your self-image.

- Living mindfully all day long can help you make the most of your life.

Meditation Power: Your Personal Mind-Body Exploration

In This Chapter

- ◆ Isn't meditation just for yogis and Buddhists?
- ◆ Enlightenment is for you!
- ◆ A self-awareness quiz
- ◆ Your personal mind-body scan

Meditation may sound pretty good here on paper, but you might be wondering how it really applies to you and your very individual life, problems, stresses, body, and mind. You're not a Zen master, you're not a yoga master, and you're not looking for a guru, so is meditation really practical, workable, and realistic for you? Will it actually help you with any of your problems? And what will your friends say? C'mon, we know you're wondering if meditation is *cool*.

Let's dive right in and take a look at exactly what meditation can mean for you—not the generic "reader" you but the real you—the one sitting here reading this book. The one who needs some help dealing with all that stress, who might be curious about meditation's spiritual benefits, or who is looking for something to improve health and enhance feelings of happiness and well-being.

Yes, you.

Who Meditates?

You? In your jeans and T-shirt and Nikes? You in your bathrobe or your business suit or your sundress and combat boots? (Hey, whatever makes you comfortable!)

Anyone can meditate and meditate well. It doesn't matter what your religion is or where you live. It doesn't matter what your job or health or wardrobe or family is like. It doesn't even matter if you have an interest in full *enlightenment, samadhi, nirvana*, or becoming a *swami*—or whether you've aspired to reach that first glimpse of enlightenment, *satori*. All that matters is a personal commitment to improve your mind, and by extension, your life.

From A to Om

Enlightenment, also known as **samadhi** in Hinduism and **nirvana** in Buddhism, is that perfect state of supreme bliss in which the self is completely absorbed into a sense of oneness with the universe. **Satori** is a brief glimpse of enlightenment, but it is not yet full, sustained enlightenment. **Swami** is a title of respect for a spiritual person who has attained a certain level of understanding and wisdom, and also implies a "mastery" of self.

Bringing the Mind Home

So how do you use meditation to actually improve your life? That depends on one thing: you. What do you need from meditation? How do you need your life to improve?

We don't like to tell you that you "should" do anything, so we'll just say that *if* you choose to meditate and *if* you stick with it, you'll notice real and unmistakable changes in your life. How long has it been since you looked inward rather than outward? "Who are you?" is a much different question than "What do you do?" You see, there's a difference between meditation and thinking.

Thinking, for most of us, usually involves the external. *Where is my appointment this afternoon? What will I wear to the seminar? I can't forget to buy milk on the way home!*

That new office manager is pretty cute. I wonder why my car engine is making that strange noise. And what on earth has the puppy done to the kitchen? Sound familiar?

For many people, the noise in the head is a continuous clamor of worries, wonders, wishes, wheres, whys, whats, whens, whos, and hows. The world is a busy and distracting place, and there it is, all around us. It isn't easy to ignore.

Bliss Byte

Rather than trying to tune out that annoying clamor in your head during your meditation practice, try simply observing it. Look at the thoughts that come and go. Don't judge them. Don't let them engage you. Just look at them as if they belong to someone else or as if they are balloons floating by on a breezy day. There goes a red one. There goes a green one. Here comes a blue one, and there it goes.

But what about your inner life? How much time do you spend dwelling inside yourself? It's quiet in there. It's peaceful. The outside world doesn't hold much influence in there, and guess who's inside there, waiting? Someone you might like to know a little better. Someone wonderful and miraculous and joyful at the core. You.

Nothing about meditation should ever worry you. However long it takes to meditate well is good, because everyone is different—whether that means seeing improvement in a week, a month, or in a blue moon! Meditating is like going home after a long and hectic vacation—going home to yourself. It's a lovely and almost luxurious foray into self-awareness. You open the door to that old, familiar house. You kick off your shoes, sink into your favorite chair, close your eyes, and know you're home at last. Ommmm. Sweet Om.

Are You Self-Aware? A Meditation Self-Awareness Quiz

How self-aware are you? Of course, most of you are probably just beginning your meditation journey, and "self"-awareness may only be a hazy notion or seem a low priority in getting through your day. But having an idea about the state of your own personal self-awareness can help you undertake a meditation practice with more purpose and forethought. Take our quiz to find out how self-aware you really are, then read on to see how meditation can help you at your particular stage in the journey of the self.

Be honest! Circle the letter of the answer that best describes you.

1. When you look in the mirror for the first time each day, what is the first thing you usually notice?

   A. My hair—ugh! Good thing no one sees me but the people who really love me a lot!

   B. All those little pores on my nose. There must be some product to get rid of those!

   C. My expression. It's a good indicator of my mood!

   D. I don't habitually look in a mirror.

2. If you had to spend an entire day alone, how would you feel about the prospect?

   A. That would be horrible! What would I do? Whom would I talk to?

   B. It would be okay if I could have a TV and lots of books and magazines or maybe get some work done.

   C. It might be interesting to spend some time thinking over different areas of my life.

   D. I'd love it! Relaxing, rejuvenating, and what else can I say—I'm great company!

3. Close your eyes and envision your ideal self. How is that self different from the you of the present moment?

   A. Better body, nicer face, and really great hair.

   B. More successful and richer.

   C. Happier and more content.

   D. We're one and the same!

4. How would you describe your health habits?

   A. I love certain foods that I probably should give up but can't. I really hate to exercise. I often feel guilty about my lack of commitment to good health habits.

   B. Pretty good. I eat right and exercise because I want to look really great.

   C. I try to take care of my body, and I find I'm usually in a better mood if I eat well and exercise.

   D. I keep both my mind and body in shape because it helps me to maximize my physical and mental potential.

5. How would you describe your health itself?

   A. I don't have any major health problems. I don't pay much attention to my health unless I come down with something.

   B. Very good. I take all precautions to avoid getting sick. Sick people can't be productive! If I do get sick, I try to ignore it.

   C. I keep up with the latest health research and try to practice preventive health care for my overall health. If I get sick, I consider all the different healing alternatives to find the most effective course of action for me.

   D. I might be healthy or I might have certain health problems, but I continually monitor my health—physical, mental, and emotional—and listen to what my mind-body needs. I strongly believe the mind can be a significant influence in healing the body.

6. What do you think is the difference between the "real" you and the you everyone sees each day?

   A. The real me is much less accomplished, talented, and in control than the "me" everyone knows or thinks they know. Sometimes I feel like a fraud.

   B. The real me is actually an idealized version of myself—smarter, better looking, more in control, more successful. I'm working hard to become the real me through whatever methods seem workable. This me you see is just temporary.

   C. The real me is the outside me, but with more vulnerabilities and fewer material concerns.

   D. The real me is a more complex and subtle version of the me everyone else sees. In essence, though, we are the same. I feel like all sides of myself are consistent.

7. What is the most significant way you've changed in the past five years?

   A. I'm a few pounds heavier with a few more gray hairs, but basically the same. My life just keeps chugging along.

   B. I'm aging fast! I hate to see my younger self fading away, but I'm fighting it at every turn.

   C. I'm older and wiser. I've learned a lot about life in the past five years.

   D. I've become much more aware of who I am and where my life is heading. I have a clearer idea of what success really means, and I'm happier and more at peace.

8. What do you hope will be the most significant difference about yourself in five years from now?

   A. I hope I don't gain too much more weight! I also hope I'll be making more money, though I doubt I will be.

   B. I'll be following my five-year plan, and with luck I can accomplish all my goals. I'll have a perfect life even if it gives me a nervous breakdown!

   C. I hope I'm in a more secure position, both externally and internally. I imagine I'll be more mature and, I hope, less stressed about daily life.

   D. I hope I will be living in, or much nearer to, a state of enlightenment.

9. How would you characterize your spiritual life?

   A. I go to my place of worship on the significant holidays most years like a person is supposed to. Otherwise, I don't think about spiritual matters very often.

   B. Who has time for a spiritual life? There are things to do, people to see, places to go, contacts to sign, and money to make!

   C. I might or might not go to a place of worship, but I think about spiritual matters fairly frequently, and I am interested in exploring the possibilities of a more spiritual existence.

   D. My daily life equals my spiritual life. Almost everything I do, I do with a sense of spirituality.

10. Who are you?

   A. You mean you want to see some ID?

   B. Here's my resumé.

   C. I am a human being striving to live a good and happy life.

   D. I am the creation of and the manifestation of universal consciousness.

How did you do? Tally your answers and see how many of each letter you chose. Then, read the section under the letter you chose most often. If you chose several letters about equally often, read all those sections. Lots of us have a little of several types within us.

 ◆ **If you chose mostly A answers:** You aren't too fond of self-analysis. You constantly doubt yourself, criticize yourself, and may assume that others share your opinions about yourself. Choosing mostly A answers says nothing about your *actual* self-worth, only your self-perception. Whether you have been overly criticized in the past or simply feel unable to get control over your personal habits, you aren't particularly content. You function in society just fine most of the time, but your life could be so much richer and fuller if you could learn to nurture yourself and treat yourself with a little more lovingkindness.

Meditation is an ideal pursuit for you because it teaches you how to look inward without a judgmental eye. Simply look. Who are you? No, don't start judging. Just look. *Who are you?* Gradually, you'll begin to recognize within yourself the miraculous and uniquely individual human being you are. The problem is, because you aren't too comfortable with self-awareness, you may find basic sitting meditation too difficult at first. Instead, try mindfulness. Mindfulness is the practice of simply being aware and noticing as much as you can during everyday life. Take a mindful walk in the fresh air or begin a regular yoga practice. Practice mindfulness when you vacuum or go to the gym or drink a cup of coffee. Meditating during daily life can be a great way to ease into a more structured and formal meditation practice. The more comfortable you become with self-awareness, the more comfortable you will be with meditation.

- **If you chose mostly B answers:** You're a go-getter. The problem is, you may tend to chase things that won't actually bring you happiness. You might be, deep down, just a little bit discontent with who you are, but you have a very detailed plan about how to change all that. Rather than accepting yourself, you've constructed an idea of another, new-and-improved you. Whether you think more money, better looks, less fat, more muscle, a more prestigious job, or finally apprehending your soul mate is the answer to reinventing yourself, chances are your plans are generally based on external concerns. If you ask people who have these things, however, most of them will tell you that the money, the looks, the job, the soul mate are great but are not the answer to true happiness. For that, you have to look inside.

Because you are so action-oriented, meditation will probably be challenging for you. How can you just sit still like that when you've got so much to do? Meditation can benefit you by peeling away the layers of your material existence, then the layers of your desires, to see what's underneath. Afraid you'll find nothing at all? Don't worry. There's something there—a precious jewel, untouched by any mistakes you've made or wrongs that have been done to you. That jewel is worth more than all the material wealth in the world. You just have to search for it with the same energy and vigor with which you attempt to reshape your external self.

Trouble is, you find just sitting there pretty darned difficult. You like to move, so movement meditation can be a perfect segue for you into the world of meditation practice. Try yoga, dancing, or sports as meditation. Move with focused and complete mindfulness in the movement. Or take a daily meditation walk, meditating as you walk quietly by yourself without talking for about 15 minutes, simply focusing inward and noticing without judging the impressions that come and go. This can be a great centering exercise for someone like you and can help you gently and gradually accept yourself for the you you are right now.

♦ **If you chose mostly C answers:** Many people who pick up this book are probably a lot like you. You live your life, doing what you need to do, but more and more often, you find yourself wondering about what else is out there for you. You aren't so much looking for material wealth as you're looking for spiritual wealth. You know there's a lot more to you than you're putting into play. You suspect you could be happier, calmer, and more alive. On the other hand, you don't want to be thought of as weird or "out there." You've got responsibilities and the necessary worldly concerns.

Meditation doesn't have to be "out there" at all. In fact, meditation is the opposite of "out there." It's all about "in here." Meditation is quiet self-reflection. It hushes up that frantic inner voice that, granted, propels you through your day, helping you to get everything done. But you can do without it for 20 minutes or so each day. You don't need that frantic inner voice all the time, and meditating will help you shut off that voice. It will help you open up the calmer self that is beneath all the frenzy. Then you can listen for what the universe, or God, or your deeper inner self has been trying to tell you all along. Wonderful secrets lie in there, waiting to whisper themselves to you. All you have to do is listen, and you are ready to listen. You've been watching the signs, and you're just not sure if you should trust them or follow them. Follow this one. We'll show you how. Start with classic sitting meditation, just five minutes a day at first, and gradually work up to more time. Twice a day is ideal. You'll love what this kind of practice will do for your life.

♦ **If you chose mostly D answers:** What are you doing reading this book? You can't fool us! You're already meditating, aren't you! Or you've been praying or practicing some form of self-actualized living. You're in touch with who you are, you cherish and love yourself, and you feel like you know your place in the universal scheme of things. You're also in touch with a higher power, whether you believe that power is outside you, within you, or both. You are making the most of your life, and you are truly alive. But go ahead and read this book, anyway. Why not? There's always more to learn on the soul's magnificent journey.

The regular practice of meditation helps you to gain a quiet centering from which to contemplate what is important to you and why it's important. As you grow more confident in your "self"-awareness, you'll be better able to deal with the complex decisions and issues that arise every day in our fast-paced, ever-changing world. Instead of reacting, you'll be acting proactively, with a centered, deeply considered belief system that's come from within your self.

Mindful Minute

The word *meditation* comes from the Indian Sanskrit word *medha*, which can be translated as "doing the wisdom." It can also be traced to the Latin root *meditari*, which means "to muse or ponder."

Do Your Own Mind-Body Scan

Maybe these quizzes have helped you define where you are in your thinking about meditation as well as your thinking about who you are and how comfortable you are with self-reflection, inner silence, and the very nature of right and wrong.

Now let's focus on your mind-body a little closer, to help you identify your areas of tension, your ability to relax, and your propensity to practice mindfulness. We can do this with a mind-body scan.

A mind-body scan is, simply, a slow and incredibly relaxing exercise in self-awareness. Mindfulness, or the ability to *pay attention* during your everyday life, isn't easy, and most people can't simply start paying attention out of the blue. It's harder than you might think! You're driving down the highway and you start to notice how the steering wheel feels, how the road looks as you drive over it, the sky's particular shade of blue, but did you turn off the coffee pot? Oh, you can't forget to buy stamps. And look— you're almost out of gas. Do you have enough cash, or will you have to stop at the ATM? Of course, the bank is still open, so you could go through the drive-thru, and it's right next to the grocery store, and you do need milk, which reminds you, you are a little bit hungry … Whoops! So much for paying attention to the present moment!

The mind-body scan is simply a technique for noticing how you feel, in minute detail. It also involves some relaxation and breathing techniques, which help you to keep your focus. There are various ways to do a mind-body scan, of course, but a few rules apply. The mind-body scan is performed lying down, making it more comfortable than sitting meditation, especially for those who aren't in the greatest physical shape. Of course, it is also an excellent technique for those who *are* in good shape.

You can do the mind-body scan on your own, in whatever way you like, but keep in mind (body) it should go slowly and take at least 10 minutes, and preferably 30 minutes or more, if you have the time. But just in case you like a little more structure,

Bliss Byte

Here is a simple exercise to help you relax and help the world relax, too. As you inhale, imagine you are inhaling pure love. As you exhale, imagine you are exhaling pure peace. Inhale love, exhale peace. Stay with this for a while, taking long, even breaths. A fun and even more productive variation: Try doing this with a group of friends. This simple technique may help prevent road rage, world rage—and your own rage.

we'll guide you through a mind-body scan. You can read the following text and remember it approximately; you can have someone read it to you (slowly!) as you try it; or you can tape yourself reading it so you can play the tape whenever you like. Feel free to edit the following in ways that make it more appealing to you or more appropriate for your particular situation, whatever that may be.

First, lie on your back on a comfortable but firm surface, such as on a blanket or mat on the floor. A bed will work, too, although it doesn't offer quite the ideal degree of support. Relax, take a deep breath, and exhale slowly. If your mind starts to wander during the body scan, gently bring it back to the place you were when it wandered away, and continue. Ready? Let's go!

Close your eyes and begin to breathe deeply. Listen to your breath. Feel it going in and out. Relax. Imagine that with every inhalation, you are bringing positive energy into your body and with every exhalation, you are releasing discomfort and stress. Feel where your body is touching the floor and where it doesn't touch the floor. Imagine your body is very, very heavy and is sinking into the floor. Relax. Breathe.

Now bring your attention to the toes of your left foot. Can you feel them without moving them? If not, move them a little. There they are! Move up to your left ankle. Feel it. Rotate it a little if you can't feel it. Then, slowly, very slowly, scan your left leg, moving up over the shin and calf and around the knee. Is your knee bent or locked? Bring your attention up to your thigh and into your hipbone. How do your hips feel? Are they centered on the floor? Are the joints comfortable or achy? How are your buttocks centered? Is your lower back swayed or pressing into the floor? Keep breathing, positive in, discomfort out. You may soon be feeling all the negative energy dissipating, releasing, disappearing.

Now bring your attention to the toes of your right foot. Can you feel them without moving them? If not, move them a little. Move up to your right ankle. Rotate it a little if you can't feel it. Next feel your shin, your calf muscle, and your knee. Is your knee slightly bent or locked? Now feel your thigh muscle and then your hipbone. Are your hips more relaxed than when you noticed them a moment ago? Keep breathing. Positive in, negative released.

Now bring your attention to your lower back, around to your abdomen, into your upper chest and upper back. How do your shoulder blades feel against the floor? Are your shoulders drawn up or relaxed? How is your spine touching the floor? Move to the base of your neck. Can you feel it? Move up your neck to the base of your skull. How does it feel at the place where your neck and skull attach? Now move your attention around your skull. Feel your ears, your scalp, and the roots of your hair. Move over your forehead, your eyes, your nose, your cheeks, and your mouth. Is your jaw tight or relaxed? Can you feel your teeth? What is your tongue doing? Feel your lips, your chin, your throat, the inside of your mouth. Now move back up your face to your forehead, then back to the crown of your head. Keep breathing, positive in, negative out. Imagine the last of the negative energy disappearing with one long exhale. Take your time with the exhale and slowly let your breath relax out.

Last, lie quietly for a few more minutes. Try to spread your attention over your entire body. How do you feel? Where is your mind? Are you focused in the physical sensations of lying on the floor, or is your mind already somewhere else? Whatever your mind is doing, it needn't engage you. Simply notice, as you have done for the rest of your body. Now, slowly open your eyes. What do you see? Sit up. How do you feel? Stand up. Here you are! Hello! Now you can proceed with your day.

If you fell asleep and missed it all, that's okay. The point isn't to fall asleep, of course, but you probably needed the cat nap.

> **Bliss Byte**
>
> Every once in a while, do a shoulder scan while driving your car. Notice where your shoulders are riding. Nice and low, or up around your ears? Take a deep breath and as you exhale, lower your shoulders and feel the stretch in your neck, freeing circulation to your head. You'll also be able to turn your head more easily to see your side mirrors, revealing all the crazed shoulders-up drivers around you.

Now how did that feel? Pretty good? Or did you find it almost impossible to lie still? The mind-body scan is simply a preparatory tool, but it can give you a lot of information about where you need to relax and where your meditative challenges will be. But believe us, all this preparation is well worth it. Life can be tough, and getting through it well is tougher still. Our bodies—and our souls—ache. Meditation nurtures the soul back to health, opens an inner dialog, and rocks you into serenity. To find that quiet space deep inside yourself where only truth exists is to find a little island of bliss in a sometimes difficult and unpredictable world. We're here to help you find that island.

The Least You Need to Know

- Anyone can meditate, no matter his or her beliefs.
- Cultivating self-awareness in everyday life can help you to define and focus your meditation practice.
- A mind-body scan helps relax the physical body and center the consciousness.

In the Spirit of Yoga Meditation

In This Chapter

◆ Meditation in the yoga tradition

◆ A look at yoga ethics

◆ More about yoga's Eightfold Path

◆ Making your own path, yoga-style

Meditation is an ancient tradition in many different cultures, from Western Europe to the Far East, a part of aboriginal cultures on every continent, and a part of philosophically complex societies throughout history.

Thousands of years ago in India, meditation was an important part of physical and spiritual development, and in the twenty-first century, we still practice many of the same meditative techniques developed so long ago and so far away.

Surely you've heard of yoga. What health club, holistic center, or for that matter, community recreation center doesn't offer a class in this mind-and-body-bending form of exercise? But did you know that yoga is based on far more than flexibility? Yoga is a practice designed to get the body under control, but it can also be a lifestyle, an ethical construct, and a technique for meditation.

Yoga Union

Westerners often think of *yoga* as a form of stretching or a relaxation exercise that includes pretzel-like poses and impossible contortions, but as more and more "regular" people try yoga, they are recognizing that it can be an excellent way to fuse mental and physical fitness.

> **Bliss Byte**
>
> **Yoga,** from the Sanskrit root *yuj*, meaning "to yoke" or "join together," is a 5,000-year-old method of mind-body health leading into "self-realization." It has many paths, or methods, including …
>
> ◆ **Karma Yoga,** which emphasizes action and service to others.
> ◆ **Bhakti Yoga,** which emphasizes devotion to God.
> ◆ **Jnana Yoga,** which emphasizes intellectual striving.
> ◆ **Hatha Yoga,** which emphasizes balance through physical and mental exercises.
> ◆ **Raja Yoga,** which emphasizes a lifestyle for controlling both mind and body—including exercises, breathing relaxation techniques, and meditation.

Yet yoga in America still tends to emphasize the physical. More precisely, most yoga in America focuses on the physical body. This is an important part of yoga. The exercises were designed to "harness" or "yoke" the wayward body so it wouldn't interfere with meditation. Yoga exercises, therefore, were a method designed to facilitate meditation, and once the body was under control, yoga was about meditating in order to attain a higher awareness.

> **From A to Om**
>
> **Patanjali** was probably born between 200 B.C.E. and 400 C.E. He is the author of the *Yoga Sutras*, a collection of succinct aphorisms in Sanskrit that have largely defined the modern practice of yoga. (*Sutra* means "thread." *Yoga Sutra* means "uniting threads.")

Yoga was first described in writing by an Indian sage, *Patanjali*, in his book of aphorisms called the *Yoga Sutras*. Patanjali lived thousands of years ago, and his *Yoga Sutras* described an eightfold path for mind-body mastery. This path includes rules for living, exercises, breathing techniques, concentration techniques, meditation, and philosophy as a process toward enlightenment.

Yoga "Ethics"

Patanjali's rules for living included a list of do's and don'ts to help the yoga practitioner live a life more in tune with natural laws and behavior that was most conducive to enlightenment. Called *yamas* (the don'ts) and *niyamas* (the do's), Patanjali gave yoga practitioners a framework for facilitating a meditation practice.

Many yoga practitioners and people who practice the yoga form of meditation also try to live by these guidelines as part of their personal ethical framework. Maybe you will want to try it, too. But first, let's look at the concept of *dharma*—no, not the television character, but the ancient Indian word that can be loosely translated as "spiritual ethics."

Whatever you think about ethics, one way to understand how the concept fits into meditation is to look at ethics from the perspective of another culture's philosophy. *Yogis* believe in something called the dharma.

Dharma, according to yogic thought, is variously translated, but you could call it the universal tendency or movement toward the good. The world is moved by it, the universe is fueled by it, and people can choose to live in it (sort of like stepping into a river) or ignore it. If you choose to live in it, certain ways of thinking and certain actions will clearly be right or good and others won't. But when you're standing there on the riverbank, how do you know if you want to step in or not? What, according to dharma, is right thinking, right action, and right speech? And if you do decide to live in the dharma, how do you know you'll know what's right?

For Westerners, the whole concept of dharma can sound a little nebulous. We like our clear-cut, no-nonsense Ten Commandments, U.S. Constitution, that sign posted at the swimming pool that says "Children under 12 must be accompanied by adults"—no doubt about the meaning of that one!

From A to Om

Yamas are five yoga abstinences or forms of discipline that purify the body and mind. **Niyamas** are five yoga observances or personal disciplines.

Dharma is that which upholds and sustains. It is sometimes translated into English as "duty" or "ethics," but it exists apart from humans, as opposed to a moral code that humans devised.

From A to Om

A **yogi** is someone who practices yoga. If you practice yoga, then yes indeed, you can call yourself a yogi. Traditionally, the term *yogini* was used to describe female practitioners of yoga, but in these enlightened times, all of us who practice yoga can call ourselves "yogis."

From A to Om

Karma is a concept that has to do with universal balancing. Every action, even every thought, will be balanced by an opposite action or thought somewhere in the universe. In other words, everything you do has a ripple effect and will come back to you. Karma is not so much a "get what you deserve" philosophy as it is a universal balancing act.

But philosophically speaking, if you live in the dharma, you'll accumulate good *karma*. You'll know what's right and what's wrong. The problem is that living in the dharma isn't easy. It takes effort (sort of like walking in a river). And those who have lived there in the past have given future dharma-seekers some rules to help make it a little easier.

You don't need to be a yogi to make the concept of dharma your own. You can take the guidelines—those rules for living we told you about that were first expressed in writing by Patanjali—and apply them to your own life without embracing any other religion or even philosophy. Read on to see what wise yogis recommend to make life easier, happier, and more fulfilling.

Rules for Living

Some of us love rules because they help us rein in our behavior. Some of us hate them because we're free spirits and think we can make rules for ourselves. But there's no denying that rules can make life easier, as long as the rules make sense and promote a better existence. If one follows the order of the universe, life is harmonious. If not, chaos reigns—in the bigger picture, as well as the personal.

Rules do something else besides nudge us in the dharma. They help us learn discipline. Now, maybe you're one of those few incredibly self-disciplined people who have no trouble eating right, exercising, and doing unto others as you would have them do unto you. But most of us have trouble maintaining discipline. But to get the most out of your meditation sessions, a little discipline helps a lot.

From A to Om

The **Eightfold Path** is a system of standards and guidelines for living (and eventually, evolving into enlightenment) recorded by the Indian sage Patanjali in his text, the *Yoga Sutras*.

When Patanjali developed his guidelines for living, he did so within the framework of his *Eightfold Path*. This was recorded as a recipe for enlightenment or self-realization. Following the Eightfold Path, you can walk the path in the speed and direction that resonates for *you*, is one way to work toward greater happiness in your life and in your soul. We like to think you can work on all the guidelines a little at a time. Just as separate threads together form a strong rope, one thread entwined with another, building upon each other, so Patanjali's eight threads weave their paths together to form the backbone of self-actualization.

In other words, you don't need to work through the Eightfold Path in order. Knowing and experiencing all the ingredients can offer you an interesting perspective and a fabulous recipe for your journey toward a better you. So why not take a look?

Yoga's Yamas

The first two steps of the Eightfold Path consist of two sublists. The first list is the yamas, or things that are helpful to avoid. The second list is niyamas, or things that are helpful to do. (The rest of the Eightfold Path will be described in Chapter 4.) You can view these lists as guidelines for living with a capital "L."

◆ **Do no harm.** The first yama (*ahimsa*) is about nonviolence. Avoiding violence in your actions, your words, and even your thoughts is the core of this yama. This includes controlling your temper and not physically harming people. It can also include avoiding negative thoughts about others and even about yourself. Not eating meat is a component of this yama for many yogis because to eat meat is to be complicit in the killing of an animal.

◆ **Tell no lies.** The second yama (*satya*) is about truthfulness. It involves more than avoiding the big lies, like not reporting that extra little $300,000 you made last year. It also means being truthful about the little things like not telling a secret you promised not to tell or telling your boss you can't come into work because you've got the flu when really you just feel like sleeping in and watching talk shows all day. Truthfulness builds character and personal integrity.

◆ **No more stealing.** The third yama (*asteya*) is about refusing to steal, whether that means a candy bar, a million dollars in jewelry, or somebody else's great idea. Give credit where credit is due, and, quite simply, don't take what's not yours.

◆ **Cool it, Casanova.** The fourth yama (*brahmacharya*) is about controlling sexual desire. Lust manifests most clearly in our

> **From A to Om**
>
> The five yamas (abstinences or forms of discipline that purify the body and mind) are: **ahimsa,** which means "nonviolence"; **satya,** which means "truthfulness"; **asteya,** which means "not stealing"; **brahmacharya,** which means "control of sexual desire or nonlust"; and **aparigraha,** which means "nongreed."

physical bodies, but lust exists on many levels. Desire for a house, a car, a body, or a mind, especially when it becomes uncontrolled, can be misleading. The unrelenting quest for the ever-changing outer desires/lusts/achievements can easily lead us further from a deeper realization of inner peace and true beauty.

- **Don't be greedy.** The fifth yama (*aparigraha*) is about simplicity and learning to live only on what you need. Greed can manifest itself in other ways, too: monopolizing conversations, jealousy of the possessions of others, and dissatisfaction with your place in the world.

Yoga's Niyamas

The next list consists of things to do, rather than things not to do. Focus your attention on the following five qualities, and you'll be feeling great about yourself in no time!

- **Purity.** The first niyama (*saucha*) is actualized through the practice of the five yamas. The abstentions cleanse negative physical and mental states of being and guide you to a state of purity. Dressing; bathing; establishing a clean environment; and eating fresh, natural, healthy foods are all good ways to practice this niyama. Meditation and mindfulness are valuable tools for leading you toward purity in thought and action.

- **Contentment.** The second niyama (*santosha*) is about finding happiness with what you have and with who you are. That doesn't mean you can't improve yourself or attempt to get a better job, become healthier, or find more productive relationships. It does mean reevaluating the obstacles in your path as opportunities and taking full responsibility for your own life.

- **Discipline.** The third niyama (*tapas*) is about discipline. Consistent daily actions to improve your health (such as eating good food and exercising, even brushing your teeth!) are disciplined. So is practicing yoga or going to aerobics class, controlling your temper, getting your daily chores completed, or finishing that assignment at work before the deadline. Discipline isn't easy, but the more you cultivate it, the easier all the other yamas and niyamas, including meditation, will become.

- **Self-study.** The fourth niyama (*svadhyaya*) is about paying attention to who you are, what you do, how you feel and think, and what you believe. Think about it. Why do you always snap at your mother when she mentions your weight? Why do you always get a little blue when it rains? Do you act according to your beliefs? If not, are they really your beliefs, or do you just accept things others have told you? Remember all that business about self-examination from Chapter 2? This niyama is about maintaining a study of the sacred texts of different religions to inspire and teach you. In other words, never stop learning and seeking! This is a productive component of a meditation practice and can give you a focus and a direction for your meditation.

◆ **Devotion.** The fifth niyama (*ishvara-pranidhana*) is about focusing on the divine, whatever that means to you. It doesn't mean you have to be religious, although that can certainly be one meaning. It can also mean simply letting go of your ego and the focus on yourself and looking outward—or inward—to the highest ideal. It can also be as simple as your devotion to nature, the soul, or the process of life itself.

> **From A to Om**
>
> The five niyamas (yoga observances or personal disciplines) are: **saucha,** which means "purity" or "inner and outer cleanliness"; **santosha,** which means "contentment"; **tapas,** which means "self-discipline"; **svadhyaya,** which means "self-study"; and **ishvara-pranidhana,** which means "devotion."

Simple, right? Well, no. Adhering to all the yamas and niyamas all the time isn't easy, but it will help you control your behavior, your thinking, and your actions. And when you've got those under control, learning to meditate is a breeze!

Meditation Is Only One Stop from Nirvana!

But what about the rest of Patanjali's Eightfold Path? We're still quilting the path. And what a beautiful quilt we're going to have!

You can also think of the Eightfold Path as limbs spreading from a growing tree. Each limb is practiced with the others and becomes part of an organic whole. As you progress along the Eightfold Path, your understanding of each element of the path deepens and flourishes. You are the tree of life!

Work Out: Control Your Body (*Asana*)

The third step (after step one, the yamas, and step two, the niyamas) of the Eightfold Path involves body control, or the practice of *asana*. Asana are the postures of yoga that most people think of when they think of yoga. Learning the postures of yoga helps control the body so it remains both steady and comfortable. It isn't easy to meditate well (let alone attain enlightenment!) if you aren't comfortable in your body. If you are flexible, strong, and feeling great, your body is less likely to "get in the way" during the special time you've reserved for meditation.

Learning the yoga poses can be a lifelong endeavor. The poses range from simple to extremely challenging, and although people of any fitness level can practice yoga, the advanced poses take remarkable strength, flexibility, balance, and control. Opportunities to learn yoga abound. Look for classes in your area, rent one of the many yoga videos available, or read a good yoga book (such as *The Complete Idiot's Guide to Yoga Illustrated, Third Edition!*).

> **From A to Om**
>
> In the yoga sutras, **asana** refers to the pose of sitting and keeping the body still for meditation. All the other poses are part of other systems—Hatha Yoga mainly.

Yoga poses can actually be a sort of meditation on their own, too. If your mind becomes calm and centered, focused on nothing but the feel of the poses, then you're practicing a variety of moving meditation. A few sitting yoga poses are particularly helpful to the practice of meditation, as well. See Part 4 for more on seated, walking, and movement meditation.

Sitting with the spine upright and aligned helps increase alertness.

(Photo by Saeid Lahouti)

Come Up for Air: Breath Control (*Pranayama*)

Breathing exercises are excellent meditation preparation. Breathing does more than give you something to focus on. According to yoga philosophy, it infuses your body with the very force of life. In Sanskrit, breath control is known as *pranayama*. *Prana* is a word for the life force that flows in, through, and around all living things and even animates the earth itself and the entire universe. It is pure energy, and the only way to fill yourself with it is to breathe—and breathe well.

Pranayama practice works to change the mind; the breath also relates directly to the mind. Our state of mind is linked to the quality of the prana within. As the mind changes, so does the quality of the prana; we influence the flow of prana by influencing the breath. These are all linked together: mind, prana, and breath. Pranayama exercises are designed to aid you in increasing the prana within you and to allow the prana to flow properly and freely. Working with the breath and mind allow you to achieve this. Just breathing in doesn't mean you're inhaling prana. You need to use both the breath and your mind to effect a positive change in your body. Then and only then does prana enter to nourish and restore you. See Chapter 12 for more on breathing meditation.

From A to Om

Prana is a form of energy in the universe that animates all physical matter, including the human body, and is taken into the body through the breath. **Pranayama** is the practice of breath control designed to help you master your breath and help infuse your body with prana.

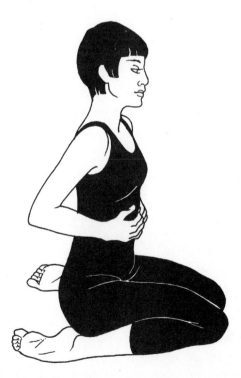

When you breathe deeply, you can feel your breath moving in and out. Concentrate and you can feel your lower back expand on inhalation, too.

Empty to Be Full: Detachment (*Pratyahara*)

The next branch of the Eightfold Path is detachment, or *pratyahara*. This step involves losing your senses. No, we don't mean going crazy! We mean learning to shut off your sense impressions—just temporarily, of course.

We have senses for good reason. They help us survive, enjoy life, and stay both safe and healthy. Who wouldn't want to be able to smell a rose garden, see a brilliant sunset over the ocean, taste a freshly picked apple, or feel a cool spring breeze? But sometimes the senses can be distracting and might even become a source of obsessive behavior. It's one thing to savor every bite of a piece of delicious chocolate cake. It's another to be so obsessed with chocolate (or red wine or bacon or taco chips or whatever) that you binge on it every day.

> **From A to Om**
>
> **Pratyahara** is the practice of withdrawing the senses and focusing inward.

Senses can also distract us from meditation, and learning to suppress them is an important skill for successful meditation. Just imagine trying to meditate in a room filled with the aroma of baking bread or the sound of blaring music or in an uncomfortably cold place. It isn't easy to focus inward, and it's even harder if your external environment continually engages your senses.

Meditation is, therefore, best practiced in an environment with as few sensual distractions as possible. But even in a quiet room alone, the senses can still be a distraction: an itch here, a sore knee there, a pang of hunger, the sound of a dog barking down the street. So practicing withdrawing the senses can help with meditation. It isn't easy, but when the external world fades away, you'll be able to look inside yourself without distraction.

> **Bliss Byte**
>
> If withdrawing all your senses at once seems overwhelming, try one sense at a time! Try this exercise with a trusted partner. One person is blindfolded, and the other person leads the blindfolded person around a garden, pausing at various places so the blindfolded person can explore minus sight and via the other senses. Have you ever felt the incredible silkiness of a white pine? Smelled the pungent aroma of a marigold? Touched a willow leaf to your cheek?

Don't Panic, Focus: Concentration (*Dharana*)

Most of us know what it's like to be unable to concentrate, especially when we're tired, hungry, or under a lot of stress. The next step, thread, or limb, in the Eightfold

Path involves the practice of concentration. Concentration isn't just something that randomly happens. It takes practice, and the more you learn how to cultivate it, the better at it you will become. Some meditation techniques involve concentrating on one thing: an object such as a candle flame or a *mandala* (see Chapter 17), a sound such as the sound of your breath or a mantra (see Chapter 16), or even a single thought. The point is to concentrate until you have dissolved all the boundaries between yourself and the object of your concentration, and can see that you and the object—and indeed, all of existence—are one. The ability to concentrate will not only make your meditation more productive, but will help you in many other aspects of your life as well.

From A to Om

Dharana is the technique of orienting the mind toward a single point in order to cultivate concentration. A **mandala** is a beautiful, usually circular geometric design that draws the eye to its center and can be used as a point of focus in meditation.

Feeling Great? Meditate: Meditation (*Dhyana*)

The penultimate leg of the Eightfold Path is the actual practice of meditation. With the ability to control your body and your breath, as well as your senses and concentration, meditation will be easier and more productive. At this stage of the game, meditation moves beyond the ability to concentrate. You are on the verge of realizing your ultimate union with the world around you. You are part of nature, part of the natural scheme, part of God or Great Spirit or love or divinity. When everything else falls away—physical and mental distractions, attachment to material things, even sensual awareness, pure being—samadhi—is what's left.

We've shown you some techniques for practicing concentration and focus and sensory detachment. These can all be meditative techniques, but the point of all of them is to get you to this point: the ability to sit in meditation.

How hard can it be? We'll get into the nuts and bolts of meditating later in this book, but to practice the classic form of yoga meditation, sit in a cross-legged position (you don't have to use the lotus position, with each foot placed on top of the upper thigh, but if you are flexible enough, go for it). You might want to sit on a pillow to make it more comfortable.

From A to Om

Dhyana is the Sanskrit word for meditation, and refers to the process of quieting the mind to free it from preconceptions, illusions, and attachments.

Place your hands, palms up, thumb and pointer finger or thumb and middle finger lightly touching to form a circle (we'll talk more in Chapter 13 about why it helps to use this hand position for meditation).

Now breathe. Relax and breathe. Look inward. Let your thoughts flow but don't hold on to them. Notice them and let them go. Keep looking inward. Inward. Inward. What's deep down in there?

Nirvana.

Last Stop, Nirvana: Pure Consciousness

And then you're there! Pure consciousness, *samadhi*, nirvana, absolute bliss—to Patanjali and to many thinkers and meditators before and after him, this is the final and ultimate experience of meditation. Can you really experience it? Of course you can—many have before you.

That doesn't mean you will experience it anytime soon, however. That's fine. But who knows … the more you contemplate, the more you study yourself, the more you learn to control your behavior, your body, your breath, your senses, and your concentration, the more you might find yourself being drawn to the idea of pure consciousness.

From A to Om

Samadhi is the Sanskrit term for the state in meditation when perfect bliss and union with all things is achieved. Consciousness alone shines forth!

How will you know when you've reached enlightenment? We offer this ancient Chinese proverb: "Before I was enlightened, I saw a tree. After I was enlightened, I saw a tree." Enlightenment is in the inner eye of the beholder.

The Least You Need to Know

♦ The Indian tradition of yoga offers a system for living and a structure for meditation that many people find helpful still today.

♦ Patanjali delineated eight steps that lead to enlightenment: certain abstentions, observances, exercises, breath control, control of the senses, concentration, meditation, and, finally, pure consciousness.

♦ You—yes, you—can experience nirvana, but it's the journey, not the destination that is the focus. It is an experience of a lifetime with a capital "L."

Chapter 4

In the Spirit of Zen Meditation

In This Chapter

- ◆ The Zen way to a better life
- ◆ The yin and yang of it all
- ◆ What the Buddha had to say about meditation
- ◆ Making Zen your own

Meditation is an integral part of many cultures and religions, but Buddhism is a religion that, while it exists in many forms and is practiced in many different countries, uses meditation as its lynchpin. More specifically, Zen Buddhism, the Japanese form of Buddhism, is based on meditation. In fact, *Zen* means "meditation."

Zen has been highly popularized in the United States. In fact, Zen has become a buzzword linked to everything from New Age-y products like miniature Zen gardens with sand and tiny rakes, "Zen" desktop fountains, and books upon books about having a Zen attitude or practicing Zen meditation. In our twenty-first-century culture, "Zen" doesn't necessarily denote meditation. Instead, it denotes a sort of attitude of living in the moment, simplifying life, and appreciating what you have. To paraphrase a popular song, the point is not to have what you want. The point is to want what you have, what you are, right at this moment. That's Zen.

But even if we don't always think of Zen as meaning meditation, that Zen attitude, even in its Westernized manifestation, remains conducive to the spirit of meditation. Zen is about mindfulness, paying attention, and letting go, instead of striving for, grasping for, or attaching to the things of the world. It is about appreciating what you have and who you are right now and being content with that. Easier said than done? Sure, but one technique makes it all possible.

You guessed it: meditation!

The Zen of Meditation

Thousands of years ago, a guy named Siddhartha Gautama (a.k.a. Buddha) practiced meditation until he got it right. In other words, through meditation, he finally apprehended the true nature of reality, attained enlightenment, and became the Buddha, or "enlightened one."

Buddhism subsequently evolved all over Asia as a reaction to this one man's experience, and Zen Buddhism—the Japanese form of meditative Buddhism—continues to evolve in America today. Thousands practice *zazen*, the Zen form of meditation, and you can, too. Zazen has been around for such a long time because it really helps center the spirit, adjust the attitude, and bring peace to the soul. It might be just the form of meditation that works for you.

Beyond zazen itself (which we'll explain in a minute), Zen can become a helpful way of living, seeing, and understanding the world. While yoga philosophy gives us a set of ethics, so does Zen: Be in the moment; love who you are right now; let yourself feel and let yourself let go of feeling. Zen preaches detachment from the grasping and grabbing and materialism and consumerism that so easily infect us in a country where many of us have access to almost everything we need. It also teaches us to let go of the people we like to think we own and control in favor of a philosophy that teaches us we can only control our own thoughts, our own actions, and our own reactions. This approach to life can help us let go of worries, stress, and anxiety over things we can't control.

Many books have been written about Zen (check out *The Complete Idiot's Guide to Zen Living* by Gary McClain and Eve Adamson, Alpha Books, 2001), but the attitude really is simple: Just be. Let the rest go. Zen meditation is similarly simple. The term *zazen* can be translated to mean "just sitting," and that's about all there is to it. Boring? It can be. Challenging? Oh yes. But does it work? You bet your desktop Zen fountain it does!

But before we talk about the how-to's of Zen meditation, let's look at some concepts that go hand in hand with the Eastern way of looking at life. Understanding these basic concepts will make Zen meditation easier to understand and practice.

Balancing Opposites: The Yin and the Yang of It

If you've ever felt imbalanced by stress, physical exertion, mental effort, anger, or even love, you know what we mean when we say that environments, whole ecosystems, individual bodies, or any kind of system in the universe has a certain homeostasis or equilibrium that helps it work at optimum capacity. When that equilibrium gets off balance, the system doesn't work as well.

In China, the concept of *yin* and *yang* originally evolved from the idea that the body is a microcosm of the world and the world is a microcosm of the universe. Therefore, qualities we ascribe to nature can also be ascribed to the body. One of the basic laws of this system is that everything in nature is balanced. Two interdependent forces exist, called *yin* and *yang*. These terms can be used to describe anything. For example, female, moon, and the body are yin; male, sun, and the mind are yang. Also, in everything that is primarily yin, there is also a bit of yang, and vice versa. The yin-yang symbol demonstrates this balance.

> **Mindful Minute**
>
> Yin and **yang** are two interconnected forces inherent in all things, and they describe the balance inherent in nature (it's we humans who get out of balance!). According to astrology, the sun signs Taurus, Cancer, Virgo, Scorpio, Capricorn, and Pisces have yin energy, while Aries, Gemini, Leo, Libra, Sagittarius, and Aquarius have yang energy.

The yin-yang symbol illustrates the harmonious balance of opposites.

Because our mind-bodies and our environment are continuously balancing themselves, we may sometimes feel out of control. After that killer test on which you wowed your teacher with your superior intellectual insights, your mind is suddenly incapable of remembering where you put your keys. When you get *too* yin, yang steps in. When you get *too* yang, yin steps in.

Of course, sometimes nature needs a little help, and Chinese medicine, for example, is based around balancing yin and yang (among other components of the mind-body) through herbal preparations and other medicines. To help you get your yin and yang in balance—you guessed it!—meditation can make you feel more balanced, no matter what terms you want to assign to the imbalance. It'll put some yang in your yin, some yin in your yang, and a spring in your step to boot!

Yin and yang can also be thought of in terms of the Western medical concept of homeostasis—the body's constant rebalancing process to achieve harmony in relation to its environment.

In other words, when we get out of balance, we don't feel well, we don't perform at our best, and we have trouble thinking clearly. Meditation is like pushing the reset button. It helps clear our minds and relax our bodies so we can regain our equilibrium.

> **Bliss Byte**
>
> Some historical figures who were spiritual leaders also sometimes tended toward extremes, whether of abstinence or self-mortification (self-punishing) or other manifestations of religious fervor and even materialistic excess. More often, however, spiritual leaders in all religions advocate moderation. The Buddha advised his disciples to avoid both extreme sensual indulgence and extreme self-mortification. According to the Buddha, sensual indulgence is low, coarse, vulgar, ignoble, and unprofitable, retarding spiritual progress, while self-mortification is painful, ignoble, unprofitable, and weakening to the intellect. Instead, the Buddha advocated the Middle Way, which he said opens the eyes and bestows understanding, which leads to peace of mind, to the higher wisdom, and to full enlightenment.

The Buddha's Journey

Thousands of years ago in India, the concept of yin and yang was known, as were the concepts of dharma and karma (which we defined in Chapter 3). There were even those who had attained enlightenment, but Siddhartha Gautama, the man we call Buddha, didn't himself attain enlightenment until what scholars guess was probably about 500 B.C.E. After rejecting a royal life of privilege, Siddhartha Gautama abandoned his family for life as a wandering religious ascetic. After six years of striving and self-deprivation, he gave up the ascetic life (to the disappointment of many of his followers) and adopted moderation as a philosophy. One day he decided to sit under a fig tree and meditate until he attained enlightenment. After some time, the story goes, he finally understood truth. He was enlightened.

Because self-deprivation, intense study, and other extremes didn't work to make the Buddha enlightened but meditation *did* work, many forms of Buddhism emphasize meditation as the way to truth, but nevertheless, different sects emphasize different meditative techniques. For instance, some say meditation is best practiced by focusing on a series of enigmatic riddles, called *koans*, until the mind is freed from rational thought to apprehend a higher truth. Others prefer chanting mantras or staring at visual centering images called *mandalas* (popular among Tibetan Buddhists), or simply sitting in complete and total awareness. (We'll talk about these options in more detail in later chapters in this book.)

But going back to the Buddha himself—after he attained enlightenment, he traveled around trying to help others do the same thing. Ironically, what he preached was that everyone had to find his own path to enlightenment and that he couldn't show them the way. On his deathbed, he is said to have told his disciples, "Be a light unto yourself."

However, to help make the path a little clearer, the Buddha did preach his own eight-fold path similar to the one Patanjali wrote about in his *Yoga Sutras*. This path also describes guidelines for living that can make meditation easier to practice and enlightenment easier to come by.

Mindful Minute

Suffering, according to yogic and Buddhist thought, is the idea that we're unhappy because we don't have something or, if we do have it, we're afraid we're going to lose it. There is no security or permanence in life as we know it. *Dukha* (suffering) is sometimes translated as "dissatisfaction" and can also be understood as incompleteness. Only enlightenment brings freedom from these human states.

Zen "Ethics"

According to the Buddha, suffering can be eliminated by adopting the Middle Way, or moderation. That means avoiding extremes—too much food, too much drink, too much spending, too much lust, too much talk, or too much of anything. The Buddha also advised working to eliminate desire because it is desire for and attachment to the things of the world that cause all suffering. It makes sense, doesn't it? What makes you most miserable—when you can't have something you want, or when you lose something you thought was yours—a possession, a person, or even something like your health or good looks? That pretty much covers it.

To get to that place where you are beyond attachment, the Buddha suggests eight steps:

◆ **Cultivate *Right Understanding*.** This step involves working to adjust your view of life. Life, says the Buddha, is impermanent and full of suffering, but understanding the nature of existence as impermanent can help you comprehend truth. In traditional Buddhism, which believes in *reincarnation*, you cannot escape the cycle of death and rebirth, death and rebirth again, until you have truly apprehended right understanding. Of course, one way to help yourself gain right understanding is through the regular practice of meditation.

◆ **Cultivating *Right Thought*.** This step is more specifically related to your thinking. To cultivate right thought, said the Buddha, you can release your mind from the tyranny of sensual desires, from the impulse toward cruelty, and from the tendency to think negatively. Right thought obliterates pessimism—and optimism, for that matter, as it helps you to live only in the moment and see everything only for what it is, not for what it might be, could be, or should be.

◆ **Cultivating *Right Speech*.** This step means refusing to lie, gossip, or speak harshly of anyone. Behind this step lies the philosophy that thought and action are inseparable. What you speak, you will eventually live. Also, right speech shouldn't be too loud or passionate and shouldn't arouse the emotions of others. It should be calm, straightforward, sincere, unprejudiced, kind, and wise. And you should listen to what others say in the same way. Talk about simplifying communication!

Bliss Byte

Reincarnation is the belief that the soul evolves in different incarnations and physical bodies or guises. Each life is uniquely individual. We are not just the same person born over and over again, but really a progression, as the Dalai Lama says, like beads on a string. Once enlightenment is achieved, the soul is released from the cycle of death and rebirth.

◆ **Cultivating *Right Action*.** This step is about how you behave and has five substeps: (1) no killing, but instead practicing love and nonviolence, (2) no stealing, but instead being generous, (3) practicing self-control and not abusing the senses, (4) speaking sincerely and honestly, and (5) not drinking alcohol or taking intoxicating drugs, but instead being restrained and mindful. Living in this way will help your body be healthy, will enable your mind to be clear, and will make the practice of meditation much easier and more natural. You won't have to keep fighting your body and your conscience when you try to meditate.

Mindful Minute

Buddhism's Five Precepts are key to understanding how to live in a way conducive to attaining nirvana and are similar to the yoga abstentions, called yamas. The five Buddhist precepts are: (1) Do no harm to other beings, (2) do not lie or speak falsely, (3) do not steal or take that which is not freely given, (4) do not engage in sexual misconduct, and (5) refrain from intoxicants that cloud the mind.

- **Practicing *Right Livelihood or Vocation*.** This step has to do with your job. The Buddha advised that anyone serious about seeking truth should only pursue an occupation that is just, nonviolent, and not misleading to others. Traditionally for Buddhists, the following jobs are considered "wrong living": arms-dealing, slave-trading, flesh-trading (whether prostitution or selling meat for food), selling intoxicating drinks, and selling poison. This would include weapons dealers, fishermen and hunters (flesh trading), and anything to do with financial greed. It isn't the making of money that's frowned upon but the motivation. Right livelihood means that the way you make your money should serve, not victimize, the sentient beings on the earth.

- **Cultivating *Right Effort*.** Right effort means working toward a better self by attempting to keep wise thoughts, words, and deeds in the forefront of the mind while attempting to banish unhealthy or unwise thoughts, words, and deeds. It's sort of a striving toward self-improvement. Yes, part of Zen is to accept yourself and the "now" as reality rather than striving for something else. On the other hand, it doesn't mean you can't keep working toward improvement. It doesn't mean you aren't on a journey, aren't moving along and evolving spiritually. It just means you can appreciate and fully realize each stage in your journey. Right effort is your journey's vehicle.

- **Cultivating *Right Mindfulness*.** Mindfulness, as we've mentioned in earlier chapters, means a sort of inner vigilance, an awareness of the state of the body, the emotions, the mind, the intellect, and the environment. When you are mindful, you will be less likely to be led astray from truth or seduced by possessions or feelings that aren't real or lasting. It is a sort of "living meditation," in which the intellect (what Buddhists believe is merely the sixth sense) is kept active in order to make the seeker more in-tune with the true nature of reality. In other words, it means paying attention and staying "awake" in your daily life.

- **Practicing *Right Concentration*.** This last step is similar to Patanjali's final step. The goal of right concentration is to be able to concentrate so wholly and completely on a single object that all desire is overcome and true knowledge of the object is attained. This is accomplished via meditation, in which one sits quietly and patiently. With practice, right concentration can be attained and the five hindrances—sensuality, ill will, lethargy, restlessness and worry, and skeptical doubt—can be overcome. Eventually, the seeker will find the way to pure consciousness, or nirvana, the traditional goal for both yoga and Zen meditation.

Desperately Seeking Samadhi

For some people who practice Zen meditation, enlightenment—nirvana, samadhi, whatever you want to call it—can become something to which we get too attached. Yet the point of Zen is to lose our attachments. Only then can we really see truth.

But for those interested in the traditional forms of meditation who practice meditation with that *goal*, meditation can be frustrating. Why can't you attain enlightenment and attain it *right now!?* Unfortunately, that's not how it works. Attachment to the idea of enlightenment, or even just to the idea of wanting immediate and dramatic results from meditation, works contrary to the very nature of meditation. Let go of your expectations, your hoped-for results, and your idea that meditation will be a panacea to your life.

Instead, embrace the *right now*. See it for what it is. Peel off all the layers of illusion—the expectations, the hopes and fears, the agendas, the big plans, the regrets, the superstitions—all that desperate stuff we like to hang on everything we think and do. Peel all that away and you've got something pretty interesting left: reality.

Meditation can be frustrating, especially at first, and it might seem like your efforts are yielding nothing at all. The more you want your life to change, the more you need some sort of enlightenment, the harder it can be to exercise the patience, will, and self-discipline it takes to reap the harvest of a consistent meditation practice. But consistent practice without expectation will indeed yield results—meditation's ultimate irony. See it for what it is, and you'll see yourself for who you really are.

How very Zen.

Bliss Byte _____

Try this concentration exercise: Look at your right thumb. Move it around. Try to sense what the thumb is feeling. Is the joint loose? Does it hurt? Where? How does it move? Now bring it to stillness. With each breath, relax your thumb a little more. Imagine going deeper, relaxing the veins and bones. Now bring your focus to one single hair on your thumb and begin again. If you feel tense and can't seem to focus on the hair, pull back to the thumb.

The Greatest Journey Begins with a Single Step

We hope you won't let the lofty sound of "nirvana" or "samadhi" or any of the rest of the philosophies of other cultures deter you. You don't have to be a Buddhist or a Hindu or a yogi to meditate, and "enlightenment" needn't be your ultimate goal in meditation. Maybe you just want a good, easy stress-management technique you can squeeze into your morning or after-work routine without having to attend a class or put on workout clothes. Great! As we've mentioned, goals of any kind are best put aside in meditation practice. Your path will become clear the more you meditate.

We're just giving you options, a little history, and the fruits of some of the great meditators to ponder, consider, discard if you like, adapt as you like, or tuck away in a corner of your mind-body for later.

No matter what your reasons for, or method of, meditation, taking that first step and making the commitment to begin a meditation practice is making a commitment to your physical health, your mental health, and your emotional well-being. It is taking care of yourself. It is akin to uttering a resounding "Yes!" to life, to living, to truly being alive. It is a decision to wake up. Good morning! It's going to be a beautiful day.

> **Mindful Minute**
>
> According to Buddhist thought, meditation is being fully aware in the current moment. It is not sitting a certain way, holding your hands a certain way, or breathing a certain way. These are simply techniques to help you become more aware of the true nature of yourself.

The Least You Need to Know

- Zen is the Japanese form of Buddhism that has been adopted and adapted by Westerners to describe a lifestyle of living in the present moment.

- Yin and yang are concepts used to describe how everything in the universe is balanced by its opposite force.

- The Buddha was a man named Siddhartha Gautama who attained enlightenment about 2,500 years ago and developed a system to help others do the same.

- The Buddha suggested moderation and eight steps to enlightenment: Right Understanding, Right Thought, Right Speech, Right Action, Right Livelihood, Right Effort, Right Mindfulness, and Right Concentration.

- You don't have to follow anyone else's spiritual method, but you can use the ideas of others to help craft your own journey of self-discovery through meditation.

Chapter 5

Say a Little Prayer

In This Chapter

- Prayer and believing
- How prayer works
- Learning (or remembering) how to pray
- Prayer and well-being

While many Eastern religions naturally incorporate meditation, Western religions seem generally more comfortable with the word "prayer." Yet prayer could be considered a form of meditation. Prayer can go hand in hand with any belief system, and it centers and calms the mind in the same way meditation does. Prayer complements meditation, and meditation complements prayer. Some consider them to be intimately intertwined practices, while others practice meditation and prayer separately.

Let's talk about prayer. The word *prayer* has a lot of connotations for a lot of people. Prayer can be as individual and unique as each human being. Just as the word *meditation* might have negative connotations to people of certain religious beliefs, the word *prayer* might have negative connotations to people who aren't affiliated with any religion or who have rejected religion for a variety of reasons. Can prayer work for you?

The Many Faces of Prayer

Although many people use the words *prayer* and *meditation* interchangeably, if you want to get really technical, there can be a difference between meditation and prayer. Meditation is inward-looking, listening, observing, and/or being present in the moment. Prayer is directed outward, toward something (or someone), whether that means talking or simply perceiving.

But perceiving what? The answers to that one are as varied as the people reading this book. Up to this point, we've used a lot of different words to express the idea of a higher power—God, nature, the universe, universal consciousness, Great Spirit, Goddess, love—all attempting to describe something we can't ever fully describe.

But why describe that higher power? It's more interesting, certainly more productive, to commune with it, speak to it, and experience it, even if you don't know what it is, can't quite agree with any particular theology or organized religion or creed, or aren't convinced anything is actually "up there" or "out there." Heck, if scientists feel space exploration is a legitimate endeavor, you can certainly send out a prayer and see what happens.

If you do have faith in a higher being or consciousness, refining and regulating your communication, communion, or conversations might work wonders in your life. Prayer can serve as a source of great inner strength, confidence, and faith.

Bliss Byte

Some people can relate better to the idea of Goddess than God. Goddess can be variously interpreted, as Mother Earth; as one of the great goddesses of mythology such as Athena, Artemis, or Persephone; or as the feminine principle in the universe. Try this goddess prayer/meditation: Sit quietly, close your eyes, and imagine the universe as the mother of the world. Imagine her taking you in her arms and rocking you. Feel her pure love, unaffected by anything you have ever done or said or become. Let her rock you in this love and feel the peace of complete acceptance. Let yourself be a child, safe in the care of the Great Mother.

You Gotta Have Faith

How can you have a conversation if you're the only one talking? Ah, but you aren't! That's the wonderful part. If you talk to the universe, the universe will talk back to you. No, you probably won't hear a booming baritone voice reverberating from the back-lit clouds. Sure, if the universe could afford his fee, it might hire James Earl

Jones to speak for it, but the universe doesn't deal in fees. It speaks in more subtle ways, and to get the message, you have to pay attention.

And to pay attention, you have to have faith. If you are one of the many out there who attended church or synagogue as a child and no longer make a habit of it, you probably remember hearing a lot about faith. "If only you had faith!" You'd be successful, loved, happy, well adjusted, and everything would go your way. Uh-huh, sure.

Well, faith isn't a meal ticket. You can't wish your problems away simply because you have "faith" they'll disappear. On the other hand, strongly believing does influence the vibrations of the universe (or so we strongly believe!). So perhaps having faith that things will work out, that you can find happiness, and so forth, can help to effect the change.

We need, though, to distinguish between faith and simply having a positive attitude. Faith is more than wearing rose-colored glasses. And it's not the same thing as hope. Faith is an abiding inner certainty. As your practice of meditation deepens and grows, so should an inner sense of belief that will lead you to have faith in what you "know," even if that faith means going against the grain or embracing something that isn't readily apparent—at least not to others.

Whether your faith is rooted in religious traditions or comes from somewhere else, meditation is a great way to explore and strengthen your own personal belief system. Faith doesn't have to be about religion, but it can be a part of spiritual growth on the path to self-actualization. When "having faith" and "knowing" begin to seem like two sides of the same coin, you may be approaching the next level of spiritual awareness.

Many religions have mystical subgroups. Kabbalah and Hasidism are two branches of the Jewish religion that emphasize Judaism's mystical aspects. Sufis and dervishes are mystical branches of Islam. Christian mystics from the Middle Ages, such as St. John of the Cross, St. Teresa of Avila, and Dame Julian of Norwich, are still well known today for their insightful writing. Many different branches of *mysticism* share similar meditation techniques, often indistinguishable from eastern techniques such as Zen or yoga meditation. Rather than externally directed prayer, mystical meditation tends to be a more internalized listening, stilling of the mind, and obliteration of the senses in an attempt to directly perceive divinity or receive guidance.

> **From A to Om**
>
> **Mysticism** is the belief in direct experience of God, universal consciousness, or intuitive truth. James H. Austin, M.D., author of *Zen and the Brain*, defines mysticism as "the ongoing practice of reestablishing, by the deepest insights, one's direct relationship with the ultimate, universal reality principle."

Bliss Byte

Saint Teresa of Avila (1515–1582) was a Carmelite nun and Christian mystic from Spain who founded the religious order of the Discalced (also called Barefoot) Carmelite nuns. Teresa of Avila's writings, all published posthumously, are still read today. They include a spiritual autobiography, *The Way of Perfection*, which consisted of advice to her nuns; *The Interior Castle*, a description of the progressive steps involved in the contemplative life; and *The Foundations*, the story of the founding of the Discalced Carmelites. According to Teresa of Avila, the soul is like a magnificent castle filled with many mansions. If you spend all your time in one room, or just walking around the exterior of your castle admiring its walls (in other words, your external self), you're missing out on adventure, delight, and joy beyond description.

Christian and Hebrew Traditions

When it comes to the dominant religions of the Western world, prayer is definitely the dominant meditative technique. The prophets of both the Old and New Testaments of the Bible practiced prayer and taught others how to pray. Both Hebrew and Christian techniques of prayer, and also of meditation, are practiced today and have much in common with Eastern meditation techniques.

Catholics meditate by chanting the rosary and other prayers. Protestants also meditate by repeating prayers such as the Lord's Prayer and the Doxology. Song, particularly in its more meditative forms such as Gregorian chanting, is distinctly meditative and reminiscent of mantra meditation. Even the quiet, reflective personal prayer of the nun in her cloister, or the minister and her family, or the regular churchgoer in the evening before falling asleep is akin to meditation. Speaking to divinity, letting oneself feel the power and faith in a certain theology, helps focus the mind on a single feeling or process, quieting the rush of daily thought and inducing feelings of serenity and even physical symptoms of increased relaxation.

In other words, if you do practice a Western religion and aren't entirely comfortable with the concept of meditation, rest assured that prayer has much the same effect and that if you do meditate, it is entirely within the realm of your religious practice. Jesus did it. The Desert Fathers did it. Monks and nuns did it (and still do). And in this increasingly global, diverse world, as traditions blend and meld and borrow the best techniques and most effective practices from each other, meditation can be the perfect spiritual practice for you.

Do I Have to Be Spiritual to Meditate?

A so-called "spiritual life" isn't for everyone, and it isn't in everyone's plan. That's fine. You are who you are, and you have your own journey. Meditation can be a boon to your life, nevertheless, because you don't have to be spiritual to meditate. You don't have to be religious; you don't have to believe in a higher power; you don't even have to believe the sun will come up tomorrow. Meditation isn't about what you believe. It's about the "now."

In meditation, you live in the now and embrace the present moment. You feel it, experience it, and live it. Maybe you will eventually end up pondering questions about your life or thinking about a religious concept, but that's highly individual. So if you are turned off by the idea of meditation because you think it's not grounded in reality or that it's too philosophical or too ethereal, fear not.

Relax _____

Some people aren't interested in meditation because they think it's too spiritual, but others avoid it because they think it is opposed to their beliefs or somehow against their religion.

The religions and philosophical systems that use meditation (and there are many!) are interesting to study in conjunction with its practice, but aren't themselves meditation. Meditation fits into *any* belief system.

Meditation is the awareness of the flow of reality in space and time. Unlike philosophy, which strives to achieve an order to reality through mental reasoning alone, meditation looks for a deep acceptance, a knowing that comes from the mind-body. And ethereal? What's more practical than a process that helps you think better and more clearly, be healthier, and thrive in life?

What often happens when someone begins to meditate, however, is that some of the "big" questions begin to materialize. What is the meaning of "good" and "evil"? What is "right" and what is "wrong"? What does it mean to be virtuous, and what are the "right" priorities? (We put all these terms in quotation marks because we don't believe they have strict definitions that are exactly the same for everyone in every culture.)

That's not to say any of these questions will *ever* occur to you before, during, or after meditation. But they might. Numerous recent studies demonstrate that people involved with a belief system or who practice a religion are generally happier, less depressed, healthier, and live longer. A little spirituality, in whatever form suits you, might make you a happier, healthier person.

But once again, we'll say that if you are diametrically opposed to things spiritual and aren't interested in anything that can't be proven using scientific methods, don't reject meditation. Plenty of scientific studies have demonstrated its benefits. Read Chapter 6 to find out more about the science and physiology of meditation.

Healing Thoughts for All Sentient Beings

You can pray for enlightenment. You can pray for insight. You can even pray that you'll win the lottery. But perhaps one of the most productive ways to pray (especially if prayers really do affect what happens in the world) is to pray for each other. Sincere yearning to help someone and thoughts or prayers directed toward that person may very well help. Hard to prove? Sure, but scientists are giving it their best shot.

> **Mindful Minute**
>
> Anthony deMello, S.J. (1931–1987), a Jesuit priest and the former director of the Sadhana Institute of Pastoral Counseling in Poona, India, wrote and lectured on meditation and enlightenment as a part of spiritual life no matter the religion. Of the path to enlightenment, he writes, "So begin to be aware of your present condition whatever that condition is. Stop being a dictator. Stop trying to push yourself somewhere. Then someday you will understand that simply by awareness you have already attained what you were pushing yourself toward."

One perspective several research studies use is the idea of *distance intentionality*. This means that someone prays or mentally tries to affect something or someone from a distance. Praying that your mother's health will improve is an example, if you are not actually with her when you pray. The concept is neither new nor uniquely Western. Many ancient cultures and indigenous peoples believed that, for example, a sorcerer or witch doctor could cure someone or, conversely, hex, harm, or even kill someone from afar.

> **From A to Om**
>
> **Distance intentionality** is a concept that refers to directing an intention toward something at a distance. Prayer is one example.

Distance intentionality defies the concept that disease—or any physical condition, for that matter—is somehow isolated within the body. Rather, it suggests that some force, energy, or flow encompasses all of us, allowing the energies of some to influence the healing of others. Imagine we are all in a river.

If you ripple the water with your hand, someone else will feel the waves downstream. Whether distance intentionality is tapping into the collective unconscious, the power of a divine force, or some universal energy, we don't claim to know. But if it works, prayer can have a very real effect. So what are you waiting for? One recent scientific study, among many, documents the healing potential of prayer: When 40 healing practitioners of different holistic disciplines prayed for advanced AIDS patients, a significant decrease in the severity of the illness was recorded for the prayer recipients over a six-month period.

The next time you are meditating, after you have relaxed and calmed your mind (see Part 3 on how to get started), imagine someone—just one person—who seems to need guidance, love, or some sort of help. Very slowly, inhale until you can't inhale anymore. Hold the breath for a few seconds and imagine suffusing it with love, positive energy, joy, and clarity. Then close your eyes, visualize the person (or animal), and very slowly exhale. Imagine the love and positive energy flowing via your breath straight into the heart of the person who needs it, filling and surrounding him or her. Repeat this several times.

Another meditation to try is the Buddhist Tongelen meditation. This meditation is a powerful breathing exercise in transforming human suffering into human joy. Breathe in deeply, and as you feel your lungs fill up with air, imagine breathing into your body all the suffering and pain of your loved one. Breathe out and in, breathing out release all your kindness, love, and healing for that person. Instead of being depleting or increasing suffering in any way (your own or your loved one's), this meditation provides healing empowerment. Its practice purifies and strengthens both the giver and the recipient. As Vietnamese monk Thich Nhat Hahn writes, applying Tongelen to a personal path of mindfulness: "Breathing in I calm my body, breathing out I smile. Living in the present moment, I know this is a wonderful moment."

 Bliss Byte _____

Who knows what changes the world would experience if everyone sent out daily healing prayers. However, let's include the physical, too. Brighten your day and someone else's life by volunteering at a soup kitchen, tutoring in an adult literacy program, giving clothes to a shelter, working on a hotline for runaway teens, helping find homes for abandoned animals, or working to heal the earth.

Form Your Own Prayer Group

If one prayer is good, a lot of prayers are great! Meditation and prayer are usually solitary pursuits, but a prayer group can be a great way not only to meet with people of similar beliefs but also boost your prayer power.

If you belong to a church, synagogue, or other similar organization, or if you are taking a yoga or meditation class, you can probably find other people who would be interested in starting a prayer group. (See Part 3 for more information on meditation groups and classes.) Groups of between 3 and 12 people are easiest to manage at first, although prayer chains can be much more widespread (in a prayer chain, prayer concerns are passed around via phone calls, e-mail, or other modes of communication to a network of people). Meet with your prayer group weekly, monthly, or however often fits your schedule. Begin meetings by raising concerns, such as someone or a community who needs help, or a world problem that needs solving. Then, pray together.

Another interesting facet of a prayer group can be discussions of prayer itself, prayer techniques, prayer and meditation, prayer-related philosophical discussions, etc. Group members can read different works on the subject and discuss them, and even try different techniques together. Refining your prayer and meditation skills in the company of your friends can be fun and spiritually rewarding—not to mention socially rewarding, too.

Remembering How to Pray

If the last time you prayed your age only had one digit and you were kneeling next to your bed with a watchful parent at your side, you might have forgotten some of the basics. Praying might feel uncomfortable at first and more awkward than simple meditation, especially if you haven't given much thought to your spiritual life lately.

Mindful Minute

As Larry Dossey, M.D. (a former internist and the co-founder of the Santa Fe Institute of Medicine and Prayer), once said, "One of the oldest men on Earth lives in Iraq; he's at least 120 years old and drinks and smokes all the time. And history is full of very spiritual people who were sick all the time. In the Bible, Job was described as perfect and look what happened to him. The Buddha died of food poisoning." Although a staunch believer in the power of prayer, Dossey emphasizes that faith and healing are not directly correlated. If you get sick, it doesn't mean you weren't praying well enough. But if you do pray, you might be able to improve your situation.

It isn't easy to jump right into a prayerful state with both knees. You need to warm up before you exercise, right? A prayer warm-up doesn't hurt, either. To help you get into the right frame of mind, we'll instruct you in prayer preparation. Then we'll guide you through some prayer exercises, too, in case you aren't quite ready to wing it or you're looking for some new strategies.

Get Ready: Prayer Preparation

Before you begin to pray, prepare your mind. Sit comfortably in a hard-backed chair in a quiet room where you won't be disturbed for at least 15 minutes. (For more on chair meditations, see Chapter 13.) Keep your back straight. Close your eyes, or, if this makes concentrating more difficult, leave them slightly open and focus on an object you can bring your attention to if your mind begins to wander.

Now, notice your breathing. Don't change it. Simply notice it. Direct all your attention to the feel of your breath moving in and out of your nostrils. Keep your attention here for a bit. Next, shift your attention to your feet. Feel the way your shoes feel on your feet or the way your feet feel against the floor. Don't move them. Just feel. Next, feel how your body is touching the floor or chair. Notice all the places it is touching. Are there places you know it is touching but that you can't feel? Keep trying to feel it.

Last, feel the air on your skin. Feel it on your face, your hair, your arms, your hands, and anywhere your skin is exposed. Does the air feel cool? Warm? Is it moving or still? Is it humid or dry? Feel the way you are placed in the air. Feel how it makes way for your presence and how it moves in and out of you. Feel how integrated you are with the air.

Bring your attention back to your breathing for another minute or two. This exercise is designed to be profoundly relaxing.

Just Say "Pray"

Now that you are relaxed, let's give prayer a try. Center your thoughts on what you want to say. Or if you aren't sure what to say, consider the following exercise:

Place two chairs together in a quiet room. Sit in one. Now, visualize someone you love who is not physically with you. A meaningful religious figure is a good choice (your guardian angel, a saint, Jesus, Buddha, a personified form of God, etc.), but it could also be someone who has passed away, or someone upon whom you wish healing or happiness. Imagine how that figure looks sitting across from you. Imagine the details of the face, the clothes, the hands, the feet, etc.

Now simply talk to that person. What do you want to tell them? Pour out your heart, ask questions you've wondered about, or simply tell the person about your day.

Bliss Byte _____

Light a candle and gaze into the flame. Imagine the flame is the universal source of divinity, love, inspiration, or creativity. As you gaze at it, feel those qualities in you awakening and recognizing their universal counterpart. Spend some time allowing your inner divinity, love, inspiration, or creativity to fully awaken. Allow the flame to spark a flow of warm, positive energy inside you; use that spark to feed the fire of the flame you are meditating upon.

The Least You Need to Know

- Prayer can complement meditation as an important vehicle in your spiritual journey.

- You don't have to believe in a specific religion or a specific higher power to pray.

- Prayer may affect actual events, such as the health and well-being of those prayed for, as well as your own health.

- Prayer is comfort food for the soul.

Part  The Physical and Beyond: Meditation Mind-Body-Spirit Union

Meditation is more than a spiritual tool. It's a great way to manage your physical health, too. When you meditate, your brain waves change and your brain chemistry changes, effecting change all over your body. Other cultures have theories for the physical benefits of meditation. Did you know you have a natural energy field, a force of life energy that runs through your body, and for that matter, three bodies and five sheaths of existence?

Meditation is also similar, physiologically, to the dream state, and working with your dreams can be beneficial to your meditation practice. Knowing the physical changes that happen in your mind-body through meditation can help you get the most of meditation's ability to alleviate your stress, calm your mind, and heal your body.

Chapter 6

Neurophysiology: This Is Your Brain on Meditation

In This Chapter

- ◆ Meditation and your brain waves
- ◆ How meditation promotes mental efficiency
- ◆ Concentration and relaxation

It might be tempting, at this point, to think that all this meditation business is happening in your mind. Well, sure it is, but not only in your mind. Things are happening in that meditating brain of yours—interesting things. Sure, studies have demonstrated meditation's relaxing effect, and everyone knows stress-management techniques are valuable allies to good health. In fact, a National Institutes of Health panel recently found strong evidence that relaxation and behavioral techniques such as biofeedback are effective in reducing chronic pain and insomnia. A 1999 NIH study showed a significant reduction in post-operative pain for patients who listened to music, practiced relaxation techniques, or did both.

The National Center for Complementary and Alternative Medicine, a division of the National Institutes of Health, continues to study relaxation and meditation as well as many other behavioral-based therapies. For example, studies are currently progressing to determine the beneficial effects of meditation on coronary heart disease, cardiovascular disease, and binge eating disorder.

For this chapter, we'd like to get physical and show you what's going on in your brain during meditation. Studies have proven that meditation does have a physical effect on your brain and body.

Meditation Makes Your Brain Stronger

Your brain isn't a muscle, so how can it get stronger? Although it isn't an actual muscle, it has similarities to a muscle. When you exercise your muscles, especially with weight-bearing exercises like weight lifting, push-ups, sit-ups, and running or jogging, you cause tiny tears in the muscle fibers. When these tears heal, they bulk up the fibers to be even stronger than before. That's why the rest period between exercise sessions is important. It is during rest that your muscles strengthen.

Your brain doesn't have muscle fibers, but it does have *neurons*, or nerve cells, not to mention *neurotransmitters*, the chemicals that deliver messages back and forth between neurons. Everyone is born with billions of neurons (approximately 12 billion in your brain alone), and although they can't be regenerated, research suggests we can strengthen the connections they make with each other. We can also slow their inevitable loss.

From A to Om

Neurons are nerve cells, and **neurotransmitters** are the chemicals produced in nerve cells that travel from one nerve cell to another, delivering marching orders from the brain to the rest of the body.

Some neurons are bound to be damaged due to aging. Injuries (such as a severe bump on the head) or illness that cuts off oxygen to the brain (a stroke, for example) may cause the loss of many more neurons. Sometimes neurons can repair themselves, and sometimes they can't.

Mindful Minute

Neurons look a little like spiders. Each neuron has a cell body, and extending from that body are "legs," or branches, called *dendrites*. Also extending from the cell body is a single long fiber called an *axon*, and at its tip are more little extensions, like tiny roots. Dendrites receive messages from the body and carry them to the center of the nerve cell. The messages are then carried away by the axon and sent on to the next neuron. Although neurons don't actually touch each other, messages "jump" from neuron to neuron, almost instantaneously in a kind of chain reaction, via an electrochemical process that utilizes chemicals called *neurotransmitters*.

But evidence suggests that we can keep our neurons more active by our own efforts. One way is to use them. Keeping your brain active into old age can be an effective way to combat senility. Another way to keep your neurons in tip-top shape? Treat them like muscles. Every day, for just a little while, give them a meditation workout.

Neurophysiology: The Brain, the Body, and Meditation

The effect of meditation on the brain and the body is the subject of much research. A number of rigorous scientific studies on the subject have appeared in scientific journals on psychology, psychiatry, psychobiology, alternative medicine, and neuroscience (the study of the brain). For example, studies have demonstrated that during Transcendental Meditation (TM), blood flow to the brain increases. Neurophysiology, or the study of brain physiology, can offer an interesting perspective to the concept of mind-body medicine.

Are the changes in the brain and body experienced during meditation due solely to its relaxing effect on the body? Certainly that is part of it. But studies on the effects of meditation have been compared with studies on the effects of resting, and the results aren't exactly the same. Resters tend to have slowed arousal responses, while meditators didn't, for example. That means that resting can dull your senses, making you slower to react to a stimulus such as a threat. Meditation, on the other hand, seems to awaken the senses, making you more easily roused by a stimulus such as a threat. Meditation doesn't "space you out," nor does it slow your reactions, as a nap certainly would. Instead, it seems to fine-tune your attention. People who are meditating, then, are not falling asleep—even if they appear to be!

There are several problems with physiological studies of meditation. Anyone being studied is likely to be more tense and self-conscious than normal, so the difference between "before" and "after" states measured in meditators might be exaggerated under the conditions of a study. Also, because the brain is so powerful, if a meditator knows what a researcher is looking for (or even suspects, not having been told), the meditator may be able, subconsciously, to influence the body to produce the desired effect. For example, if you suspect a researcher wants to discover that meditation lowers your blood pressure or oxygen consumption, your body may oblige by lowering your blood pressure or oxygen consumption,

Mindful Minute

Researchers have discovered that meditation shares many of the physiological qualities of Stage I non-REM sleep. This is the stage where you begin to become drowsy. However, they agree that sleep and meditation are two separate phenomena. Different studies show that people who meditate regularly have more efficient REM sleep, the sleep stage during which dreams occur, making your sleep more restful and rejuvenating.

even if you aren't trying, consciously, to cause that change. For rebellious types, the effect might be the opposite. "So those researchers think they'll find that meditation relaxes me? I'll show them!" And tension sets in!

Another problem is that meditative experiences are largely subjective. You can measure all the bodily processes that you like, but no instrument, no matter how fine-tuned and precise, can measure the full spectrum of an enlightenment experience.

Kensho: Seeing the Essence

Is there any way, then, to objectively prove an enlightenment experience? As an example, consider *kensho*. Also called insight-wisdom, kensho is like a pre-enlightenment experience. It is a moment of profound wisdom or insight where truth and the essence of all things are suddenly clear. An example is suddenly discovering the answer to a koan, one of those Zen "riddles" that help your awareness to "pop" into a new way of seeing. One of the most famous Zen koans is "What is the sound of one hand clapping?" We Westerners have thought similar concepts, too, such as, "If a tree falls in the forest when nobody is there, does it make a sound?" Some are even more enigmatic, such as "Does a dog have Buddha nature?" or (to paraphrase), "Why doesn't the bearded man have a beard?"

> **From A to Om**
>
> **Kensho,** also called insight-wisdom, is a sudden-understanding experience of seeing into the essence of things. It is considered a step toward true enlightenment.

Kensho is temporary and short-lived, one of those "ah-HA!" experiences. But does it register in the brain?

For one thing, you never know when kensho will occur, so it isn't easy to be ready to "measure" it. But those who have experienced it can talk about it, and there do seem to be some patterns. Kensho seems to happen more frequently:

- In the early morning hours (in fact, the Buddha was said to have attained enlightenment upon seeing the first morning star)

- When in an unfamiliar surrounding

- In the spring, specifically May and June

Morning and spring are both awakening phases of cycles, and unfamiliar surroundings may force chemical reactions in the brain that wouldn't normally occur. But the neurophysiology of kensho is still mostly theoretical. We don't yet have the means or the information to pin down the elusive experience of enlightenment, but that doesn't mean we can't continue to study the subject. Considering the positive changes meditation invokes in the body, scientists will certainly keep trying!

Mindful Minute

Meditation can give you control over bodily functions you never knew you could control, including your temperature. Dr. Herbert Benson, M.D., of Harvard University, visited a Tibetan monastery in northern India and filmed a group of Tibetan monks meditating. The temperature in the meditation room was 40°F and the monks were wrapped in sheets that had been dipped in ice-cold water. Reportedly, the monks generated such heat while meditating that steam quickly began to rise off their bodies, and the sheets were completely dry in 40 minutes.

Riding the Brain Waves

Brain waves are caused by electrical activity in the brain, and they can be measured by a test called an electroencephalogram (EEG). This test involves recording the brain waves via electrodes placed on the scalp, or even sometimes on the brain itself, as during surgery.

The brain doesn't produce a lot of electricity—maybe enough to light a 25-watt bulb. But the brain waves are nevertheless revealing. They can come from different parts of the brain and occur at different frequencies. Delta waves are the slowest, cycling $1/2$ to 2 cycles per second. Alpha waves cycle about eight to 12 times per second. Theta waves cycle at four to seven times per second. Beta rhythms cycle 14 to 30 times per second, and gamma waves cycle 30 to 50 times per second.

Each type of brain wave can be attributed to certain types of mental states (although not always reliably). Studying the brain waves during meditation, then, can give us some clues about what's going on during different phases of meditation. Here are some generalizations:

- **Alpha waves** are generally associated with relaxed, attentive states. When you think, mostly nonvisually (such as thinking about a concept rather than day-dreaming), your alpha waves may tend to increase. Alpha waves usually slow when you fall asleep or when you engage in complex thought. Alpha waves are often dominant in the first stages of meditation when you attempt to concentrate on the sound of a mantra, the feel of your breath, or an object (you're looking at it, which is visual of course, but that's different from visualizing in your mind). However, alpha waves have been detected in people reporting a wide range of mental states, from happy relaxation to attentiveness to internal reflection.

- **Delta waves** are the slow waves that are characteristic of very deep sleep.

- **Theta waves** aren't usually present in normal waking states, but they begin to replace alpha waves as consciousness gives way to sleep. Theta waves may also appear during daydreams and during activity that requires mental effort when the subject is relaxed. Theta waves don't always appear consistently, though, so they are hard to categorize.

> ### Mindful Minute
>
> Many studies have measured the brain waves of experienced and inexperienced meditators alike. One study showed that during walking meditation, about half the recorded brain waves of Zen monks were alpha waves, while only 20 percent of the brain waves in inexperienced meditators were alpha waves. A control group of non-meditators exhibited no alpha waves during walking. This study could be evidence for a state of increased attentiveness in daily life bestowed by practicing meditation.

◆ **Beta waves** might appear when people are feeling the effects of stress, whether in a negative way (such as anxiety) or a positive way (such as excitement). They may also be present during states of alertness or concentration, or even when subjects are feeling very happy and content. Typically, beta waves increase when we are paying close attention to something, but the increase doesn't last (maybe because it's hard to pay close attention to something for a long time). After an hour or two, alpha and theta waves take over again. Beta waves sometimes occur in the deepest, most advanced stages of meditation.

◆ **Gamma waves** are the fastest waves and can be found in many parts of the brain. They are difficult to attribute to any particular state, but one study showed an increase in gamma waves when subjects were asked to respond quickly to clicking sounds.

Something else interesting that happens to brain waves during meditation is that they tend to synchronize. Several studies on Transcendental Meditation have demonstrated that brain waves tend to synchronize their peaks and valleys. In normal states of awareness, brain waves appear randomly, with each peak and valley occurring seemingly independently of the others. What does it mean, then, that brain waves tend to organize themselves during meditation? Scientists aren't sure, but intuition suggests some sort of enhanced centering, tranquility, and an inner sense of order.

A Tibetan Monk's Brain on Meditation

Aside from your brain waves, what does your brain actually look like during meditation? Does it change? Apparently. A study sponsored by the Institute for the Scientific

Study of Meditation (ISSM) used a brain-imaging technology called SPECT imaging (single photon emission computed tomography) to take pictures of the brains of Tibetan Buddhist meditators who were seasoned practitioners of meditation. The images show which areas of the brain are more active by showing where blood flow increases.

Images were taken of the Tibetan Buddhists' brains during meditation and when not meditating. The images taken during meditation clearly showed two things:

- The front of the brain, which is the area typically involved in concentration, is more active during meditation. Because meditation requires focused attention and concentration on something, whether the breath, a visual point, or a sound, increased activity in the frontal lobe makes sense.

- The parietal lobe shows decreased activity. This area typically governs our sense of where we are in space and time. For example, you know you are sitting in a chair in your living room reading this book or perhaps standing in a bookstore flipping through the pages. You know what day it is, what year, what city you are in, what state, what country, what planet, etc. Meditators sometimes describe the feeling that their orientation in space and time becomes suspended during meditation. Decreased activity in the parietal lobe would correspond with this sensation.

What does this mean for you? Even if you aren't an experienced Tibetan Buddhist meditator (we're guessing you probably aren't, though we could be wrong!), does your brain show similar changes during meditation? More research has to be done before that question can be answered accurately, but chances are that although the changes in a novice meditator are probably less dramatic, they are also probably similar.

> **CAUTION**
>
> **Relax**
>
> According to some, wearing metal on the body (such as metal jewelry) affects the body's energy field. You might want to consider removing all metal jewelry while meditating. Also, try and have the energies around you be as natural as possible. For example, sit on a cotton or wool rug instead of a polyester one.

Blending Ritual: The Spiritual and the Scientific

Whether your tendencies and preferences fall on the religious or the scientific side of the spectrum, you can still find a meditation principle, practice, and ritual that makes sense for you. If you tend to be more scientific in your approach, focus on the brain-boosting benefits of meditation, the research, and the way it can improve your health. If spirituality is your mode, approach meditation from a more transcendent standpoint. Maybe prayer is your favorite mode, or perhaps you like the idea of giving yoga or Buddhist methods a try.

Something else to consider is stretching your focus to encompass, at least to a small degree, the aspects of meditation that go against your natural inclination. You can't grow, whether intellectually or spiritually, if you never challenge yourself.

> **Bliss Byte**
>
> The idea of balance is an important aspect of most meditation traditions. In Chinese, the yin/yang symbol represents balance. In Hatha Yoga (the yoga emphasizing the practice of physical postures), *Ha* is male and *tha* is female. Hatha Yoga also includes postures requiring balance of the body. When meditating, consider the idea of balance. If your mind is overwhelmed with mundane details, clearing it can put your mind-body (your life!) back into balance.

Meditation may be a joy; however, it may also be tempting to desire instant enlightenment, and when this doesn't occur, you may become frustrated by the very mundane and boring process of getting "good" at meditation. Try a systematic, scientific approach to your meditation practice, even if it goes against your nature. Meditate at a specific time each day, for a set length of time. Rather than letting your mind get caught up in dreams of enlightenment and spiritual awakening (which actually is a fairly common hindrance to the real business of meditation), be pragmatic and disciplined in your approach. Focus on your breathing or whatever your choice of focus is, and dutifully bring your mind back to your focus—and nothing else!—for your allotted time. You'll contend with boredom. You'll contend with tedium. You'll contend with the very real *fact* of just sitting. Why aren't you enlightened yet? Let meditation teach you its lessons.

Meditation and Neurotransmitters: Getting the Message Across

But back to the science. Another compelling aspect of meditation and neurophysiology is that the activity of neurotransmitters, those chemical messengers shooting back and forth between nerve cells, can actually change nerve cell metabolism and even the structure of the cell membranes. Specifically, neurotransmitter release can make nerve cells more easily excitable or more resistant to stimulation.

If processes in the brain can change the brain, and if meditation creates processes in the brain, then meditation can change your brain. Not dramatically, of course. You may find yourself tapping into a wellspring of psychic intuition you never realized you had. Meditation does indeed make you more sensitive to subtler and subtler vibrations.

For example, meditators' quickened reaction times may be due to the brain learning to make the most efficient use of its speedier neurotransmitters, such as *acetylcholine*. It appears meditation can actually make your mind work more efficiently!

Building Concentration

Meditation also has a measurable effect on your ability to concentrate. According to researchers, concentration can, to an extent, be cultivated. As we saw in the section on brain waves, beta waves are often dominant during periods of intense concentration, but don't last for more than an hour or two. After that, concentration levels seem to drop no matter what the subjects do, and alpha and theta waves kick in, signaling that intense concentration is at an end.

If something interests you, you'll be more likely to concentrate on it, of course. If something is boring, boring, boring, you'll have a much harder time concentrating. In fact, most meditation techniques are concentration techniques. That's why meditation is such a great way to cultivate concentration. It can get boring, and there's your opportunity to practice! Just like anything else, the ability to concentrate does improve with practice, and daily meditation is the perfect venue.

We heard a story about a meditation student who complained to the teacher that just focusing on the breath was boring. The teacher (a Zen master, we're sure!) plunged the student's head into an icy-cold river and held it down. The student struggled for a while until the teacher let him up and said, "Now, tell me how boring the breath is!" American religious thinker Thomas Merton wrote this about boredom (we're paraphrasing): If you find something to be boring, keep doing it more and more until you get so bored that eventually it becomes interesting!

Perhaps the abilities of experienced meditators intimidate you. You could never concentrate that well, for that long! You probably couldn't

 Bliss Byte

Try breathing into your arms. It might sound strange, but your skin breathes, too. Imagine helping your skin to release what it doesn't need. Visualize inhaling deeply through your upper arms and exhaling slowly through your lower arms. Repeat for a few deep breaths. Since your skin covers your entire body, you can do this exercise with any area of your body. Really get into that skin!

perform as a circus acrobat or understand an esoteric physics theorem, either—certainly not without training and practice! People can accomplish amazing feats with directed practice. You can, too.

> **Bliss Byte**
>
> Another effective way to learn how to improve your concentration is *biofeedback*. Biofeedback is a technique through which you learn to control various internal processes, such as brain waves or blood pressure, by seeing them displayed on a monitor. Subjects who suffered from chronic anxiety were taught to control and increase their alpha waves (the brain waves associated with relaxed attention, as in the first stages of meditation). They reported a subsequent sense of well-being, compared to subjects who were unsuccessful at the technique and whose anxiety remained unchanged.

Meditation: The Ultimate Natural High

Stress, anxiety, even insecurity are often treated with drugs and in this day and age, although excellent drugs have been developed to treat chemical imbalances, nothing beats the natural high attained through diligent meditation. From pain relief to union with the universe, meditation has a natural high for everyone.

The Least You Need to Know

- Meditation strengthens your mental processes in ways that can be both objectively measured and subjectively experienced.

- Your brain waves and brain blood flow change in response to meditation.

- Meditation seems to encourage the neurotransmitters that improve reaction time.

- Science and spirituality need not exist in separate camps. Meditation can encompass both views.

Chapter 7

Prana, Chi, the Force: Meditation Is Energy Central

In This Chapter

- ◆ Your mind-body's energy fields
- ◆ Energy blocks and obstacles
- ◆ Getting to know the chakras and recognizing auras

What *animates* you? What makes the "machine/computer" of your mind-body move, act, react, and interact? What possesses you to think, respond, dream, listen, contemplate, ruminate, and meditate? What spark pops you into *being?*

Different cultures have different answers to these questions, but the answers are largely similar. We each seem to have a unique energy that manifests itself in us. But is the energy *really* unique? Is your energy the same as your friend's energy? You might say no, but perhaps your energy only *seems* different. Perhaps your energy moves in and out of you, in and out of all of humanity, around and through the whole world, and even the universe. Perhaps that animating energy is what ties us all together.

Prana, Chi, the Force: Whatever You Call It, Get with It!

According to yogic and Buddhist thought—as well as many other schools of thinking such as those associated with traditional Chinese medicine (TCM), acupuncture and acupressure, Shiatsu massage, feng shui, and tai chi—the universe and all its inhabitants are joined by a life-force energy. This energy runs through meridians in the body, is inhaled with each breath, pools and stagnates, and flows and releases like an intricate universal river system. Yogis call it *prana*. The Chinese call it *c'hi* or *chi*. The Japanese call it *ki*. Many cultures have names for this energy. If you've seen any of the *Star Wars* movies (or even if you haven't), you surely heard of the Force. There it is again! The Force is always with you.

Is this life-force energy real? When we look around us, we don't see energy waves and flows in the air. We can't measure it. Certain scientific instruments can measure electrical fields on the body, and a few studies have measured electrical changes over the areas of the body called *pressure points* through which chi can be manipulated. The concept would seem to be merely theory. Yet many have made compelling arguments for its existence:

> **From A to Om**
>
> Prana, c'hi, chi, and ki are all names for life-force energy that animates the body and the universe and which, when unblocked and properly directed, can help the body heal itself.

> **From A to Om**
>
> Pressure points are points along the energy channels in the body where energy tends to pool or get blocked. Pressing, massaging, or otherwise manipulating these points can help rejuvenate energy flows through the body, facilitating the body's ability to balance and heal itself.

- Many of the world's cultures—today and throughout history—have independently come up with the concept of life-force energy.

- Acupuncture, an ancient Chinese technique that works on the principle of life-force energy and manipulating it by inserting needles into pressure points, works so well to treat chronic pain that many insurance companies cover treatment.

- Energy-based bodywork treatments designed to enhance healing and well-being are immensely popular and have a large body of anecdotal evidence to support their effectiveness. In many of these treatments, such as with Reiki (an energy-manipulation therapy), the subject is never actually touched by the practitioner. Only his or her energy is manipulated by the movement of hands just above the body.

- Most people can feel their own energy levels. Sometimes they are high; sometimes they are low.

Mindful Minute

In recent years, the National Institutes of Health (NIH) has lent increasing approval to the use of acupuncture by mainstream physicians as a complementary medicine technique effective for the treatment of many common conditions, from arthritis and back pain to attention deficit/hyperactivity disorder in children. The American Association of Medical Acupuncturists (AAMA) has created a board certification for medical acupuncturists, and there are currently 40 acupuncture schools in the United States offering Master's degrees. Ask your doctor about including acupuncture in your treatment plan.

And is life-force energy something you can use? You bet! Many ancient systems have formulated methods for unblocking chi, filling the body with prana, and suffusing your whole being with life-force energy. Yoga, massage, bodywork, Chinese medicine, homeopathy, and meditation are some of the main methods for getting in tune with your life-force energy and using it to your best advantage. Start thinking in terms of how best to facilitate your life force, and pretty soon that light saber will fly right into your hand when you need it most! (Well, maybe not—but you'll probably feel like it could!)

Life's Animating Quality

This life-force energy isn't just in your body. It emanates from you, flows in and out of you, and animates every sentient being and, according to some theories, every object—trees, rocks, mountains, clouds, buildings, cars, and even the earth itself.

Learning to use and enhance your life-force energy can do more than improve your health and well-being. It can also connect you to the earth, your fellow humans, and nature. It *does* join you to all those things and makes you part of them and them part of you. Breathe it in, unblock it, move with it, and recognize it in yourself and in the world around you. Meditate on it, with it, and in it.

Bliss Byte

Life-force energy is said to run not only through the body but through the world, and the now-popular art of feng shui for home and building placement and arrangement is based on manipulating the environmental life force energy to maximum effect.

Are You Blocked? A Self-Quiz

Of course, meditating on, with, and in your life-force energy is easier said than done, especially if you are blocked. Blockages can create emotional paralysis or physical illness. Not many people are completely unblocked in every way. Are you blocked? Take our quiz to determine if you are and in what way. (*Note:* We aren't using any particular established theory of energy blocks, but instead are using the term more loosely to refer to blocks that could both cause or be caused by physical or emotional states.)

Answer each question yes, no, or not sure/maybe/sometimes:

1. Do you suffer from allergies? _____

2. Do you find it difficult to express yourself in writing? _____

3. Do you feel as if you remember little about your childhood? _____

4. Do you experience pain at least once a week (for example, headaches, backaches, or joint pain)? _____

5. Do you suffer from depression or sometimes feel a noticeable lack of emotion? _____

6. Do you feel like you don't have an outlet through which to express yourself creatively? _____

7. Do you feel uncomfortable with casual touching, such as a hug from a friend or a pat on the back? _____

8. Would you describe quantitative thinking as more "comfortable" than creative thinking? _____

9. Do you suffer from chronic muscle tension? _____

10. Do you feel more negative than positive emotions in the course of a typical day? _____

11. Did you enjoy creative tasks such as writing, drawing, dancing, or playing an instrument or sport as a child but felt obligated to give them up as an adult? _____

12. Do you have high blood pressure? _____

13. Do you feel like you could have been a great *something* (artist, musician, parent, philosopher, humanitarian) but instead chose a path that involved less commitment or was "safer"? _____

14. Do you suffer from insomnia? _____

15. Are you addicted to nicotine, alcohol, caffeine, or drugs? _____

16. Has it been more than a month since you experienced a feeling you would describe as "inspiration"? _____

17. If you were given a professional massage for a gift, would you avoid getting the massage because it would be too uncomfortable, embarrassing, or intimidating? _____

18. Are you chronically tired even when you've had enough sleep? _____

19. Have you tried repeatedly to keep a journal to record your thoughts and feelings and are you always unable to keep it up for more than a few weeks or even days? _____

20. Do you seem to get colds more often than other people you know do? _____

21. Would you describe yourself as unpleasantly overweight or underweight? _____

22. Are there people in your life you haven't forgiven? _____

23. Do you think you are untalented? _____

24. Do you have a general feeling of unhealthiness or unwellness, even if you can't describe any particular symptoms? _____

25. Do you feel guilty about spending time doing something creative that isn't related to your job, your household duties, or what you see as your other obligations? _____

26. Do you dislike who you are? _____

27. Do you eat a lot of processed foods? _____

28. Do you sometimes feel inexplicably angry? _____

29. Do you feel like you are more your mind than your body? _____

30. Do you have any phobias (irrational fears)? _____

Give yourself two points for every yes answer, one point for every not sure/maybe/ sometimes answer, and zero points for every no answer.

◆ **If your score was between 31 and 60:** You're experiencing some major blocks, and whether they are based on physical or emotional problems, they are almost certainly causing some health problems for you, even if minor ones. If you remain blocked, these physical problems might worsen, might disappear and reappear as more serious problems, and/or might expand into your emotional realm. They may already be affecting your emotional life, personal relationships, and self-esteem. Try improving your diet and exercise habits, receiving periodic massage or other bodywork, and consulting a physician or qualified holistic health practitioner for advice on your physical symptoms. Also consider seeking a counselor or receiving some type of bodywork that manipulates energy. Moving meditation may be just the ticket for shaking those blocks loose. Sitting or prone meditation, particularly in the form of the mind-body scan, can help you get back in touch with your body to determine where any physical blockages are located. But when you are feeling at your worst, exercise or practice moving meditation rather than sitting and dwelling.

◆ **If your score was between 10 and 29:** You have some blocks, like most people do. Some of them might be serious and causing you some physical and/or emotional problems. But you can deal with these blocks, and you can get rid of them. Meditation can be a great way for you to get back in touch with your inner self. Remembering who you are and learning to trust your instincts can help you become unblocked; meditation is a great technique to facilitate this. It can also clue you in to other worthy avenues to pursue such as bodywork, counseling, or medical treatment.

◆ **If your score was between 0 and 9:** Compared to most, you are relatively unblocked. You are in touch with your inner feelings, you take care of your body, and your energy is flowing freely. You still might have an issue or two in your emotional life or a physical problem or two that, although not life-threatening, affects your health. Meditation might be easy for you, and you can benefit from it immensely. You have fewer barriers than most in your path, so meditate whenever you can. Sitting meditation, moving meditation, creative visualization, mindfulness meditation—try it all! Become an expert. You might just attain enlightenment!

CAUTION

Relax

Energy blocks are complex. Blocks due to physical causes can create emotional problems, blocks due to emotional problems can cause physical problems, and any number of factors can influence many aspects of the mind-body simultaneously. Rather than trying to diagnose your energy blocks yourself, see a qualified healthcare practitioner who is knowledgeable about energy therapy.

Meditation for the Body Chakra

According to yogic theory, the body contains seven primary energy centers called *chakras.* These psycho-spiritual energy centers roughly correspond to certain glands and/or nerve centers along the spine.

The *Saturn chakra,* or first chakra, is located at the base of your spine, and in it lies a powerful but often dormant energy source. Yoga philosophy calls this source of energy *kundalini energy* and compares it to a snake lying coiled and sleeping inside every person. Awakening this energy causes it to rise up through the chakras along the spine. When kundalini energy reaches the top chakra, located at the crown of the skull, you will be most open to the realization of your full potential and can most readily understand the nature of reality.

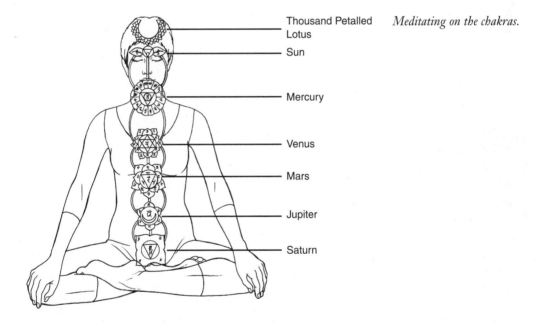

Thousand Petalled Lotus

Sun

Mercury

Venus

Mars

Jupiter

Saturn

Meditating on the chakras.

The seven major chakras are …

♦ **The Saturn, or Muladhara, chakra** at the base of the spine (source of dormant energy).

♦ **The Jupiter, or Swadhishthana, chakra** behind the lower abdomen (source of creative energy and passion).

Mindful Minute

Kundalini is often compared to a sleeping snake that, when awakened, is said to travel up through the chakras to the crown of the head. Once there, it can effect spiritual changes, such as enlightenment, and even, according to some, physical changes in the body, such as the ability to control previously involuntary bodily functions like your heartbeat. It is the energy of self-actualization.

- **The Mars, or Manipura, chakra** behind the navel (source of action energy and of the digestive fire, called *agni*).

- **The Venus, or Anahata, chakra** behind the heart (source of compassionate energy and emotion).

- **The Mercury, or Vishuddha, chakra** in the throat (source of communication energy).

- **The Sun, or Ajna, chakra** on the forehead at the site of the urna, or third eye (source of intuitive energy, unclouded perception, and intuition).

- **The Thousand Petalled Lotus, or Sahasrara, chakra** at the crown of the head (source of enlightenment energy and self-realization).

Each and every chakra can become blocked, and certain exercises, such as yoga postures, can help open them. Meditation, too, can help open them, particularly when the point of focus for meditation is a particularly troublesome chakra. If you're feeling blocked (or even if you would just like to enhance your energy in a certain area), try one or two—or all our chakra meditations.

Saturn Chakra Meditation: Coiled Energy

The Saturn chakra lies at the base of your spine, where kundalini energy waits to be awakened.

While sitting comfortably, close your eyes and focus your attention on the base of your spine. Sense the earth beneath you. Feel the connection between your Saturn chakra and the ground below. Feel the earth's energy powering your Saturn chakra and merging with your kundalini energy. Imagine this energy flowing slowly up your spine and out each of your limbs. Imagine it flowing upward and out the crown of your head. Imagine the energy pulsing and flashing, flushing and suffusing you with crackling, spectacular power. Now, allow the energy to dissipate slowly, falling back, leaving you energized but calm. Bring the energy back down into your Saturn chakra, ready to be activated when you need it. Feel again your connection with the earth's energy. Breathe.

The Saturn chakra connects you with the earth beneath you.

Jupiter Chakra Meditation: Creation Energy

Your Jupiter chakra is located in your lower abdomen, the pelvic area. It is the seat of your creative energy.

Sitting comfortably, close your eyes and focus your attention on your Jupiter chakra. Imagine your life-force energy concentrating in your lower abdomen. Imagine it intensifying, looking for an outlet. The energy builds, then transforms into pure creativity. Imagine this creativity mobilizing and flowing through your body, into your brain. Imagine it filling and activating your brain, preparing you to use it for whatever purpose you require. You become pure creativity. You can do anything. Breathe and imagine that creative energy stilling, holding, waiting for instructions. Open your eyes. Now go create something!

The Jupiter chakra is associated with creative energy and passion.

Mars Chakra Meditation: Action Energy

Your Mars chakra is located behind your navel. It is the seat of action energy and the digestive fire.

Sitting comfortably, close your eyes and focus your attention on your Mars chakra. Breathe deeply, and with each breath, imagine energy is flowing from the air around you and from the earth below you into your Mars chakra, where the energy accumulates. Imagine the warmth of your digestive fire stirring and sparking. Consciously release this fire energy into the rest of your body. Feel it flowing down your legs and into your feet, warming and readying you for action. Feel it flooding your chest and streaming down your arms. Feel your hands and fingers tingling with readiness. Imagine it flowing into your head and awakening your brain. Imagine your hair standing on end, energy streaming out of your scalp. Feel the energy straightening your spine, activating your muscles, and sharpening your mind. Now, open your eyes slowly and feel how energized you are. Time to accomplish something great!

The Mars chakra is the seat of action energy.

Venus Chakra: Heart Energy

Your Venus chakra is located behind your heart. It is the seat of compassionate energy.

Sitting comfortably, close your eyes and focus your attention on your Venus chakra. Breathe, and with each breath, imagine pure love streaming from your heart into the world. With your first 10 breaths, send compassion and love into the room where you are meditating. With the next 10 breaths, imagine the compassionate energy flooding out the doors to fill your entire house or apartment. With the next 10 breaths, imagine the love energy overflowing your house or apartment, spilling out the windows and doors and encompassing your neighborhood. The next 10 breaths flood your town or city with compassionate energy. The next 10 breaths fill your state. With the next 10 breaths, compassionate energy flows over the entire country, then the continent. With the last 10 breaths, embrace the entire planet in love. You can even extend out beyond the earth to the other planets, galaxies, and realms of existence. Feel how strong and far-reaching your energy can be. Before you know it, compassionate energy will start bouncing back to you.

The Venus chakra is associated with compassionate energy.

Mercury Chakra: Communication Energy

Your Mercury chakra is located in your throat. It is the seat of communication.

Sitting comfortably, close your eyes and focus your attention on your Mercury chakra. Breathe and imagine your throat opening. Consider how you tend to communicate, then imagine that when your Mercury chakra is open, you can communicate effortlessly, saying exactly what you mean. Imagine the power of communication flowing from the universe, God, or whatever source makes sense to you, into your Mercury chakra, then back out of you. Contemplate the way Ghandi, Buddha, Moses, Mohammed, and other gifted spiritual leaders were able to communicate with divine and inspirational simplicity. You, too, have the ability to communicate honestly, directly, and with great meaning.

The Mercury chakra is associated with communication.

Sun Chakra: The Third Eye

Your Sun chakra, or third eye, is located in the area of your forehead, between and just above your eyes. It is the seat of perceptive energy and unclouded thinking.

Try this one outside on a sunny day, if possible. Sitting comfortably (try a blanket, quilt, or mat on the grass), close your eyes and tilt your face toward the sun. Focus your attention on your Sun chakra and imagine yourself communicating with the sun. Feel its rays flowing directly into your Sun chakra. Imagine your Sun chakra opening, and instead of being blinded by the sun, imagine you can suddenly see everything with a clarity you've never experienced before. With your eyes still closed, imagine looking around you and seeing your house, your yard, or whatever your surroundings are in an entirely new light—the light of the enlightened sun and the light of un-clouded perception. How do things look? Sharper, more beautiful, radiating energy? How would you see the people in your life when looking at them through your Sun chakra? Now, open your eyes slowly. Do things look different than before? You might actually be seeing more clearly.

The Sun chakra, or third eye, is the seat of perceptive energy and unclouded thinking.

Thousand Petalled Lotus: Enlightenment

The Thousand Petalled Lotus is the chakra located near the crown of your head. It is the seat of enlightenment energy.

Sitting comfortably, close your eyes and focus your attention on your Thousand Petalled Lotus. Imagine it opening slowly, like the petals of a flower just beginning to bloom. Quietly repeat to yourself the words "All is one." Say them slowly, hearing the way they sound, contemplating what they mean. Say it again and again until you feel as if your Thousand Petalled Lotus is opening in full and magnificent bloom. Ommmm.

The Thousand Petalled Lotus is the chakra of bliss, the enlightenment energy.

Oops, Your Aura Is Showing!

With all this energy flowing around and through you, wouldn't you think you'd be able to see it? Actually, according to some, you can. Anyone can. All you have to do is develop your auric sight.

Auras are considered the visual result of the vibrations that surround every material object. People have them; objects have them; plants, animals, and trees have them; even articles of clothing, kitchen utensils, and bodies of water have them. Scientists will tell you that everything is made up of atoms, molecules, electrons, etc. and that these subcomponents of existence are by no means solid or still. They are filled with space and they move. So it makes sense that we are vibrating creatures, down to the atomic level.

We also emit electromagnetic energy. We emit heat. And some of that energy is emitted as ultraviolet light. According to auric theory, the part of our energy emitted as ultraviolet light is the part related to our consciousness, emotions, intentions, and spirituality. Auras, especially around the head, can reveal someone's basic character, mood at the moment, level of spiritual attainment, and even whether or not they are telling the truth.

The color of an aura is indicative of a person's basic mental, emotional, and spiritual state. Bright, clear colors mean a person is well intentioned, has a good nature, and is spiritually advanced. Dark, muddy, or cloudy colors denote bad intentions, materialistic natures, dark or depressed thoughts, pain, or anger. Auras can also contain little shoots and bursts of color within them. For example, bursts of purple are indicative of spiritual thoughts.

Although your instinct about a color can be more accurate than somebody else's list, use the following table as a guideline for interpreting the auras you see.

Aura Color	Qualities
Blue	Calm, relaxed, tranquil, maternal, attentive, and caring
Brown	Unspiritual, unsettled, anxious, nervous, and distracted
Gray	Depressed, pessimistic, negative, and repressed anger
Green	Intelligent, straightforward, a natural healer, quick thinker, close to nature, and a doer
Orange	Creative, inspiring, compassionate, powerful, and able to inspire and/or manipulate people
Pink	Protected and dominated by pure and radiant love

Aura Color	Qualities
Purple/violet	Spiritual, intuitive, psychic abilities, and dedicated to leading humanity toward the next step in higher consciousness
Red	Physical, materialistic, passionate, easily excited, an emphasis on the body, and intense emotion
Sulfur-colored	Discomfort, pain, irritation, and festering anger
Turquoise	Full of energy, a natural leader, and organized
White	Innocence, purity, and spirituality; or serious illness or altered state due to artificial substances
Yellow	Joyful, playful, and blissful; when gold, rare spiritual development and highly evolved

A Special Way of Seeing

Learning to see an aura isn't difficult, but it becomes even easier with practice. Experienced auric-seers barely have to concentrate to see someone's aura, and the colors and subcolors are obvious and clear. Like to give it a try? We'll teach you how to see your own aura. Then, you can also apply the same technique to look at someone else's aura.

Here's how it works:

♦ Stand about four or five feet from a large mirror. The wall or surface behind you should be white or off-white (any solid, unmarked light color will do, but white is easiest). Lighting should be adequate but not too bright, and the surface behind you should be evenly lit without bright spots or shadows.

♦ Fix your eyes on the reflection of your Sun chakra, that point between and about one or two inches up from your eyes (the third eye).

♦ Gaze at that point for one full minute without moving your eyes away. You can blink, but don't look anywhere else. Then, still without moving your eyes away from that point, survey the area around your

CAUTION

Relax _____

If you're having trouble seeing auras, try squinting slightly, or adjusting your eyes into a soft focus. Squinting makes it easier for some people to master the technique. Also, when looking at someone else's aura, have them wear a muted or pastel color. Bright clothing can interfere with a person's aura, as it has a bright aura all its own.

head via your peripheral vision. It might be hard to see at first, and you might be tempted to look directly at it, but don't. It works best if you keep your eyes fixed to your third eye. Eventually, you should see a sort of halo or illuminated area around your head. That is your aura. Notice the color or colors you see.

♦ The first time you try this exercise, you might only be able to keep it up for a couple minutes, but if you gradually increase your time to 10 or 15 minutes per day, you'll get better and better. You'll be able to see auras everywhere.

But what do the aura colors mean? Maybe your aura was a beautiful sky blue, a pale turquoise, or a sunny yellow. Different sources interpret colors in different ways, and so to some extent, only you can interpret the color of your aura and what it means (even though many people out there will be happy to interpret your aura for you, for a fee, of course). There are a few basic characteristics that many people agree belong to different colors, however, as listed in the table earlier in the chapter.

Some aura theorists believe that all young children and infants can clearly see auras, but they lose this natural ability as they age. Another theory is that in past ages, more people could see auras and that in paintings, halos around saints and religious figures such as Jesus and the Buddha were actually auras perceived by the artists. Aura theorists often advise that anyone claiming to be a spiritual leader should have a bright golden-yellow aura. If they don't, they shouldn't be trusted as spiritual guides. Legend has it that both Jesus and the Buddha had large golden auras around their heads and expansive pink auras around their entire bodies, suggesting spiritual perfection.

The Least You Need to Know

♦ We are all surrounded by, suffused with, and animated by life-force energy that also permeates and fuels the universe.

♦ Chakras are energy centers in the body, each governing certain types of energy and serving as portals for energy to enter and exit the body and be transformed.

♦ The electromagnetic field around all objects and living things is called an aura. You can learn to see auras, and their colors can reveal a person's inner nature, mood, and intentions.

Chapter 8

Sleep, Dreamwork, and Meditation

In This Chapter

◆ Are you real, or is this just a dream?

◆ Dream wisdom from Freud, Jung, and the Dalai Lama

◆ Meditation, sleep, and dreaming

◆ Remembering your dreams for self-exploration

◆ Lucid dreaming: living the dream

Who are you in your dreams? If you're like most people, sometimes you are *you*, sometimes you are watching yourself do things, and sometimes you are someone else altogether. You might have places you visit over and over again in your dream landscape that don't exist in real life; perhaps you know people in your dreams who don't exist in real life. But wait—when it comes to dreams, what is real life and what is dream life? Can we be sure which is which? And what does any of it have to do with meditation?

Self or Lack of Self—What Is Real?

One of the goals of meditation is to lose subjectivity in favor of an objective appre-
hension of truth. But you are you. You are yourself. How can you *not* perceive everything around you from your own point of view?

Eastern philosophers, especially, advocate losing the self and attachments to the
world, which are all products of subjective thinking, through the process of meditation which is not an easy task. Some might argue that such a task is impossible and
that any sense of the loss of self during meditation is just an illusion. Eastern philosophers would counter that instead, the self *itself* is the illusion, and that any sense of
self, or even of worldly reality, is the artificial construct.

Of course, at this point in our human evolution, we can't prove either hypothesis—
that self or lack of self is the "true" reality. Who is to say what truth is? We don't yet
know what truth is … at least not objectively. Many philosophers and scientists have
speculated and theorized, but humanity has yet to agree on the nature of truth when
it comes to the self.

But what about when we dream? Dreams and sleep have been studied extensively.
Have we come to any conclusions that are more concrete when it comes to the dream
realm? We know a few things. For example, brain waves exhibited during dream sleep
are almost indistinguishable from brain waves exhibited when awake. That's why
dream sleep (or *REM sleep*) is often called *paradoxical sleep*. Yet dream sleep obviously
isn't the same as being awake. Falling asleep is, in a sense, losing the self, or at least,
the conscious self. Conscious control takes a break, allowing the *unconscious mind* to
take over. Dream sleep is like being awake with the unconscious mind behind the
wheel. The unconscious mind consists of the thoughts, feelings, desires, and impulses
that, although the individual is unaware of them, influence his or her behavior.

From A to Om

Paradoxical sleep is another name for the stage of sleep usually referred to as
REM (rapid eye movement) sleep, the stage of sleep at which dreams occur. During
this stage of sleep, brain waves resemble brain waves when the individual is awake,
yet muscles are completely relaxed, producing a paralyzing effect (so we don't get up
and act out those dreams). This lack of muscle tone is called *atonia*.

The unconscious mind is a vast, unexplored territory. Who knows how subjective,
objective, or even "real" the unconscious is? Many philosophers/psychologists have

also speculated on this question—Plato and St. Augustine, Freud and Jung, to name a few prominent thinkers—but the workings of the unconscious mind can't be measured. The best we can do is try to remember our dreams, those leftover symbols, landmarks, and glimpses of the topography of our unconscious mind.

So dare we turn French philosopher Descartes's idea, "I think, therefore, I am," on its head and say, "I dream, therefore, I am not"? Or "I dream, therefore, for a short while, I am not"? Our dream lives might be as close as we can get to peering over the edge of reality and seeing what else is out there, because only in sleep is our conscious mind no longer able to exercise its subjectivity.

Separating the Dreamer from the Dream

Let's explore that dream world a little further. Let's say you have a dream that you're a bird flying in the sky, looking down on the earth. Are you quite sure, after you awake, that you dreamed you were a bird? Could you, perhaps, be a bird dreaming you are a person? Chinese philosopher Chuang-tzu once dreamed he was a butterfly who was very happy with himself. When he awoke, he, too, wondered whether he was a man dreaming he was a butterfly, or a butterfly dreaming he was a man. You'll probably agree that in both cases (yours and Chuang-tzu's), the first scenario is probably the "real" one. But then, why did you dream you were a bird, or a cow, or someone of the opposite gender, or even someone a lot like you but not exactly the same? Or for that matter, why did you dream that you did something you would never do or experienced something you've never experienced?

Theories abound. Perhaps you're working out emotional dilemmas by acting out different realities in your dreams. Maybe your brain is simply sifting through the huge amount of sensory stimuli you accumulate each day to keep the important stuff and discard the unimportant stuff, like some ethereal secretary cleaning out your mental file cabinet. Or maybe all that neuron firing is totally random.

Whatever your personal opinion, your dreams can be a tool to help you know yourself better. They can also be a tool for your meditation sessions, just as meditation sessions can be a tool for dreamwork. Together, dreams and meditation can be the key to unlocking the secrets of

> **Mindful Minute**
>
> René Descartes (1596–1650) was a French philosopher and mathematician who is sometimes called the father of modern philosophy. Descartes attempted to apply rational, inductive reasoning to philosophy using principles inherent in science and math. He once said, "In our search for the direct road to truth, we should busy ourselves with no object about which we cannot attain a certitude equal to that of the demonstration of arithmetic and geometry."

your unconscious, and unlocking that least-known part of yourself can lead to greater self-knowledge.

Dreams have traditionally been of great inspiration to artists. Salvador Dali, William Blake, Henri Rousseau, and Jasper Johns all used dream imagery in their paintings. George Frederic Handel reportedly heard the ending of his famous work, *The Messiah*, in a dream. Ingmar Bergman, a renowned Swedish director, frequently used his own dream imagery in his films. Orson Welles used his own dream imagery in his film *The Trial*. Mary Shelley created the Frankenstein monster from a nightmare. Edgar Allen Poe, Robert Louis Stevenson, William Burroughs, Jack Kerouac, Franz Kafka, and Charlotte Brontë all used dreams for inspiration and imagery in their writing.

Freud: The Royal Road to the Unconscious

Sigmund Freud's book *The Interpretation of Dreams* is arguably the most important and influential text on dream interpretation. Freudian theories on dream interpretation as a key to the unconscious mind are widespread and have influenced Western culture to an immeasurable extent. Freud called dreams the "royal road to the unconscious." He saw them as important keys to unraveling the unconscious aspects of the human psyche. He believed dreams contained symbols that represented inner conflicts, repressed emotions, and often angry, violent, or "inappropriate" sexual thoughts. In fact, Freud has been widely criticized for asserting that human nature is not essentially good at its core, but essentially driven by base instincts.

Because of societal structure, however, base instinct is often inappropriate. We can't walk around grabbing food whenever we want it, dropping to the floor to sleep whenever we are tired, lashing out and hurting people whenever we are angry or threatened, or ravishing anyone who catches our fancy. Instead, according to Freudian theory, we repress these desires into our unconscious, along with memories of our past experiences (particularly from childhood), things we do that we wish we hadn't done, and things that were done to us that angered, scared, or hurt us.

> **Mindful Minute**
>
> Sigmund Freud (1856–1939) was an Austrian physician, neurologist, and the founder of psychoanalysis, a technique of talk therapy for investigating unconscious mental processes and treating psychological disorders and illnesses.

In our dreams, the window to the unconscious cracks open, and we get little peeks of what we've pushed down there, manifested as symbols and stories our psyche weaves out of all the bits and pieces, wishes, and fears. Interpreting our dreams, ideally with the help of a trained therapist, can explain many of our otherwise inexplicable problems in life: phobias (fears, such as of heights or enclosed spaces), depression, self-destructive feelings, obsessions, fantasies, or problems with relationships and self-esteem.

Freud also once said that we don't have dreams so they can be interpreted, and that dreams were merely "guardians of sleep," keeping internal conflicts from awakening us. But perhaps they can also be used to solve problems and to understand ourselves better.

Jung: Universal Archetypes

Carl Jung was a colleague of Freud's who later went his own way, broadening upon Freud's theories. Jung interpreted mental and emotional disturbances as attempts by an individual to find personal and spiritual wholeness. He believed in the unconscious, but divided it into two types, personal and collective. In the collective unconscious, Jung theorized, lie the archetypes shared by all humankind. These archetypes represent societal or human beliefs and morals, and are represented in ancient mythology, fairytales, and other universal stories.

> **Mindful Minute**
>
> Carl Jung (1875–1961) was a Swiss psychiatrist who founded the analytical school of psychology. Jung coined many common psychological terms used today, such as "complexes" (as in "inferiority complex") and the notion of extroverts and introverts. He believed dreams were attempts to work toward wholeness by integrating the different levels of the unconscious.

To Jung as well as Freud, dreams are keys to the unconscious. But for Jung, dreams from the collective unconscious represent our basic human beliefs. When we face dilemmas in life, these archetypes tend to arise with greater frequency, helping us along our road to personal fulfillment.

Jung believed that each of us is seeking wholeness and that integrating our personal unconscious and our collective unconscious was the way to achieve this wholeness. Because both the personal and collective unconscious can be represented in our dreams, interpreting those dreams, even if just for ourselves, can be a way to begin this integration. To Jung, life was a journey of growth and self-examination was the vehicle.

The Dalai Lama: Finding the Clear Light of Sleep

In Tibetan philosophy, sleep is like a mini death, a sort of practice for death. The period of time between death and rebirth when the soul is in a sort of transition (known in Tibetan Buddhism as the *bardo*) is comparable to the period of time between deep sleep and dream sleep, called the Clear Light of Sleep. Ideally, although asleep, the soul is conscious, yet this kind of consciousness is marked by complete clarity of mind, inner peace, and understanding. While some Westerners consider sleep as an unconscious time, Tibetan Buddhists believe sleep is ideally a superconscious, super-aware period.

Mindful Minute

The Dalai Lama is believed by Tibetan Buddhists to be a reincarnation of the Buddha. When the Dalai Lama dies, his soul is thought to enter a new body who, after being identified by traditional tests, will become the next Dalai Lama. The current and fourteenth Dalai Lama, Tenzin Gyatso, was forced into exile in India on March 16, 1959, by the Communist Chinese government occupying Tibet. In 1989, he received the Nobel Peace Price for leading nonviolent opposition to Chinese rule of Tibet.

Maybe that doesn't sound too restful. How can you relax if you are superconscious? Actually, this state is also the ideal meditation state, and many religions and philosophies that advocate meditation believe meditation is more restorative than sleep. In fact, many seasoned meditators are said to require only a few hours of sleep each night because they derive such profound rest from a deep meditative state.

Bliss Byte

For those who find it too difficult to sit in silent meditation, try studying your dreams for further self-knowledge. Keep a dream journal and a small light by your bed. When you have a dream, jot it down before you forget what happened in the dream. It's amazing the new insights dreams will supply you with. Thinking about and understanding your dreams helps you transform current problems, joys, and encounters in ways you never dreamed of!

About dreams and meditation, the Dalai Lama once said, "Tibetan Buddhism considers sleep to be a form of nourishment, like food, that restores and refreshes the body. Another type of nourishment is *samadhi*, or meditative concentration. If one becomes advanced enough in the practice of meditative concentration, then this itself sustains or nourishes the body."

As you can see, the lines between sleeping, dreaming, and meditating sometimes blur. The goals are similar, the results are similar, and the brain-wave patterns are similar. The philosophies on these subjects vary widely but also have their similarities. Dreaming, meditating, and self-study corresponding with both are all roads to greater self-knowledge and, ideally, greater bliss.

Meditation, Sleep, and Consciousness

But let's get back to science for a bit. Many people have compared the sleep cycle to the meditation process, and the similarities are striking. Meditation seems to be like a fusion of unconscious and conscious states. Brain waves look like the meditator is asleep (and admittedly, sometimes meditators do fall asleep). But even in studies where the meditator had to press a button to signal each progressively deeper stage of meditation and was able to do so successfully, brain-wave patterns still were similar to those of sleep.

Understanding the Sleep Cycles

To best compare the states of sleep and meditation, it will help to have a little background on the sleep cycle. Although sleep cycles vary in different people, most of us go through several sleep cycles of between 90 and 110 minutes every night.

The sleep cycle consists of four stages plus dream sleep. In stage 1, the sleeper becomes increasingly drowsy and drifts into sleep. Brain-wave activity changes from random, fast waves to regular *alpha waves* as drowsiness sets in. Then, when we fall asleep, even slower *theta waves* dominate.

> **From A to Om** _____
>
> **Alpha waves** are brain waves that cycle up and down on an EEG about 8 to 12 times per second and usually correspond with a drowsy state or, in meditation, a very relaxed yet alert state. Slower **theta waves** cycle between three to seven times per second and usually correspond with light sleep or deep meditation. The slowest **delta waves** cycle between one half to two times per second and usually correspond with deep sleep.

In stage 2, sleep becomes deeper, though the sleeper is still fairly easy to awaken. EEGs during stage 2 reveal regular waves with occasional bursts of energy, indicating brain activity is still sporadic. In stage 3, brain waves become slower and more even while body temperature and heart rate slow down. During stage 3, the sleeper is difficult to awaken and brain waves are dominated by large, slow *delta waves*. In stage 4, the deepest level, brain-wave patterns are also dominated by delta waves. This deepest level of sleep usually begins about an hour after the commencement of stage 1.

After reaching stage 4, the stages reverse. When the sleeper reaches stage 1 again (or sometimes stage 2), he or she enters REM sleep. REM stands for rapid eye movement (so called because the eyes move visibly during REM sleep), and it is dream sleep. During REM sleep, brain waves resemble waking brain waves, becoming faster, more active, and more random. Blood pressure, heart rate, and breath rate all increase as well. Muscles, however, become temporarily paralyzed. This paralysis keeps us from physically acting out our dreams (so the theory goes), and when this mechanism malfunctions, sleepwalking may result.

After REM sleep, the sleeper usually awakens, even if very briefly or not fully. Then the cycle starts again. The time each stage lasts varies in individuals and also throughout the night. In the first few cycles, REM sleep is comparatively brief but takes up a larger portion of the cycle toward morning. Naps taken in the morning, or an hour or two after awakening from a night's sleep, are often primarily REM sleep. Afternoon naps contain less REM sleep. Then the whole process begins again in the evening.

Meditation, too, is thought to occur in four cycles of progressively deeper concentration. Meditators don't dream, however (unless they fall asleep). Instead, they seem to be able to remain in a state that is not really sleep yet not really waking, either, at least according to EEG readings. One study showed experienced Zen meditators exhibiting a mixture of alpha and theta waves, the characteristic brain-wave patterns of light sleep.

> **CAUTION**
>
> **Relax**
>
> Never practice meditation while driving! Falling asleep is common during meditation, so you certainly don't want that to happen as you speed down the interstate. The only kind of meditation to practice while driving is mindfulness meditation, during which you become acutely aware of what you are doing. Everyone should drive mindfully!

Fusing the Sleeping and Waking Consciousness

Meditation is essentially a fusion of sleeping and waking consciousness. What does all this have to do with dreaming? If dreaming is the key to unlocking our unconscious minds and meditating is a way to sleep while staying awake, meditation might also be able to reveal our unconscious minds while conscious.

Meditation can also be an arena in which we can consider our dreams, open our minds to their meaning, and perhaps gain new insights about ourselves.

Some cultures, as in Tibetan Buddhism, believe dreams are essential in our life experience. According to these beliefs, we transcend into our dream world upon death. Understanding and working with your dreams is important not only to your life, but also to your death, which will become your life … which will become your death … which will become your life …. Get the picture?

Bliss Byte

Have you ever thought you heard someone call your name just as you were falling asleep? What about hearing music playing or a phone ringing? Do you remember a fragment of someone standing in the doorway, a chair next to your bed starting to move, or even seeing brightly colored shapes? You've had a hypnogogic experience. The *hypnogogic state* is the transitional state between waking and sleeping; it has the quality of a hallucinatory fragment. The *hypnopompic state* is a similar experience but occurs in the transition between sleeping and waking.

Do You Remember Your Dreams?

Although most people remember their dreams, a few people typically don't, and some even claim they don't dream. Even though people who sleep experience REM sleep, no one has definitively proven that they always dream during REM sleep. This period is considered dream sleep because in research studies, when people are awakened during REM sleep, most of the time they can vividly describe a dream—but not always.

If you're like most people, however, you do remember your dreams some of the time. Would you like to remember them more often? Like anything else, remembering your dreams is just a matter of practice. People who study dreams suggest that keeping a dream journal next to your bed is one of the best ways to train yourself to remember your dreams. Dreams are always freshest right after awakening because awakening typically occurs just after REM sleep.

To begin using a dream journal …

   ◆ Find or buy a blank notebook. On the first page, write the following statement (or a different statement about your purpose that you create):

   > My dream journal contains clues to myself. By recording my dreams each day, I am making a commitment to know myself better. By meditating on the contents of this dream journal, I am moving toward self-actualization.

   ◆ Keep the dream journal and a pen next to your bed so you can quickly jot down the impressions you remember from your dream whenever you awaken. (Dream memories usually fade very quickly, so write them down immediately, even if you are still drowsy.)

   ◆ Every morning for two weeks, try to piece together the night's dreams immediately upon awakening and without opening your eyes. Recall the imagery, the sequence, the characters, and the setting. Then, open your eyes and immediately write down everything you can remember.

♦ Can't quite find the words to describe your dream or a part of it? Draw a picture.

♦ Whenever possible during these first two weeks, take a nap one to two hours after you wake up in the morning. REM sleep is most prevalent at this time of the day. Don't forget to keep your dream journal by your side. (Most of us can't afford to nap at this time, of course, but if you have the kind of schedule that allows it, give it a try. If nothing else, maybe you can squeeze in a nap on the weekend.)

♦ Each night before you go to bed, or whenever you're about to take a nap, spend 5 to 10 minutes meditating by relaxing and repeating the mantra: "I will dream, I will remember." Or if you are facing a particular decision, ask yourself what you should decide and leave your mind open to answers. Don't try to answer your own question consciously. Just let the question hang there as you fall asleep.

> **Mindful Minute**
>
> For more on dreams and keeping a dream journal, read *The Complete Idiot's Guide to Interpreting Your Dreams* (Alpha Books, 1998).

♦ After two weeks, go back and read your dream journal, then write freely about any patterns, symbols, or meanings you perceive. You should be in the habit of recording your dreams by now. Keep it up!

♦ Dreaming + recording = self-actualizing!

Dreamwork Meditations

Once you are used to recording your dreams, you'll find you remember them more often and their meanings come to you more easily. Sure, sometimes it helps to have a professional psychoanalyst interpret your dreams, but you may be able to discover their meanings on your own. Who knows what's in your subconscious mind better than you do? You are best equipped to imagine what your dreams say about you.

> **Bliss Byte**
>
> If you find it difficult to grab a pen and write legibly when you first awaken, try tape-recording your dreams instead. Keep a tape recorder by your bed, and whenever you awaken from a dream, gab to your heart's content about all the details you can remember. You can transcribe your dreams later, or simply keep a library of dream tapes for your listening pleasure. Label tapes with dates and the titles you give your dreams.

If you want to try dreamwork, the following meditations can help you get started. Before any dreamwork meditation session, relax, sit comfortably with your back straight, and begin by focusing on your breathing.

◆ Consider an image, place, or person you've seen in more than one dream. Imagine all the details. How does the image, person, or place look? Fill in the things you can't remember by letting your imagination produce the details. For example, if you have recurring dreams about a house, picture the house in your mind. What color is it? What are the details of the architecture? Does it change from dream to dream, even though you know it's the same house? Imagine each of the rooms. What is the furniture like? Are there people at home? Who owns the house? Why are you there or not there? Keep digging by asking yourself as many questions as you can about your chosen image, place, or person, even if you aren't sure you know the answers. Maybe you know the answers subconsciously, which is where you are trying to go. If thoughts occur to you about the meaning of the dream or what it represents, great! If they don't, don't press it. Just keep filling in the dream with your imagination and see where it takes you. When your unconscious is ready to reveal the meaning, it will reveal the meaning.

◆ Think of a good or pleasant dream you had. Go through the sequence of your dream in your mind, reliving the order of events. Does the chronology make sense to you in any way? Now consider the characters of the dream, if any. Are they people you know, strangers, or a combination? Are you in the dream as you, or are you watching yourself in the dream? Now imagine the setting. Where did the dream take place? Did the setting change? Why do you think the dream was set where it was set? Now, consider why the dream is pleasurable to you. Did the dream give you a secure, comfortable feeling? Was it about love, success, or happiness? What does the dream say about you? What did you do in the dream: fly, dance, relax? Pleasant dreams are not inherently "good" dreams or "better" dreams than dreams that have more challenging or disturbing content. All dreams are meant to help us work through subconscious issues, and we should avoid labeling any dream as "good" or "bad."

◆ Think of a disturbing dream you had. Break it down into all its elements. What bothered you about it? Was it the way you were in the dream or the way someone else was? Was it scary, sad, or tragic? Now imagine what the dream could represent. Are you nervous about something that is going to happen? Are you feeling like one of your relationships isn't right? If the dream was about death or destruction, these things usually symbolize change rather than something necessarily negative. Are you anticipating, dreading, or even wishing for a major change in your life? How could you interpret the dream in a positive way, as instructing you about how you feel and what you should do? Disturbing dreams are not inherently "bad," but can be profoundly beautiful and provocative sources for positive personal growth.

> **Bliss Byte**
>
> *Boo!* Do you have scary dreams? Although nightmares are more common in children, adults have them sometimes, too, especially during stressful times. Learning how to dream lucidly—that is, to realize you are dreaming during your dream—is an effective way to take control of your scary dreams and turn them into empowering dreams during which you face your fears and challenges. *Note:* If your nightmares don't let up or are very disturbing and are affecting your waking life, explore them with the help of a licensed therapist or mental health professional. Your subconscious mind could be trying to bring something important to your attention.

Using Your Dreams to Empower Meditation

As you seek to know yourself better through meditation, your dreams can be a powerful tool. Use them in your meditation as if they are secret passwords allowing you access to ever-new, hidden levels of yourself. You say you keep dreaming about a friendly dog? A waterfall? A dark castle? An attractive stranger who holds you in his or her arms? Clues! What do they mean? There's your meditation. Focus on the clue. Examine it. Dissect it. Name it. Describe it. Look at it from all sides. Apply it to yourself, to your loved ones, and to your dilemmas. Where does it fit? Which lock does it open? Eventually, you'll find the answer.

Or maybe you won't. Plenty of people will argue that some dreams are just dreams, that they are random images or discarded, insignificant experiences your brain is simply processing before tucking them away. But trust your intuition. Some dreams just "feel" meaningful or seem like they hold answers for you. Focus on those dreams.

Lucid Dreaming

Wouldn't it be fun if, while you were dreaming, you could *know* you were dreaming? Maybe this has actually happened to you before. All of us daydream occasionally, allowing our minds to drift off to fanciful places we create with our imagination. During daydreams we are awake and consciously aware. Lucid dreams, however, are not daydreams.

Lucid dreams occur during the sleep state. When lucid dreaming, you become aware that you are dreaming although you are still asleep. For some, lucid dreaming, the conscious awareness that you are dreaming, is a lifelong goal. According to one survey, about 58 percent of people have had at least one lucid dream, but only about 20 percent have them frequently. But dreaming lucidly is a skill that can be developed and refined. Lucid dreaming can then be harnessed as a further way to direct the mind. Lucid dreaming is itself a sort of meditation wherein the mind has powers it doesn't have while awake.

Lucid dreams have been proven to exist. Subjects hooked up to an EEG were instructed to move their eyes in a specific pattern using right-left motions when they became aware during their dreams that they were dreaming. (The eye movement was the only movement they could make because other muscles are in temporary paralysis during REM sleep.) In several studies, while the EEG revealed that subjects were indeed sound asleep and dreaming, the subjects did give the appropriate signal and, when awakened, described remembering to give the signal in their dreams. Lucid dreaming can allow you to confront and conquer fears, enjoy supernatural abilities or situations you could never actually experience like flying or breathing underwater, and even explore symbolic representations of yourself and your life challenges. What a great opportunity for fun and personal growth!

Some people find lucid dreaming difficult, and it is definitely a skill to master, especially for adults (children find it easier). In Tibetan thought, it is important to study your dreams so that you will have some understanding of how to face your dreams and work with them rather than have them control you. For example, if the elevator is going down in your dream, you can be aware that you want it to go up and help your dream along. Of course, you take with this the consequences of your actions. You can find incredible paths in the choices you take. For example, if you choose for the elevator to go up because you believe you will reach new heights of understanding, there is nothing to fear, even if it seems fearful. If you fear your choice of making the elevator go up, your dream will reflect this and help you to see your indecisiveness and its consequences more clearly.

The cultivation of lucid dreaming is about building consciousness in your dreams, so that eventually there is no separation between the two worlds. Your waking and dreaming states are both profound and meaningful. When you learn to dream lucidly, both waking and dreaming states become less stressful because you, in all your dimensions, are an active part of this miraculous life, in all its many forms.

Now, this is different from "control." Lucid dreaming isn't a chance to control every facet of your dream, for example, purely to derive pleasure. You probably won't be able to force yourself to dream, every night, that you are flying, or a millionaire, or married to a supermodel. Lucid dreaming is more about being an active participant rather than a passive observer in the workings of your subconscious. As in the practice of meditation, where eventually you merge with the object of your meditation, in dreaming, we merge with our dream. For this reason, dreams can be an important part of developing and refining our meditation practice.

To help yourself dream lucidly, or simply to dream with more clarity and to remember your dreams better, try the following tips:

- Meditate! People who meditate are more likely to dream lucidly.

- Pick a symbol from your memory that represents something significant to you but is easy to visualize—a star, a statue, or an ordinary object, for example. Decide this will be your lucidity object, and when you see it in your dream, you'll know you are dreaming.

- When you awaken in the middle of the night from a dream, keep imagining the dream to get yourself back into it again. Tell yourself that when you return, you'll know you are dreaming.

- Before you go to sleep, tell yourself you will be on the lookout for things that couldn't happen in reality. When you recognize these absurdities in your dream (for example, incongruous environmental elements like a fish swimming through the air, or something impossible occurring, such as being able to float or change locations instantaneously), you might realize you are dreaming.

Mindful Minute

According to one study, people who meditate are more likely to experience lucid dreams than people who don't meditate. Children are also more likely to experience lucid dreams than adults, and the ability seems to diminish with age. Another study showed that 63 percent of 10-year-olds experienced monthly lucid dreams, while 58 percent of 11-year-olds and only 36 percent of 12-year-olds experienced monthly lucid dreams.

- Slow down the pace of your waking life.

- Spend some quiet, reflective time before going to sleep. Turn off the TV!

- Practice falling asleep more slowly, gradually lengthening breaths and the time between waking and sleeping.

- Try to increase your awareness upon first awakening. See if you can become conscious of your very first waking breath.

♦ Avoid using alarm clocks. If you have to, you have to, but they aren't the kindest way to awaken. There are alarm clocks available that waken you by a soft bell (or music) that gradually increases in loudness so as to gradually waken you from your sleep.

♦ Get enough sleep! You may need more or less than other people in your family, but get as much as you need (few people in our society today get enough sleep). Research shows that the average adult needs about $7^1/_2$ hours of sleep each night. But you might need more or less than that, depending on your individual circadian rhythm. Between seven and nine hours nightly is usually sufficient for most adults.

So put on your safari garb and go take a nap!

The Least You Need to Know

♦ Philosophers from ancient times to modern times have speculated on the nature of reality, the self, and dreams.

♦ The sleep cycle, when measured on an EEG, contains similarities to meditation.

♦ Meditation contains elements of both sleeping and waking states, making it seem to be a fusion of the two states.

♦ Remembering your dreams and meditating upon the themes, images, symbols, and stories in those dreams can aid you in your quest for self-knowledge.

♦ Lucid dreaming is the ability to know you are dreaming during your dream and act accordingly.

Chapter 9

You and Your Three Bodies

In This Chapter

- ◆ How many bodies can a body have? (three)
- ◆ How many sheaths of existence can a body have? (five)
- ◆ What happens to the body after death?
- ◆ Past-life meditation

We've been talking a lot about how meditation can improve the health and functioning of your mind-body. But we could just as well have said that meditation improves the health and functioning of your *subtle body*. According to yoga philosophy, we are much more than our physical bodies and our mental processes. We actually have three bodies—the physical, subtle, and supersubtle—and only one of them shows up in the mirror.

A Glimpse of the Three Bodies

Yoga philosophy states that when we consider all our physical, mental, and spiritual layers, they contribute to what are called the three bodies. The three bodies consist of the *physical body* you see in the mirror plus two other layers that include and extend out from it: the *astral*, or subtle body, and the *causal*, or supersubtle body. Throughout the subtle body are energy channels through which our life-energy flows.

Your physical body is the body you see in the mirror, the body you can learn to control through self-discipline. The rules for living (yamas and niyamas) in Chapter 3, physical exercise such as yoga postures and breath control, are ways to get your physical body under control so it doesn't interfere with your attempts to know your higher self.

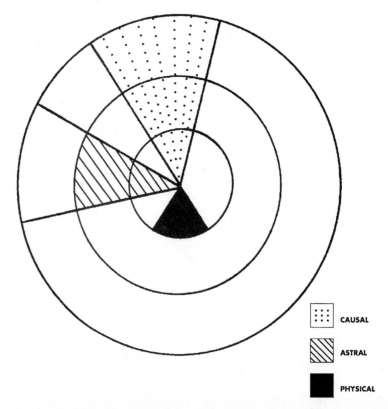

From A to Om

The **physical body**, **astral body**, and **causal body** are all aspects of the whole self, including all its various layers and energy fields. The physical body is the body we see in the mirror. The astral body contains the realm of the mind and emotions, the chakras, and life force. The causal body contains the spirit.

The astral, or subtle, body is the realm of your mind and chakra energy system. The subtle body penetrates down though the physical body. Breathing exercises can also help control the subtle body, as can the practice of sense withdrawal and concentration.

Last is the causal body, which is the finest body, the supersubtle body. The causal body contains the spirit itself and is your connection to the universe, God, and/or bliss. It penetrates down through the subtle and physical bodies. It's the body that understands the concept of "all is one." You can communicate with this body through meditation and the attainment of samadhi, or enlightenment.

The causal body (the spirit) is the finest and penetrates down through the astral or subtle (mind) and physical (gross) bodies. The astral or subtle body penetrates only down through the physical (or gross) body. So the three bodies are interpenetrating—from the finest to the grossest levels.

CAUSAL

ASTRAL

PHYSICAL

Just as knowing ourselves includes delving into our unconscious minds, it also includes becoming familiar with and learning to maintain the three bodies.

Balancing Your Five Sheaths of Existence

But you are even more complex than your three bodies! Within these three bodies are five sheaths of existence, which are like envelopes or layers of energy, each containing and governing different aspects of your body. Learning to control these layers, one by one, will eventually clear the way for productive meditation. The five sheaths of existence are as follows:

- The *physical sheath*, or actual physical body

- The *vital sheath*, or layer of prana surrounding and flowing through and from the body

- The *mind sheath*, or your emotions and thoughts, with energy extending slightly beyond the vital sheath

- The *intellect sheath*, or realm of higher knowledge and unclouded thought, which extends beyond the mind sheath

- The *bliss sheath*, or realm of divine energy that houses our potential for inner peace and happiness

The five sheaths of existence are similar to the three bodies—each of the finer sheaths penetrates down through the less-fine, all the way through the physical. See the following table to discover how the three bodies relate directly to the five sheaths of existence.

The Three Bodies	The Five Sheaths of Existence
Physical body (*Sharira*)	Physical sheath (*Anna-maya-kosha*)
	Prana sheath (*Prana-maya-kosha*)
Astral body (*Sukshma Sharira*)	Mind sheath (*Mano-maya-kosha*)
	Intellect sheath (*Vijnana-maya-kosha*)
Causal body (*Karana Sharira*)	Bliss sheath (*Ananda-maya-kosha*)

Meditations for the Physical Realm

First let's look at the most familiar of your bodies, your physical body. The physical realm contains two sheaths of existence: the physical sheath and the vital sheath. The physical body is your body itself. The Sanskrit word for the physical body, *sharira*, can literally be translated as "food envelope." The vital body is your breath sheath, or layer of prana that flows through and from you. This second, vital sheath extends slightly beyond the physical sheath. The vital sheath is often paired with the mind sheath as well; you can think of the vital sheath as a bridge between the physical and astral bodies, existing partly in each.

Diligent practice to keep each of these layers in check will make meditation easier, but you can also use these sheaths of existence as subjects of focus (concentration) for your meditation sessions. Need some suggestions? Keep reading.

1. The Physical Body: Housekeeping

Sit comfortably with your back straight and your eyes closed. Turn your attention to your feet and say or think the following words:

- *Feet, be calm and tranquil. Wait here in peace until I need you again.*

- *Legs, be calm and tranquil. Wait here in peace until I need you again.*

- *Hips, be calm and tranquil. Wait here in peace until I need you again.*

- *Stomach, be calm and tranquil. Wait here in peace until I need you again.*

- *Chest, be calm and tranquil. Wait here in peace until I need you again.*

- *Back, be calm and tranquil. Wait here in peace until I need you again.*

- *Arms, be calm and tranquil. Wait here in peace until I need you again.*

- *Hands, be calm and tranquil. Wait here in peace until I need you again.*

- *Neck, be calm and tranquil. Wait here in peace until I need you again.*

- *Head, be calm and tranquil. Wait here in peace until I need you again.*

- *Face, be calm and tranquil. Wait here in peace until I need you again.*

Bliss Byte

To keep your physical body in control, it helps to emphasize personal hygiene. We're sure you are perfectly clean, but a little extra attention to cleanliness, including a good daily scrub down, a high-fiber diet to keep your insides clean, breathing exercises designed for cleansing, and keeping your clothes and external environment clean will help keep your body maintained and less distracted during meditation.

Now, scan your body and feel how relaxed it is. If any part of you isn't "being" calm and tranquil, ask it again. Now, say the following:

◆ *Body, as you rest and wait, reveal your wisdom to me.*

Rest and wait. Be aware of your body. Is any part presenting itself to your attention? Listen to what your body has to tell you. Did you notice until now that your knee aches? It needs your attention. Is your neck revealing its stiffness? It needs your attention. Are you hungry or tired? You need to eat or sleep. Now, say the following:

◆ *Body, I will attend to you. Now, I need you again. Thank you for your wisdom.*

2. The Vital Body: The Breath

Sit comfortably with your back straight. Close your eyes. Imagine your vital body, the body of life-force energy emanating from your physical body. Imagine the life-force energy flowing in and out of you through your nose, your mouth, and your skin. Imagine it swirling and dancing around you.

Now, visualize your physical body. Imagine how good it would feel if it were even more intensely suffused with life-force energy. You can fill yourself with this beautiful and vibrant energy simply by breathing.

Slowly inhale through your nose to a count of five. Imagine the life-force energy flowing into you as you inhale, filling your legs, your body, your arms, your head, and gathering up all the stagnant energy that's been lingering in the corners and crevices of your physical body for too long. Now, to a count of 10, exhale even more slowly through your mouth with pursed lips. Let the exhale make a whispering sound, and imagine you are shooting out all the stagnant energy that is now transformed, purified, and revitalized in your body as positive life-affirming energy that you are releasing for the benefit of others. Breathe in again in the same manner to a count of 10, and exhale in the same manner to a count of 20. Now, let your breathing return to normal again and feel the life-force energy swirling and dancing inside you, healing and freeing the systems of your body and filling your being with joy.

CAUTION **Relax**

If you're overweight, you can use breath meditation as a "vital" part of your fitness program. Concentrating on the breath promotes mindfulness and helps increase your lung capacity. Let that diaphragm muscle gently but fully expand and contract during deep-breathing exercises. As this area grows stronger, you'll notice your body's vitality beginning to change.

> **Bliss Byte** _____
>
> As we age, our breathing tends to become more shallow and we use less of our lung capacity. Conscious practice of deep breathing—filling up the lower chest first and not involving the shoulders during the inhalation—can help maintain efficient and effective breathing through our entire lives. Watch your profile in a mirror as you breathe. If your shoulders rise and fall, your breathing is too shallow. Place your hands on your lowest ribs and, as you breathe in, consciously expand the lowest part of your lungs with air. Some experts believe that deep breathing itself increases longevity. So use those lungs—all of them!

Meditations for the Astral Realm

The astral body is the realm of your mind and emotions. It's your *feeling* body, and it extends slightly beyond your vital body. Everything you think and feel lives as energy in you and around you, out as far as the astral body. Perhaps that is why people can sometimes "sense" each other's feelings. When you stand next to someone, you are closer to that person's astral body than you are to his or her physical body.

The astral body contains two more sheaths of existence, the mind sheath—the layer of thoughts and emotions—and the intellect sheath—the layer of higher understanding through which you can begin to see the true nature of reality. Just as the vital sheath is considered a bridge between the physical and the astral bodies, the intellect sheath is considered a bridge between the astral (subtle) body and the causal (supersubtle) body. You can learn to control the mind and intellect sheaths through breath control (which helps to center the mind), the practice of sense withdrawal, and concentration exercises. You can also include these layers as the subject of concentration for your meditations.

3. The Mind Sheath: Feeling

Try this exercise with a partner. Sit facing each other. One person places his hands, palms up, on the knees. The other person places her hands, palms down, over but not touching the other person's hands. Do not touch knees or hands. Keep them just slightly apart.

You and your partner may now close your eyes. The person with palms facing down will be the energy sender, and the person with palms facing up will be the energy recipient. After you try this exercise one way, switch palm positions and do it the other way:

The person with the palms facing down concentrates on expressing joy. Imagine joy radiating from your palms and flowing into your partner's hands. Take your time with this. After a few minutes, slowly shift your emotion to sadness. Feel sadness in your body, radiating into your hands and into your partner's hands. Take your time with this. Then, try other emotions: playfulness, anger, hope. Take your time with each feeling.

After you are through experimenting, let your partner place his or her palms face down over yours and your partner will try expressing various emotions this way. After this experiment is over, discuss your findings with your partner. Discover what this experience was like for both of you. Were you able to sense the emotions your partner was sending? How did the feeling in your hands change? The feelings in your body? Your mind? The more you practice this exercise, the better you'll get at sending energy.

Bliss Byte

Some people find color easy to work with during meditation, but for others, sound makes more sense. Others find the sensation of touch an easier point of focus, while for others, a thought works best. Chinese meditation balls or stones are a good tactile source of focus (see Chapter 16 for more). It all depends on your particular orientation. Experiment to see which of your senses provides the most effortless point of concentration.

4. The Intellect Sheath: Understanding

Sit comfortably with your back straight. Breathe normally and notice your breath. Now, close your eyes and casually notice your physical body. Visualize where it starts and where it stops. Next, recall your vital body, how it extends beyond the physical body in a swirling dance of energy. Next, recall your mind sheath, a glowing pink encompassing your physical and vital bodies.

What is beyond the mind sheath? Visualize the edges of the mind sheath. What do you see? Nothing at first, but then you begin to see a pale yellow color extending beyond the mind sheath. What is it? You can't quite see it. You can't quite get there.

Bring your attention back to your mind sheath. Visualize tiny bright green shapes floating around inside your mind sheath. Some are circles, some are triangles, some are squares, and some are random polygons with no names. Sometimes they bounce against the edges of the mind sheath, but they seem to be stuck inside it as if in a bubble.

These green shapes are your thoughts and feelings. They live in the mind sheath but can't go beyond it. They are content to live there. But wait—one triangle doesn't seem content. It keeps bouncing against the mind sheath, as if trying to break through the bubble. Follow this triangle. Is it a thought or an emotion? What is it about?

Suddenly, the triangle breaks through the boundary of the mind sheath and the intellect sheath shows itself in sunny yellow. *Ah-ha!* you think. *Now I understand!* You've reached a new level, a new understanding of some aspect of reality you've been struggling with. The true nature of your problems, your self, and your world are suddenly clear. You've encountered the intellect sheath.

Meditations for the Causal Realm

The causal realm is so called because this is the realm where everything originates. Although you might be able to access it last, it was the first "you" before you descended into the physical body (according to reincarnation theory). Think of the causal realm as your spirit. It pervades you and extends from you, beyond all the other bodies. It is you, the whole you, and the you who you will be after your body has worn out. It is also the you who is the same as the universe, as God, as nature, and as all being. It is the universal, divine you. Yes, right there in front of you (and behind you and above you …).

The only sheath within the causal realm is the bliss sheath. To get in touch with this sheath of existence is to gain true inner peace. Unlike the other sheaths of existence, this sheath is thought to be beyond space and time, pervading all reality.

5. The Bliss Sheath: Om

The following meditation is the most advanced of all the five-sheath meditations. With practice, including the practice of many of the other meditations in this book, the bliss meditation will become a blissful reality.

Sit comfortably with your back straight. Close your eyes and breathe normally. Focus on your breath. Listen to it. Visualize it. Feel it moving in and out of your nostrils. Stay with the breath for five minutes or more.

Now, visualize the word *om*. According to yogic theory, om is actually a sound meant to represent the original sound of the vibrating universe. Om is like the sound of the origin of all things and the continuing sound of all things that are one. It is the sound of divinity, unity, and the only true reality.

To further open the chakras and free the breathing in the astral body, try the pose illustrated here. A soft pillow on the floor under your head and upper back allows your breath to flow without constriction. Feel your chest and your heart chakra relaxing and opening. Place your hands in prayer pose over your heart and concentrate on the way your heart lifts on every inhalation. Feel your breath and your mind clear and expand.

Open the Saturn and Jupiter chakras by allowing your knees to fall open, supported once again by soft pillows. Let your legs open only as far as they can comfortably go—don't press them toward the floor to the point of a painful stretch. This should feel good and liberating, not stressful!

As you breathe, feel the energy of your chakras opening.

Now, try the sound. Begin softly, and let the *mmm* part of the word vibrate and linger. Repeat the word in a slow rhythm. As you murmur it, imagine the slow turning of the earth, the galaxy, and the entire universe. Imagine you are making the sound of the universe breathing. Feel it expand and contract with every breath, feel it rotate with every *om*. Focus on nothing but the sound of the origin of the universe. If other thoughts surface, blow them away gently with the sound of *om*. Listen, speak, listen, speak, listen, and speak, until you see how you are able to make the sound of *om* because you are the universe and the universe is

Mindful Minute

The more you read and study meditation, the more often you might notice that many concepts having to do with meditation are expressed in Sanskrit, an ancient Eastern Indian language. Yoga philosophy and Buddhism originated in India, and meditation is more central to Indian philosophies than most others. Even though Sanskrit is not used today as a conversational language, many sacred texts were written in Sanskrit and so the terminology survives.

you. You are divinity and divinity is you. You have always made the sound of *om*, and you will always make the sound of *om*. You are the sound. And look—the bliss sheath isn't a sheath at all. It is everything.

Be a Buddha

To reach the realization that all is one—not just to think it or know it intellectually, but to truly realize it—that's what it means to be a Buddha. It can happen to you. It has happened to many before you and will happen to many after you. Experiencing this realization doesn't mean you cease to exist, of course. But typically, it results in an overwhelming and abundant sense of compassion for all sentient beings. The compassion is so strong that it becomes the focus of life and duty to relieve the suffering of others.

Maybe you don't want to be a Buddha. Still, we'd like you to know that if Buddhahood is something you feel is the right path for you, it is an attainable goal. If you are of some other religion, you might not feel comfortable saying you are journeying toward becoming a Buddha, but perhaps you can feel comfortable saying you are seeking true knowledge through service to humankind.

The Transforming Experience of Death

Some cultures compare both sleep and meditation to the experience of death, and in some ways, depending on your personal beliefs, meditation can be like a rehearsal for death. Why rehearse for death, as the *Bardo Thödol* or *Tibetan Book of the Dead* suggests one should do? Because death, whether or not it leads to rebirth or reincarnation (as Tibetan and many other Buddhists believe it will), is an amazing opportunity for the soul.

Mindful Minute

The *Bardo Thödol* or *Tibetan Book of the Dead* is an instruction manual for death meant to be read to someone as they die and move into the *bardo* (the intermediate state between life, death, and rebirth into the next life) so they know what to do. According to this book, which gives a detailed explanation of what happens after death, the soul moves through several stages in the bardo, then back through the same stages toward rebirth. During sleep, the sleeper goes through four progressively deeper stages of sleep then back up to stage 1 into dream sleep. The *Tibetan Book of the Dead* likens these two states, referring to sleep as a rehearsal for death, and also compares these two states to the stages through which one progresses during meditation.

Death is a profound (we won't say final) lesson in nonattachment and the futility of materialism, mundane concerns, and the illusion of possession. In death, we gradually loosen our hold on the world and on the temporary reality we experienced as life. Our senses fade, and we move to a new stage of existence. The experienced meditator already knows what it is like to let go of attachments, escape the hold of the senses, and become one with the universe. How like death, yet how fulfilling and wonderful! If death is like enlightenment, then we have nothing to fear.

Reincarnation: Our Lives Are Like Beads on a String

But what about reincarnation? Is it true? Have we really been here before? Some say yes; some say no. Some have very strong opinions on both sides. We leave the question to you to decide for yourself.

But those who believe in reincarnation compare us to beads on a string (the Dalai Lama's simile). We are the same evolving soul—the string—through our many lives, but the outer trappings, including the body and mind (the beads), change with each new life. Our souls learn something new with each life. We have free will and sometimes we make good choices, sometimes bad choices. Our choices determine what we learn and how much our soul grows (or loses) in each life. This, in turn, determines how we come back next time.

Some believe we are only reincarnated as people. Others believe we can come back as animals, birds, insects—just about anything. Belief in reincarnation isn't necessarily specific to any religion. Have you lived before? Try our past-life meditation and see what comes to you. If you do "remember" a past life, you might consider that it is another side of your personality, a part of you in your unconscious mind, a side of yourself you have yet to encounter—or maybe you just have a vivid imagination. On the other hand, also consider that you might actually be remembering a past life. Either way, the experience will be instructional and teach you a little bit more about who you are, because no matter what you discover, it will have come from inside you.

> **Bliss Byte**
>
> Do you recycle? Are you concerned about pollution, waste, and living an earth-friendly life? Consider the possibility that you will be coming back to this earth for many more lifetimes, and you might have to reap the consequences of environmental destruction. The time to start caring about the future of your environment is now.

Do Your Preferences Equal a Previous You?

Before we start the actual meditation, consider the following questions and whether they might be clues to past lives you've experienced:

♦ Have you always been particularly interested in a certain country, culture, or region of the world, such as ancient Greece, medieval Spain, or turn-of-the-century Paris, although you never really knew why?

♦ Is there a place you feel sure you would never want to visit, although you aren't sure why?

♦ Have you ever met someone and had the feeling you knew him or her from somewhere, even though you had never met before?

♦ Do you have unexplained fears, such as drowning, small spaces or crowds, or storms or heights?

♦ Is there a specific time in history that interests you more than others, such as the Victorian era or the Middle Ages?

♦ Have you ever visited a place that was very familiar even though you'd never been there?

♦ Have you ever dreamed you were someone else?

Any of these could obviously occur for reasons other than past lives, but maybe they are evidence after all. Maybe someday we will know for sure, but in the meantime, it's fun—and perhaps soul-enriching—to speculate.

Remembering a Past Life

If you would like to try to remember a past life, even if you don't really think they exist, try our past-life meditation. If nothing else, it will tell you something about yourself.

> **CAUTION**
>
> **Relax**
>
> Past-life meditations can be fun, fascinating, and yes, even addictive. Some people become so obsessed with finding out the details of their past lives that they completely miss the point of the exercise: how to improve this life and help your soul grow in this stage. Don't forget to live the life you have!

Sit comfortably with your back straight and close your eyes. Imagine yourself walking through a beautiful green field bordered by forest on all sides. The grass is brilliant green and dotted with small blue flowers. Suddenly, in the middle of the field, you come upon a rise of hill. A massive wooden door with a heavy, round, gold door-pull is set into the hill. You approach the door and put your hand on the heavy, glossy wood. There you see your name carved in the door. You must be meant to enter!

You open the door to feel the air become damper but also lighter, like fog or mist. You feel as if you are walking through a cloud as you step into a round room. The room is encircled with doors, and each door has a gold nameplate on it. Turning in circles, you wonder which door you should open.

Suddenly, one door begins to glow, and you notice a light on behind it. You go to the door and look at the nameplate. It has your name on it, and beneath it, another name. You know this was your name in a past life. Look closely until you can read it. (It might be in another language or alphabet you don't understand.)

You open the door and step into a small chamber filled with blue mist. In front of you is a large wooden table holding a large book with a blue silk cover. You open the book and look at the page. At the top of the page is the name of a place. At the bottom of the page is a date. Look at the page until you see the place name and date clearly. Then, a picture forms in the middle of the page. It is a portrait of a figure with a half smile. You gaze at it and realize it is you in a past life. Study the picture until you can see it clearly.

When you look up from the book, you see the room is filled with shelves, cabinets, and drawers. Each one contains things that belonged to the person in the book, things that were meaningful, things from that person's life. Explore the room for as long as you like. Pick up objects, feel them, smell them, examine them, and remember their stories. Get to know the past you.

Now, go back through the door and into the room with the many doors. Know that you can return and work through all the doors at your leisure. When you open the door that leads into the field, open your eyes. Write about your experience so you don't forget the person you met there!

The Least You Need to Know

- The physical body is only one of three bodies. It is interpenetrated with the astral body—the realm of the emotions, thoughts, and understanding—and the causal body, the realm of the spirit.

- The three bodies contain five sheaths of existence within them: (1) the physical sheath, (2) the vital sheath, (3) the mind sheath, (4) the intellect sheath, and (5) the bliss sheath.

- Meditation can be a rehearsal for the release of the material world we will eventually discover in death.

- You can explore the possibility of your past lives, or other sides of yourself, through past-life meditation.

Part

Get Ready to Meditate

How stressed are you? Perhaps more than you realize. It's easy to mistake a stressed state of being for "normal" when stress is present over long periods of time. In this part, we'll help you to determine your own stress level and offer you some coping strategies, including a technique called mindfulness, that can help wake you up to your life and really enjoy what you do each moment, even if you are washing the dishes or commuting to work.

We'll also give you some tips on where to meditate and how to create a meditation space in your home. Then we'll actually get you meditating, and we'll show you how to use your breath to enhance your meditation, your health, and even your longevity.

10

Stress: Is Your Mind *Too* Full?

In This Chapter

- ◆ Stress: living with it or without it
- ◆ How stressed are you? Take our quiz
- ◆ The physical and mental effects of stress
- ◆ If stress is the question, mindfulness is the answer

Spiritual layers or no spiritual layers, sometimes you might feel like you're nothing more than an exhausted heap of overtaxed muscles, joints, and emotions. Meanwhile, your brain is running at 110 miles per hour. What do you need to do today? When do you need to do it? How are you possibly going to do it all? Did you forget anything? Did you do a good job? Are you capable? *How does anybody get through the day?*

Are you stomped by stress? Most people are, at least some of the time. The responsibilities and challenges of life sometimes overwhelm even the laid-back types. Knowing how to let life's challenges roll off your back isn't easy, and sometimes it isn't practical, either. Stress helps you take action when action is required. But sometimes, you might feel like screaming "Enough is enough!"

Relax

Stress can cause serious health problems, so if you suffer from chronic stress or severe acute stress that you can't seem to relieve through meditation, don't hesitate to see a doctor or holistic health practitioner. You might need medical treatment.

It's Not Stress, It's Just Life!

To some extent, stress is a necessary evil (and sometimes, a necessary good) of modern life. But it isn't, or at least shouldn't be, the dominating force in your life. If acting under stress seems to be your modus operandi, it's time to reevaluate your responses to life, your overloaded schedule, your stress-management techniques (or lack thereof), and your routines for mental maintenance (or lack thereof).

But first, let's evaluate how stressed you really are.

How Stressed Are You? A Self-Quiz

Choose the one best answer for each of the following questions to determine your stress level (for question 10, choose as many answers as apply):

1. Find a mirror and look into it. What is your facial expression at this moment?

    A. Slightly clenched jaw and slightly furrowed brow.

    B. I look tired.

    C. I look like I'm concentrating on something interesting.

    D. I've got a half smile and look relaxed.

2. What is your first reaction when the phone rings?

    A. Expectation.

    B. Thank goodness for caller ID.

    C. Panic. What if something awful has happened?

    D. Disinterest. I'll answer if I'm not busy, but if I'm involved in something, I'll check my messages later.

3. Who do you feel is dependent on you for their basic needs?

    A. Nobody.

    B. Just my children (even if they're 30).

    C. One or more adults (spouse or partner, parents).

    D. My children and my parents—I'm responsible for the generations on both ends!

4. How do you feel about your job?

    A. It pays the bills, but I have other pleasures in my life.

    B. I hate going to work each morning.

    C. I feel I have found my true calling, and my work is a joy.

    D. It's often unpleasant, tedious, or stressful, but at least it gives me status and money.

Bliss Byte

Sometimes the fastest and easiest way to defuse a stressful situation is with laughter. Laughter is healing, relaxing, and a great way to put things into perspective. In fact, there is even a form of meditation, aptly named laughing meditation, that is based around laughter. In India, large groups of people gather together in parks and common areas, make funny faces, stretch, move, and laugh together. Some advocate waking up each morning and laughing for five minutes before the day begins. The laughter might be forced at first, but will soon become genuine as you realize how wonderfully funny life can be. Revel in it!

5. Are you …

    A. Single but looking.

    B. Happily unmarried.

    C. Divorced or separated.

    D. Happily married.

    E. Unhappily married.

6. During the time when you are home and awake, what percentage would you estimate you have the television turned on?

    A. 75 to 100 percent.

    B. About 50 percent.

    C. I watch maybe an hour a day.

    D. I rarely watch television.

7. How would you describe your financial situation?

    A. I have all the money I could ever spend and then some.

    B. I could always use more, but I get by just fine.

    C. I never have enough left by the end of the month.

    D. I try to live simply and get by on less. I make enough to meet my needs and that's all I need to make.

    E. I can barely get by, have already filed or am considering filing for bankruptcy, have huge debts, and/or worry about money constantly.

8. I feel …

    A. Content with who I am.

    B. Deeply dissatisfied with who I've become.

    C. Okay about myself but striving to become a better person.

    D. I like the inside me but not the outside me.

    E. I like the outside me but not the inside me.

9. I also feel …

    A. Like I have no control over my life and what happens to me.

    B. Like I have only a little control over my life and what happens to me. I tend to blame circumstances, bad luck, or other people for consequences I've had to face.

    C. Mostly in control of my life, though major life events often give me the feeling I've lost control.

    D. I understand that I reap what I sow. I make my own luck and my own choices, and in general, I know that the consequences are my own responsibility. I like it that way.

10. How many of the following have you experienced in the last year?

    A. A move to a different state

    B. Pregnancy, childbirth, or adoption of a child

    C. A job change, including a hiring or firing

    D. A major change in financial circumstances (good or bad)

    E. A trip out of the country

    F. The death of a parent

    G. The death of a child

    H. The death of a friend or other relative

    I. The death of a beloved pet

    J. A major health problem

    K. Major surgery

    L. An accident resulting in serious injury

    M. A marriage

    N. A divorce

    O. A separation

    P. Divorce or separation of your parents

    Q. Health problems of your parents if they are under your care

    R. Graduation

    S. Being the victim of a crime

    T. A natural disaster (flood, tornado, hurricane, etc.)

    U. A bout with depression

    V. More than two panic attacks or episodes of severe anxiety

    W. The development of an irrational fear

Now, score your quiz by giving yourself points according to the following:

  1. A: 3   B: 2   C: 1   D: 0

  2. A: 1   B: 2   C: 3   D: 0

  3. A: 0   B: 1   C: 2   D: 3

  4. A: 1   B: 3   C: 0   D: 2

  5. A: 2   B: 1   C: 3   D: 1   E: 3

  6. A: 3   B: 2   C: 1   D: 0

  7. A: 1   B: 1   C: 2   D: 0   E: 3

  8. A: 0   B: 3   C: 1   D: 2   E: 2

  9. A: 3   B: 2   C: 1   D: 0

10. One point for every answer circled.

If you scored between 25 and 40 points: If your stress level hasn't already affected your mental and/or physical health, it might well affect either or both very soon. Get help immediately. Delegate responsibility to other family members or friends. Find someone to talk to (friends and/or a licensed mental health professional or counselor) about your feelings. Realize you can't shoulder the burdens of the world on your own. If you aren't involved in one already, begin a program of moderate physical exercise like mindful walking or movement meditation such as yoga. You need to engage in some serious mental and physical maintenance that slows down the pace. (But remember, in times when you're feeling very low or depressed, physical activity through movement meditation might be better than sitting meditation.)

If you scored between 10 and 24 points: You certainly have stress in your life, and your stress levels are probably comparable to those of most active, involved people. Sometimes you feel completely overwhelmed by what life throws your way. Other times, you feel proudly in control of your life and circumstances. Meditation is the perfect mental maintenance activity to incorporate into your daily routine. It will strengthen your reserves and help you handle those over-the-top days with grace and serenity. It will also help you appreciate and live your life more fully, since you sometimes tend to switch on the auto pilot to function.

If you scored between 0 and 9 points: Somehow you've managed to create a life of ease and relaxed attention. You feel good about yourself and your life, and when stressful events happen, they don't usually make you feel out of control. Maybe you're already meditating and that's your secret! If you aren't, give it a try. Your frame of mind is such that you are primed for spiritual growth. All that daily junk isn't getting in the way. Also, you never know what the future has in store for you. Adding resources to your already formidable stress-management arsenal will assure continued success in dealing with the challenges of life.

What Stress Does to Your Body (and Your Mind!)

People experience two types of stress: chronic and acute. Chronic stress is experienced over a long period of time. An unhappy relationship or long-term financial problems are examples of situations that can cause chronic stress. Acute stress might be triggered by a sudden event, such as a car accident or getting fired from a job (if you become seriously injured or can't find work again, you might suffer from both acute and chronic stress).

When we experience either type of stress, our bodies react in what we call the *fight-or-flight reaction*. This reaction can be observed in nature. When an animal is threatened by a predator, it has two choices: stand up and fight, or run for its life. Which method it chooses has to do with a lightning-fast appraisal of the situation. Would fighting be worth the risk? Could the animal flee fast enough? What is the size, strength, and nature of the threat?

We do the same thing. Although the development of stress in humans doesn't usually involve being chased by wild animals anymore (like it once did), it's just as real. Work deadlines, family members in trouble, life changes—physical or emotional crises of all kinds confront us, often on a daily basis. What happens to your body when the fight-or-flight response kicks in?

From A to Om

The **fight-or-flight reaction** refers to the body's response to extreme stress, allowing it to react more quickly and with greater strength and speed so it can fight or flee from a perceived threat (see Chapter 6).

Lots of things, all designed to help you act more quickly and with greater strength. Even when your stress response is triggered by a threat that doesn't require a physical response, such as the death of a loved one or losing your job, the result is the same. Your body doesn't know the difference, and here's what happens:

◆ Stress hormones such as adrenaline and cortisol are released into your system and heighten your perception of a situation and your ability to react.

◆ Your heart beats faster and harder to deliver more nutrients and blood to muscles in case you need to perform some physical action.

◆ Blood is diverted away from the gastrointestinal system and toward muscles (have you noticed you are often completely without an appetite when you are under a lot of stress?).

◆ Your pupils dilate so you can see better.

◆ Your hair stands on end, and your skin becomes more sensitive to vibrations.

◆ Your breathing rate quickens, delivering more oxygen to your body.

If you've forgotten that your presentation is due tomorrow, stress will serve you well, revving you up to get the work finished. But if you live under stress all the time, your *autonomic nervous system*, the source of all these changes, can easily become overtaxed. The signs of an overtaxed autonomic nervous system are chronic muscle tension, often in the form of tense shoulders and neck, furrowed brow,

From A to Om

The **autonomic nervous system** is responsible for bodily functions such as heartbeat, blood pressure, and digestion.

clenched jaw, and hunched posture; sweaty palms; elevated heart rate and/or blood pressure; and digestive problems.

There are, of course, effective ways to manage chronic stress, but people don't always choose them. Instead, they might choose stress-management techniques that, although temporarily effective, eventually result in increased stress and decreased vitality, even compromised health. Consider your own stress responses. Do you engage in any of the following?

- **Denial.** "Problem? What problem? I don't have a problem," or "This kind of thing might bother most people, but it doesn't affect *me*."

- **Workaholism.** It's easier to throw yourself into your work than to face problems in your personal life.

- **Chemicals.** A cocktail after work, a pot of coffee in one-mug doses during the workday, cigarette breaks, sleeping pills, and over-the-counter stimulants can all alter your mind-body in a way that can keep you functioning during periods of stress. Plus, the effects, side effects, and after-effects of drugs can desensitize you to your own energy, making body scans ineffective and deflecting efforts at mindfulness. If you can't read your own body energy, you can't know as easily what needs fixing, and your meditative focus will suffer, too.

- **Food.** Even though your digestion tends to shut down during periods of stress, that doesn't mean you'll stop eating altogether. In fact, the reverse might be true: Compulsive eating under stress is a common problem and might result in excess weight gain, ill health due to the low quality of foods consumed, and even eating disorders.

What coping mechanism should replace these less-than-ideal stress responses? We suggest *mindfulness*. We've mentioned mindfulness before in this book, but let's take a closer look at exactly what it is and how it can work in your life.

Let's say you're reading a magazine instead of balancing your checkbook, when you really "should" be balancing the checkbook. That's not mindful, because you are doing one thing and thinking about something else. If you aren't balancing your checkbook and have chosen, for whatever reason, to read a magazine instead at that moment, *read the magazine!* Or *go balance your checkbook.*

From A to Om

Mindfulness is a way of being. It means being completely aware of, though not necessarily emotionally involved with, the present moment.

The point is to really do exactly what you are doing, fully addressing and experiencing each moment as it comes rather than letting part or most of your mind linger in the past or future, the "should be" or "could be." Live, and everything you do will have more meaning, more punch, and more energy. If you go through life making conscious decisions to do things and then do them, your stress will fall off dramatically. Sure, you'll still have some when major life events occur, but you'll handle stress much better because you'll actually be *handling stress* rather than letting it overwhelm and distract you from the task at hand.

> **Bliss Byte**
>
> Pick a daily chore you would normally find tedious, for example, filing, paying bills, folding laundry, filling the car with gas, or commuting to work through rush-hour traffic. Decide to do that chore today with complete and total mindfulness, without thinking of getting it finished and out of the way, and without looking forward to what you'll do after you are done. Really *do* the work and feel the pleasure in performing the task—note how the papers or clothes or steering wheel feel in your hands, noticing every detail of your task. See it anew, and find the fun in it.

Mindful Miracle

But what are you supposed to do when stress really has you in its grip? How are you supposed to remember that only the *now* matters? You've got a job to do, perhaps a family to support, and obligations to fulfill. You've got to keep it all in your head at once. You've got to plan for the future, learn from the past, organize, schedule, and network. You can't just drop everything and live only in the *now*, can you?

Yes ... and no. Living in the *now* doesn't mean forgetting the past or remaining oblivious to the future or "dropping" anything you need to be responsible about. Whatever you are doing in the present moment can be fully experienced, even if what you are doing is mapping out a retirement plan or writing in your journal how you feel right now about neglecting to help that kid who fell off his bike. Whatever you are doing, whatever you have to do, you can make that the most important thing to do *now*, *at that moment*, whether it's doing the laundry, paying bills, washing the dog, preparing that expense report, eating dinner, waiting for a bus, planning for the future, or reconciling yourself with the past—you get the picture. Meditation helps you become more aware of what is most important.

Living mindfully takes some training, however. Mindfulness meditation is the perfect training. It might also be the most powerful meditative technique for dealing with stress. Touted as an effective treatment for pain relief as well as an eye-opening way to live every day of your life, mindfulness has many proponents and many incarnations.

Mindful Minute

A study conducted by the Stress Reduction Clinic at the University of Massachusetts Medical Center followed 23 people in two groups, all with psoriasis (a skin disease) undergoing ultraviolet light treatments. One of the groups practiced the technique of mindfulness meditation taught in the clinic, which required them to focus on their breath and physical sensations during the treatment, eventually visualizing that the ultraviolet light was slowing down the disease process. The other group received the treatment without the mindfulness meditation. After 12 weeks, the skin patches on the group of meditators were healing much faster. Of the 13 meditators, 10 had clear skin after 40 sessions. In the group of 10 nonmeditators, only 2 had clear skin.

Bliss Byte

Mindfulness while performing the simple tasks of life will help to cultivate mindfulness that can get you through the more stressful events of life—major life changes, tragedies, etc. Much of the stress of major events involves dwelling on the past and the future. Because mindfulness deals only with the *now*, your list of worries diminishes.

But medicine is only a small part of the mindfulness gift. According to Thich Nhat Hahn, an exiled Vietnamese monk and peace activist (nominated for the Nobel Peace Prize by Martin Luther King Jr. in 1967), living mindfully is the only way to live. Each task of life should be performed with the sole purpose of performing that task. Hahn uses the example of washing the dishes (he can imagine a machine to wash clothes, but can't imagine why anyone would want a machine to wash dishes ... perhaps he's never hosted a dinner party for 12). When a visiting friend once asked him if he could do the dishes after a meal, Hahn agreed on the condition that he do the dishes in the right way. He must do the dishes *to do the dishes*, not to get them finished and get on with something else.

Mindfulness, Buddha-Style

The Buddha has provided us with a special meditation to help attain a mindful state. The following Sutra of Mindfulness exercise is part of a longer sutra, the *Sutra on the Full Awareness of Breathing* (translated by Hahn) and provides a means to help you increase mindfulness by calming and centering the breathing. Memorize it and use it to help you relax when life becomes overwhelming:

Breathing in, I know I am breathing in.

Breathing out, I know I am breathing out.

Breathing in a long breath, I know I am breathing in a long breath.

Breathing out a long breath, I know I am breathing out a long breath.

Breathing in a short breath, I know I am breathing in a short breath.

Breathing out a short breath, I know I am breathing out a short breath.

Breathing in, I am aware of my whole body.

Breathing out, I am aware of my whole body.

Breathing in, I calm my whole body.

Breathing out, I calm my whole body.

Repeat the Sutra of Mindfulness for 10 to 20 minutes, and you'll soon experience a pervading calm. As Thich Nhat Hahn says, "Your thoughts will have quieted down like a pond on which not even a ripple stirs."

Listening to Your Body: Crafting Your Stress Response

Remember all the things we told you about that happen to your body when you experience stress? Muscle tension, increased heart rate, increased breathing, blood flow away from the stomach and into the muscles, etc., are natural responses, but if you're living mindfully—and experiencing stress mindfully—you can moderate these responses in an effective way so they don't become the cause of chronic conditions. Here are some keys to crafting your stress response:

◆ Whenever you feel yourself becoming overwhelmed by stress, stop what you're doing and take a few deep breaths, then focus your attention on what your body is feeling. Don't judge or try to change anything just yet. Just notice. Is your heart beating fast? Have you lost your appetite? Do you have "butterflies" in your stomach? Is your mind racing?

◆ Now, turn your attention to the cause of your stress. What is the trigger? Did your teenager just tell you he'll have to repeat the ninth grade? Did your boss tell you your presentation is moved up to tomorrow morning? Did you realize you forgot to pay the electric bill? Did someone criticize, insult, or ignore you?

◆ Next, consider what would happen if you simply didn't let it bother you. What would happen if you were able to care and express yourself without getting your emotions all riled up in negative swirls of expression? Would that be possible?

◆ Or consider how you could modify your thinking about the event. Is there another way to see the problem? Your ninth-grader will just have to deal with the consequences of his actions. Now you'll get that presentation over with sooner and won't have to worry about it. Everyone forgets things sometimes. That person who insulted you was having a bad day, and it had nothing to do with you. Remember, most stress triggers are only stressful because of the way we see them and the emotions we attach to them. Where can you revise?

- Next, think about action strategies. Could you talk to your son about attending summer school or getting a tutor, or about learning to live with consequences? Could you ask your partner to take over dinner and the kids tonight so you can prepare your presentation? Call the electric company and explain that you forgot, and see if you can maybe pay over the phone. Talk to the person who has hurt your feelings or angered you, or just ignore it. Again, list the possibilities in your mind or write them down.

- Now, do another quick mind-body scan. If you've got any tension left, imagine breathing into the area to relax it.

Now doesn't that feel better?

Vipassana: Insight Meditation

Vipassana meditation, also known as *insight meditation*, is a popular form of mindfulness meditation anyone can learn easily. Originating in India with the Buddha, the technique became the basis of the Southeast Asian Theraveda Buddhism tradition. However, it is a technique—and a fairly easy one—not a theology. Anyone can practice it.

The most important key to remember is that Vipassana meditation doesn't involve concentrating on one point of focus, like the breath, a mantra, or a candle flame. It is simple awareness, noticing everything you feel and everything in your environment, letting your mind drift around toward whatever catches your attention, but without becoming emotionally involved with it.

From A to Om

Vipassana meditation or **insight meditation** is a type of meditation grounded in the meditational aspect of Southeast Asian Theraveda Buddhism. *Vipassana* means "insight," and the technique is considered a meditation method the Buddha himself taught. It is simple, requiring only mindful awareness, which leads to insight.

Insight Exercise

Although you may want to take a class with a reputable teacher of insight meditation, you can try meditation, which follows the basic concept on your own:

Sit comfortably with your back straight. Relax and breathe normally. Imagine the word *I*. What does it mean? What is I? Become the I. Open your awareness as an I. Observe. What do you feel, hear, see, and smell? Imagine that your awareness is one of those wispy dandelion seeds that blows through the air. Don't attempt to concentrate on any one thing. Simply let your mind go where it will. Don't become emotionally involved with anything you observe, just observe.

Also observe your feelings and consider how they are a part of you, but do not define you. As you observe your emotional landscape, put your observations into words (even if you don't speak them out loud). For example, if you notice that you are feeling sad, instead of thinking, "I am sad" (which defines you), say to yourself, "I am observing a feeling of sadness." Instead of noticing, "I am anxious" (which defines you), say to yourself, "I am observing an anxious feeling." Putting your emotions into perspective, as only one small part of the qualities that shift and change around the unchangeable and essential *you* can help you to manage them.

Observe the sadness, the anxiety, the anger, the fear, the hunger, even the relaxed feelings, the happy feelings, the in-love feelings, the contented feelings, as feelings and feelings alone. See them, watch what they do, but don't let them overwhelm you, engage you, control you. You'll gain a new mastery and self-possession over your emotions without having to give them up.

Practice this type of meditation each day, and soon you will see your thoughts and feelings as small parts of you, but not *you*. They'll be manageable because they won't define you. They'll be of some interest, but they won't control you. *You* will control you.

Feeling more centered? We are! And we hope you are, too. Now that you've tried some techniques and really gotten your feet wet, let's get structured. Read on to learn how to integrate meditation into your daily life.

The Least You Need to Know

◆ Stress might be inevitable, but it doesn't have to compromise your health or clutter your mind.

◆ Mindfulness meditation can teach you to live in full awareness, experiencing every moment.

◆ Mindfulness meditation can also relieve pain, restore a positive attitude, and help you accept who you are right now.

◆ You can control your stress response through mindfulness meditation.

◆ Insight meditation—following your awareness without a point of concentration (other than your own awareness!)—can help you gain self-knowledge and control over your thoughts and feelings.

Chapter 11

Starting Your Meditation Practice: When, Where, and How

In This Chapter

◆ When to meditate and how to get ready

◆ Meditation paraphernalia

◆ At-home indoor and outdoor meditation spaces

◆ Choosing a meditation class

◆ Due diligence will get you there

So you've discovered you are indeed under stress. What a shocker! What else is new in the modern world? Let's get down to some practical details that will help you establish a regular, structured meditation practice.

In this chapter, we'll help you determine when you should meditate, how you should get ready, and how to find the perfect place to meditate. Technically, you can meditate anywhere, but there's no question that some places are more conducive to meditation than others.

When to Meditate

Now that you've decided you want to meditate, some careful planning will help to make you more successful. First, decide when meditation will fit best into your schedule.

Meditating at random times each day is better than no meditation, but it isn't ideal. Many philosophies postulate that a regular schedule is best for a calm mind and good health.

If you're schedule-resistant, adopting a regular schedule might seem impossible and even undesirable. Maybe you like your free-wheelin' lifestyle! But a regular time for meditation, if for nothing else, will help keep you grounded and centered. Although you might, at first, dread anything you have to do every day at a certain time, look at it as a welcome oasis rather than a chore or a burden. Sure, sometimes you won't feel like it. But discipline is the first step to freedom. (Really!)

> **Mindful Minute**
>
> Many cultures consider the time between 5 and 5:30 A.M. the perfect time to meditate. This time, just before or at sunrise, is a time when peacefulness, awareness, and a calm state of mind are easiest to uncover. Think you can't possibly get up that early? Try going to bed an hour earlier, then setting your alarm. It might be hard at first, but it's largely a matter of habit.

Consider when your energy is at its peak. Early morning? Late morning? Afternoon or evening or late at night? Also consider when you have free time. Do you have to be at work very early, or until late at night?

Believe it or not, it is better to meditate during times of peak energy than during times of low energy. Even though your meditation practice might involve sitting or lying down, you'll need a lot of energy to channel into the effort of mindfulness, concentration, and awareness. If you are in an energy slump, you'll probably just fall asleep.

But time, of course, is the crucial factor. When it comes to energy, it doesn't matter if you are a morning person if you already get up before dawn and immediately launch into an award-winning effort to get everyone in your family, including yourself, dispatched to their proper locations before school buses and carpools leave, meetings begin, and time clocks hit their designated hours. If your only possible free time is your lunch hour or that precious interval between when the kids are asleep and when you collapse in bed, you'll probably find that evening is your best meditation time. Ideally, of course, your energy peak and your free time coincide, but we recognize that it isn't a perfect world.

Whatever time works, pick a time and stick to it whenever possible. Keep that time sacred and instruct the people who live with you to respect your meditation time. Turn on the answering machine, go to your meditation space, leave all other responsibilities behind, and be at peace.

Start Slow

If we are driving you mad with the details of preparation, it isn't on purpose. We want you to be successful, and that's less likely if you rush in and start too quickly without a plan. But we do recognize you are eager to get started. That's great! Just remember to take it slow.

When you first sit down (or lie down or stand up or whatever form you are trying) to meditate, make your goal a good five minutes of meditation. For first-timers, this might be the longest five minutes you've ever experienced! Your nose might itch, your muscles might twitch, and you'll probably run down every to-do list on your agenda before you remember to remind yourself that you are meditating. Don't worry. That's usually how it is at first. It will get better.

Stick with 5-minute sessions for 3 days, then move up to 7 minutes the next day, 8 minutes the following day, 9 minutes the next day, then on the seventh day, 10 minutes. Stick with 10-minute sessions for one week, then move up to 15 for a week, then 20 minutes.

Twenty minutes twice a day is the recommended meditation schedule according to many instructors, but if you can only manage it once, that's great! In one month, you're there! If you can eventually work up to 30, 45, or even 60 minutes, that's great, too. Eventually, the goal is to be able to maintain a mindful, meditative state all the time, but even then, two 20-minute sessions of sitting meditation will keep your mind in peak operating condition.

CAUTION

Relax

Don't let your back be your enemy! Posture is important, even when seated. An erect spine keeps the energy circulating through the body and keeps the chest open, allowing for fuller breathing. Imagine a string gently pulling the crown of your head toward the sky. Bring your shoulders back to open your chest, and breathe.

To keep track of the time while you meditate, set a timer. If you're looking at a clock every minute or so, not only will the time seem interminable, but the clock will also keep you from concentrating on your point of focus, and time will become too high a priority in your awareness. With a timer (a simple kitchen timer or egg timer with a bell will do), you can forget about the time until you hear the signal. Try to use a timer with a gentle ring instead of a blasting alarm and without a loud tick, tick, tick, to distract you.

Bliss Byte _____

If you are having trouble keeping your mind focused on your breath, your mantra, or your visual point of focus, try counting. According to Zen master Thich Nhat Hahn, counting is a great meditation technique for beginning meditators. Breathe in and count "one," breathe out and count "one," breathe in and count "two," breathe out and count "two," etc. Counting helps keep the mind from wandering but varies just enough to keep the novice meditator involved.

Dress for Success

Once you've got your schedule mapped out, what else do you need to do to get ready? Dressing appropriately for meditation is very important. If your clothes are binding or uncomfortable, you'll be much less likely to successfully focus during meditation. Wear loose-fitting clothes that breathe, preferably in natural fabrics like cotton or silk. Watch out for tight waistbands or anything that limits your circulation. Other ways to prepare for meditation include the following:

♦ Take a shower or a bath first so you feel clean.

♦ Drink a big glass of water to feel clean on the inside.

♦ Don't eat for at least a half hour before meditation. Meditation is tough on a full stomach. It's difficult for your body to work on both digestion and mental focus at the same time.

♦ Meditate with intention. Decide what you want to accomplish today during your meditation session. Relaxation? A calm mind before a test? A resolution to a problem? An escape from your mental chatter? What will your focus be today?

Creating a Meditation Space in Your Home

Ideally, you could devote an entire room in your home to meditation, making it into a spiritual sanctuary. Unfortunately, not many people have an extra room to spare for this purpose. (If you happen to be in the process of designing a house to build, however, why not consider adding a small meditation room?) If you live in a limited space like most of us do, you can still carve out the perfect spot for your daily meditation.

First, consider what spaces are available in your home. At first you might not think you have any space at all you can dedicate to meditation, but let's take a closer look:

- Is your living room or den L-shaped? Could one end of the L be set apart with a curtain or stand-up screen for meditation?

- Do you have a spare walk-in closet? Do you really use it, or could coats, old clothes, and other stored items be relocated to a coat rack, a garage, another closet—or maybe you can give away all that stuff you don't use?

- Do you have any small areas like nooks, window seats, or other small unused spaces?

- Do you have a home office, separate den, dining room, or guest room that isn't full or that you only use occasionally?

- Do you have an enclosed pantry? Could you clean it out, throw out all the junk, and relocate food to the kitchen cabinets?

- Do you have a breakfast nook set off from the main kitchen?

- Any window seats, nooks, or extra floor space in your home you could surround with a drape or screen?

- What about outside? Do you have a beautiful garden, group of trees, corner of a hedge, or water source that would make an aesthetically appealing spot for meditation?

Think about which area you'd like to use, talk to other family members about it if necessary, and get to work making the space your own.

Relax

Not having a designated meditation space is no reason to give up on the idea of meditation. You can always sit on your bed, on the floor in the middle of the living room (with the TV off!), in any comfortable chair, or even on top of the kitchen table, if it will hold you.

Bliss Byte

Sometimes you might find yourself meditating in a less-than-ideal environment. If distracting sensory stimuli seem impossible to tune out, try an exercise in sensory withdrawal. Close your ears with your thumbs, your eyes with your index fingers, your nostrils with your middle fingers, and your lips with your ring and pinkie fingers. Open your nostrils for each inhalation and exhalation, closing them in between for a few seconds. Keep this up for 5 to 10 minutes. Turning off the senses gives your mind nowhere to turn but inward.

Meditation Doesn't Mean Deprivation!

Once you've chosen a meditation space, the next step is personalization. Maybe you thought meditation was the stuff of ascetics and your meditation space must be spartan. Far from it! In fact, for the beginning meditator, comfort is extremely important. Otherwise, you might give up before you even get started.

How do you make your meditation space comfortable? First, it would help if you could regulate the temperature. If you can't or if you like to meditate outside, keep a soft blanket or quilt nearby to wrap yourself in. Hypothermia during meditation might help keep you awake, but it sure isn't conducive to sitting in one place for 20 minutes or more!

Likewise, if your meditation space is too hot, the heat will probably become distracting. Make sure the area has sufficient ventilation. Although natural cooling is preferable (open windows and fans, for example) during midsummer, especially in warmer climates, we'll admit the A/C can feel really good. If blasting the air conditioner is the only way you can stand to sit there, then by all means, blast away.

> **CAUTION**
>
> **Relax**
>
> Don't get *too* comfortable! If you feel too cozy in your meditation space, you might fall asleep before you can say "Om." If it helps, keep the temperature a little on the cool side and sit up straight.

> **From A to Om**
>
> A **smudge stick** is a bundle of dried herbs (sage is one of the most common) tied together and burned for the purpose of purification. The burning and purification process is called *smudging,* and it is a traditional Native American purification technique.

Finally, consider aesthetics. Maybe the only space you can find to be alone is the attic, the basement, or the garage. That's great—unless just looking at these places depresses you. If your meditation space is cluttered with junk, you'll have a hard time clearing your mind. Our surroundings are often reflective of our internal housekeeping, and changing our surroundings can alter our internal sense of ourselves. So before you meditate in your meditation space, make sure the space is ready.

First, clean your space really well. Get rid of cobwebs, sort through junk and organize, then scrub, polish, and shine.

Next, clear the energy of the room. Open a window or a door to let in the fresh air and let out the stale. Walk slowly around the room with a burning incense stick or a sage smudge stick, waving it into all the corners and crannies where energy could get "stuck." (You can buy smudge sticks at many organic grocery or health food stores and other shops and boutiques that carry meditation tools.)

After your space is clean, make your space comfortable. Cover hard cement or cold linoleum floors with soft, comfy throw rugs. Clean, fluff, or even recover old, lumpy furniture and pillows. Make sure your room has lots of pillows, mats, bolsters, or whatever else will make meditating more comfortable. Several companies sell meditation mats, meditation pillows and cushions (traditional kinds are called *zafus*), and small meditation benches. These can help take the stress off knee joints and sensitive backs as your seated time increases.

For a meditative ambience, light candles, burn incense, play relaxing instrumental music. (When actually meditating, though, silence is best so as not to distract your thoughts with the music. You might want to play the music only at the start of your session to help relax and prepare you for mediation.) Decorate with colors that make you feel tranquil (blues and greens are good) or joyful (orange and yellow are good). Hang tapestries or pictures showing symbols, figures, or scenes that relax and inspire you on the walls. You can even construct a personal altar on which you keep items of spiritual significance to you.

Making an Altar Your Own

Personal altars can provide you with a sense that your meditation space is truly yours. They can also provide items to use as points of concentration during meditation and can inspire you to maintain a reverent and spiritual frame of mind. All your altar need be is a small table, shelf, or cabinet. Fill it with items that mean something to you:

♦ If you feel close to nature, keep pinecones, seashells, fresh flowers, pine branches, glass bowls of seawater, a miniature fountain, or even a small fish tank on your altar.

♦ If you're devoted to a specific religion, keep statues, sacred texts, symbols, or other representations of those beliefs on your altar. (For example, statues of Buddha, of Hindu gods like Krishna or Ganesha, a crucifix or picture of Jesus, a Bible, a cross, a picture of the om symbol, etc.)

♦ If you are inspired by music, keep a collection of instruments on your altar: small flutes, chimes, gongs, drums, whistles, rattles, and bells. Or for those visually inspired, cover your altar with prints, photos, sculptures, or paintings you find meaningful and inspiring.

♦ If you admire and emulate a particular spiritual leader, include a picture of him or her on your altar.

♦ If you feel centered and grounded by considering the four elements, keep a bowl of water, a stick of burning incense or a burning candle (for fire), a bowl of salt or a beautiful crystal (for earth), and a wind chime (for air) on your altar.

Sounds, Sights, and Smells

Ideally, meditation involves withdrawal of the senses. Complete sense withdrawal isn't easy, however, especially for beginners. In fact, your senses can actually work for you, to help you train yourself to concentrate. The trick is not to bombard them, but to focus on them one at a time.

To help with this pursuit, you can fill your meditation space with tools and equipment that can help you with concentration techniques. You can spend thousands of dollars on fancy meditation and relaxation tools, but you needn't spend a penny. Consider some of the following:

- A wind chime hung near an open window or in the current of a fan

- A small mechanical fountain to provide the peaceful sound of flowing water

- A bell used as a point of meditation focus or to start or end your meditation time

- Candles, candles, candles, for use as a point of focus and also to give the room a warm glow

- Mandala or other spiritually inspired artwork

- Incense and incense burner or essential oil warmers or diffusers

- Tranquil-colored fabrics draped on the walls (But keep any draped fabric away from candles and incense!)

> **Bliss Byte**
>
> For the perfect portable meditation space, find a beautiful stone somewhere outside. Make it sacred by blessing it. For example, you could hold it between your palms and bring your palms to your heart, saying, "I fill this stone with tranquility." Carry the stone with you so that whenever you pull it out of your pocket or purse, you create your own sacred space, wherever you are.

Honoring Your Meditation Space

Once you've created your meditation space to be a true embodiment of you (not of some generic idea you have about meditation), it should feel comfortable, not foreign or strange. Entering it should fill you with tranquility and satisfaction. If your intention is to have a relaxing space, your space should make you feel relaxed just stepping into it. If your intention is to have a spiritual haven, you should feel spiritually inspired by your space.

This is Joan's meditation room. Joan wanted to feel surrounded by sky, nature, beauty, simplicity, and love. Her meditation space is large enough for practicing yoga, or to be used as a healing space for Joan's massage clients—using a massage table or chair. The room is blue in color to evoke the peacefulness of a natural setting and sparsely furnished. Candles for soft lighting, plants, and moveable pillows create a functional and calming environment. A window allows for fresh air. Joan removes her shoes before entering her meditation room. You'll want to craft your own meditation space—one that's just right for you!

Now that you've crafted your space, honor it. Keep it sparkling clean. Periodically replace burned-down candles and wilted flowers. Clean up incense ash, shake out pillows and mats, and dust your altar. Also, every so often, especially when you seem to have hit a meditation plateau, cleanse the energy of your space again. Remember to open the windows and doors.

Also, when in your meditation space, you can honor it and maintain the atmosphere by behaving with reverence. Take your shoes off at the door. Speak softly. You might even consider saying a blessing each time you enter or exit the door or entrance to the space. A few to try:

- ◆ *I honor this space.*

- ◆ *Thank you for this haven.*

- ◆ *May truth be present here.*

Choosing a Meditation Class

If, in despair, you just can't find a good meditation spot, or if you've created the perfect spot but you'd like a little in-person guidance about what to do there, you might consider taking a meditation class. Although meditation is a highly personal experience, a meditation class, or even a simple meditation group, might give you just the motivation you need to sit still in silence for a significant length of time. Being in the company of others who are also interested in the "inner journey" can inspire you to stick with your program. Discipline is an important aspect of meditation and is sometimes easier when you've got like-minded friends around you: *Satsung*.

> **From A to Om**
>
> *Satsung* is a Sanskrit word used to describe the company of like-minded spirits and the strength possible through their companionship.

A meditation class "in action."

Meditation classes might be difficult to find or might be short-term or even single-session classes designed to teach a specific technique. If you can't find a meditation class that appeals to you or makes you comfortable, consider starting your own meditation group. If you attend a place of worship, you can likely find people who would be interested in joining you. Or ask people in your yoga class, ask around at your natural food store or alternative bookstore, or ask your massage therapist. Chances are someone near you either knows of something like what you seek or knows others who would be interested in meditating together.

If you do take a class with a teacher, be wary of anything that seems overly costly, requires more money to learn additional "secrets," or makes you uncomfortable in any way. Many wonderful meditation teachers exist to help you in your journey, but like any other field, there are always a few who are not so well intentioned. Keep your eyes open (figuratively), use your common sense, and sprinkle that with a healthy dose of intuition. When you've found someone you can trust, learn all you can. A good meditation teacher is a great gift.

Be Diligent

Last, let's consider your attitude toward meditation. You can have all the equipment in the world, the perfect meditation space, and an hour a day to devote to meditation, but that doesn't mean you will keep it up. You need something else, something from inside. You need diligence.

Without diligence, perseverance, and discipline, you'll soon give up. Maybe your parents used to tell you that nothing worth having comes easily. That's usually true, and it's true here, too. Meditation takes time to yield its benefits.

In many ways, our modern society is an undisciplined one. We don't want to wait for anything. We have drive-thru fast food, banks, dry-cleaners, pharmacies, even drive-thru convenience stores! (As if "quick shops" aren't quick enough.) We want everything that might be a little tedious done for us and done fast. We're glad to pay money for it, but what spiritual price—not to mention financial price—are we paying as we shell out the big bucks so we can get daily life behind us?

But you can change all that, at least for yourself. (And perhaps the world can change, too, slowly, person by person.) One step at a time, one aspect of your life at a time, cultivate discipline. Be diligent about the very task of living. Meditation can be the groundwork of that diligence. You can do it! You can change your life, one om at a time.

A Little Progress on a Long Road to Samadhi

The road to enlightenment—whatever enlightenment means to you—is a long one, fraught with obstacles. But you can find your bliss, little by little. Although meditation won't result in immediate, dramatic benefits, it does yield tiny treasures along the way. One day, you might suddenly realize that your work demands don't get to you the way they used to. Or your spouse's annoying little habits aren't so annoying. Maybe you find that you are seeing a brilliant sunset or a snowy forest or a bed of pink tulips for the very first time, and the sight fills you with sudden joy.

CAUTION

Relax

Expectation can be a hindrance to meditation. If you are expecting drastic change after just a few sessions, you'll be disappointed and might discontinue your meditation practice. Live in the moment when meditating, rather than looking forward to the future benefits.

Maybe you will look in the mirror one day and will, quite unexpectedly, love what you see, and it will have nothing to do with your external appearance. Maybe your movements will develop more grace, your speech will become more relaxed, or your demeanor will suddenly radiate composure. Maybe one month, day by day, your life will look more and more like a garden every day. Then you'll see how worthwhile a daily meditation practice can be and how important it is to tend to the garden of your soul.

The Least You Need to Know

◆ Fit meditation into your schedule and synch it with your cycle of energy during the day. Wear something comfortable.

◆ Create a personalized meditation space in your home, indoors and/or outdoors. Keep it clean and honor it.

◆ Consider the variety of meditation classes available, for a meditation space away from home and a new perspective on meditation.

◆ A diligent inner commitment to meditation is the best way to uncover the treasures within.

Focus on the Breath of Life

In This Chapter

- Breathing is boring? Guess again
- How breathing works in your mind-body
- Finding out how well you breathe
- Breathing exercises to enhance meditation

Before we jump into the actual meditation process any further, we'd like to cover one more very important process. We've talked a lot about meditation techniques that involve following the breath or focusing your attention on your breathing, but are you breathing the right way?

You might be skeptical that there is a right way to breathe. If your breathing is keeping you alive, you're doing it right, right?

Not necessarily. As infants, most of us were able to breathe effortlessly, deeply, and in the way that best nourished our bodies with oxygen. As we grow older, however, tension, stress, bad posture, diet, and other factors begin to hinder proper breathing. According to many proponents of breath-work and natural health care in general, the breath might be the most important factor in increasing and maintaining good health and longevity.

The Breath of Life

Remember all that talk about prana, the life-force energy that can suffuse our bodies more fully if we learn how to draw it into us through the breath? Prana is one reason why breathwork is so important.

Many languages and traditions have linked breath with spirit, divinity, wisdom, and the creative spark. The word *inspiration* literally means "to breathe in," while the word *expiration*, meaning "to breathe out," is sometimes used as a synonym for death. Here are some other meanings for breath in other languages and traditions:

◆ In Tibetan Buddhism, breath is sometimes called "the vehicle of the mind."

◆ In Sanskrit, the word for breath is *prana*, which also denotes universal life-force energy.

◆ In the Bible, God breathed into clay to create man, and the Holy Spirit is said to "inspire."

◆ In Judaism, the word for breath also means "spirit of God."

◆ In Greek, the word *pneuma* meant "breath," "soul," "air," and "spirit."

◆ The Chinese character for breath consists of three different characters that mean "of the conscious self or heart."

◆ In Latin, *anima spiritus* means both "breath" and "soul."

◆ In Japanese, *ki* means both "air" and "spirit."

Breathwork is also important because of the benefits more oxygen brings to all the systems of the body—the muscles, heart, lungs, brain, digestion, and even our attitudes, emotions, and energy level. Have you ever wondered why children have so much energy? Perhaps it is because they still know how to breathe. Perhaps that kind of energy could be yours.

And So I Asked My Teacher, "How Do I Breathe?"

Maybe you are under the impression that breathwork is for amateur meditators. Meditation 101, right? Actually, although breathwork is an excellent way to ease into meditation, it's nothing less than a lifetime pursuit. Zen masters are still working on perfecting the nuances of breathing. Breathing might be easy, but breathing *well* is another matter. Even experienced meditators will tell you that learning to breathe can be a lifelong journey.

Breathing is, in itself, both a beginning and a highly advanced form of meditation. The breath is a multi-layered, highly complex, yet pure and simple process. It suffuses the soul with vitality. It delivers oxygen to the brain. It is as mundane as panting; as sublime as the nature of reality. To control the breath is to control life itself. You could simultaneously ponder it and practice it for a lifetime. And many have.

Relax

When you realize you're under stress or overwhelmed, simply tell yourself, "Breathe."

The Psyche, the Breath, the Soul

Breath is life. We can live for a number of weeks without food, about two or three days without water, but only a few moments without breath. Breathing properly will fill you with vitality. Allowing your body, your mood, or anything else to interfere with right breathing only interferes with your vitality. Guard your breath, master the breathing process, and you will be filled with life, energy, and inspiration.

Breath has plenty of physical benefits, but it has benefits for the psyche, as well. Conscious deep breathing has the amazing capacity to calm us, even in the most stressful situations. From calming the nerves before a test to bringing tranquility to the mind of someone who is dying, deep breathing transforms us. Or perhaps *transform* is the wrong word. Actually, deep breathing *reminds* us of how we are meant to feel.

Bliss Byte

Try this simple calming exercise: Double the length of your exhalation to your inhalation. For example, breathe in to a count of four, then breathe out to a count of eight. Work up to an inhalation on the count of 6 and exhalation on the count of 12, 8 and 16, 9 and 18, 10 and 20, etc. Never strain the breathing process. If you feel strain, intersperse the rhythm with some normal breaths.

That feeling is the source of a new sort of self-control. Deep breathing reminds us that although we might not be able to control the world, we can control our reaction to the world. We can control our selves. Consider a newborn baby. Newborn humans have less control over themselves and are less able to survive on their own than any other newborn animal. They are helpless for longer than any other newborn, as well. Yet are they stressed out about it? Nope. Sure, they'll make a fuss when they want something, but as soon as their needs are met, they are calm and happy again. (As long as their needs are met, which might be a key as to how we all lose this ability to breathe mindfully.) Infants know how to breathe, and with each breath, their bodies experience the present moment, wherein everything is just fine.

Just think how much more self-control you have than a baby and how much more control you have over your own circumstances! If, in addition to this added skill, you could retain the ability to breathe like a baby, you'd probably find yourself sleeping like a baby, smiling like a baby, eating like a baby, loving like a baby, and … happy as a clam.

The Physiology of Breathing

Why does breath have such a pervasive influence on your mind-body? For one thing, our entire body is made up of cells, and cells are nourished through breath (as well as through the food we eat).

To truly understand how significant breath is for life, it helps to know a little bit about the actual process of breathing and what happens in the body with each breath. When you inhale oxygen, it flows into your lungs and attaches to *hemoglobin* (part of red blood cells). It then travels into the capillaries of the body, where it diffuses into your body tissue to nourish and replenish it. The blood cells, having dumped their oxygen load, pick up a load of carbon dioxide, travel back through the capillaries to the veins, and flow into the heart, where they are pumped back to the lungs. The carbon dioxide is expelled by the lungs via the exhalation of the breath. Another inhalation delivers more oxygen to the lungs, and the cycle continues. It's one small manifestation of the life cycle.

From A to Om

Hemoglobin is a molecule in red blood cells responsible for carrying oxygen from the lungs to the tissues and carbon dioxide from the tissues back to the lungs.

The oxygen is able to keep entering this lung-heart-lung system because your body has certain muscles, including the diaphragm muscle and abdominal muscles, that keep moving it in and out of the body. For deep breathing, the diaphragm may be the most important muscle over which you can exert a great deal of conscious control.

Actually, you've got several diaphragm muscles, but the largest one and the one most instrumental in breathing (although the others play a part, too) is the large, bowl-shape muscle that lies at the bottom of your chest just above your abdomen. When you inhale, the diaphragm expands downward to give your lungs and chest more room to hold breath. Imagine the cup of the bowl filling up and dropping downward to make more room for air. With each exhalation, the bowl inverts, its cup pushing upward to push air out. Ideally, this process comes off without a hitch. Realistically, however, we often manage to get it all wrong. Sure, we keep breathing. We stay alive. But we no longer maximize our breath potential.

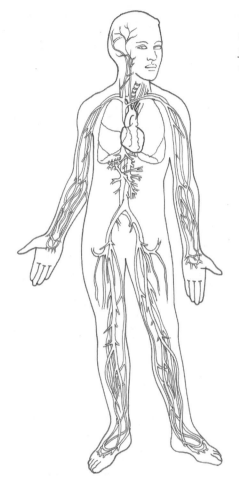

The cardiovascular, respiratory, and circulatory systems flow oxygen through its circle of life.

Breathing at Its Worst

Life has taught us to mess with a good thing. Most adults have developed breathing patterns that restrict the flow of oxygen, and the inevitable result is undernourished tissue, including muscle tissue and brain tissue. Restricted oxygen flow might also result in a greater sense of anxiety, a lower tolerance for stress, and an inability to think and react quickly. Unhealthy breathing patterns come in several forms.

Mindful Minute

Deep breathing is being used more frequently as an actual medical therapy. The Stress Reduction Clinic at the University of Massachusetts Medical Center teaches its clients deep-breathing exercises and uses breathing as a focus for mindfulness meditation.

One of the most common forms of unhealthy breathing is shallow deep breathing. This kind of breathing is what many people do when they *think* they are breathing deeply, as in, "Everybody take a *deeeeeep* breath!" As they suck in air, these misbreathers hike up their shoulders and raise their chests. But what do your shoulders have to do with breathing? If anything, they should be moving outward, away from your body, not up around your ears. Even our diaphragm muscles can become involved in this pseudo–deep breathing. If you're accustomed to holding your stomach in all the time (as do many of us, conditioned as we are to try to look thinner), your diaphragm may get confused, thinking that upon inhalation, it should push upward, forcing air into the upper chest. Upon exhalation, it then collapses downward.

> **Bliss Byte**
>
> Breathing can be more interesting than simple inhalation and exhalation. During meditation, try a variety of powerful breathing techniques:
>
> - Inhale with a series of small breaths, then exhale with a *sss* sound.
> - Inhale through pursed lips, and exhale with a whistle.
> - Breathe in through one nostril while holding the other closed, then switch and exhale through the opposite nostril. Repeat the other way.
>
> These techniques can increase your vitality and alter your consciousness. Deep breathing can even create a natural buzz! A drug is defined as any substance taken into the body that effects change. Oxygen is no different.

But this is backward and counterproductive to an efficient intake of oxygen. When this kind of breathing becomes chronic, it interferes with the workings of the whole mind-body system. Common problems associated with this type of breathing are indigestion, muscle tension in the upper body, confusion, and a feeling of being uncoordinated. If your very breath is uncoordinated, it is only natural that your mind-body will follow suit.

> **From A to Om**
>
> **Hyperventilation** is "overbreathing," or breathing too rapidly and shallowly. It is characterized by a feeling of not being able to get enough air, as well as dizziness, racing heart, fainting, and muscle cramps.

We block our breathing in other ways, too. Chronic muscle tension and chronic pain can tend to make people hold their bodies in a chronic clinch. Overall muscle tension doesn't allow the entire body to expand and contract with the breath. Bad posture doesn't allow the lungs and diaphragm to expand and contract sufficiently. Stress can cause rapid, shallow breathing, which brings in less oxygen and causes the loss of too much carbon dioxide. The system becomes out of balance and in the extreme, *hyperventilation* occurs.

The hunched shoulders and collapsed chest characteristic in poor posture restrict breathing and inhibit the correct action of the diaphragm muscle. Lift and open your heart chakra, creating space for the flow of breath into and through the body and allowing the diaphragm muscle to function at its best.

Breathing at Its Best

Nobody wants to hyperventilate, of course, but who wouldn't want to maximize their physical and mental power through something as easy as breathing? But how do we regain our ability to breathe fully, deeply, and with the whole body?

Correct breathing comes in many forms, depending on what you are doing and what your body's needs are. Your breath will necessarily change with each passing moment. All in all, the deeper your breath, the deeper your life experience.

During deep breathing, your diaphragm presses downward and your abdomen extends on the inhalation, rather than your chest rising and shoulders lifting. Also, your lower back expands outward (this movement is subtle but real), and your rib cage expands to allow room for your expanding lungs. On the exhalation, the diaphragm should rise, causing your abdomen to fall inward, your lower back to contract slightly, and your rib cage to move back to its normal position. Your shoulders shouldn't move at all during proper deep breathing, and you might have noticed we don't mention your upper chest. Try to keep it still and focus your attention lower. If you focus on your upper chest, you might tend to begin breathing more shallowly again. Remember: inhale, lower lungs, lower back, and rib cage expand. Exhale, lower lungs, lower back, and rib cage contract, returning to normal position and helping to push the breath out of the body.

Breath pours in, diaphragm moves down. Breathe pours out, diaphragm moves up. It's a mantra!

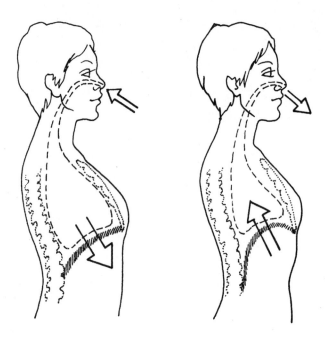

This action is contrary to how many adults are used to breathing, because shallow breathing is a common malady of adult life. In shallow breathing, the chest rises and falls, and sometimes the shoulders follow. In deep breathing, the shoulders stay still and the abdomen and stomach move first from the compression of the diaphragm. The lower lungs fill up before the upper chest.

If you are a shallow breather (like many people are), you may find deep breathing, counterintuitive and extremely difficult at first. It helps to lie down and put your hand on your floating ribs, next to your stomach. As you inhale, try to push your hand out with your stomach as you feel your lower back and rib cage expanding, too. As you exhale, push your lower ribs and stomach in with your hand, all the while trying not to engage your shoulders, but instead focusing on the lower half of your torso and rib cage contracting. Eventually you'll get the hang of it. Then you'll be able to try it standing up, and before long it will be second nature once again.

Another way to encourage proper deep breathing is to concentrate on breathing "out of" your entire body. Rather than visualizing air filling your lungs and moving back out, visualize that with each inhalation, air flows in through every pore on the surface of your skin and expands your entire body. With the exhalation, air flows out through your skin again. Feel your entire body slowly inhaling, exhaling, inhaling, exhaling—your feet, your legs, your stomach, your back, your shoulders, your arms, your head. Now you're breathing!

> **Mindful Minute**
>
> Holotropic breathwork is a psycho-spiritual bodywork technique developed by Stanislav Grof, M.D., and his wife, Christina, in 1976. It combines rapid breathing with loud music, meant to invoke an alternate state of consciousness that loosens psychological barriers and frees repressed memories and emotions.

How Do You Breathe? A Self-Quiz

For this quiz, wear clothing that allows you to see your body shape (or if you are comfortable, strip down to your skivvies or wear no clothes at all!). Stand in front of a large mirror, preferably a full-length mirror. Pick the one best answer for each question.

1. Take a deep breath without thinking too much about it. As you inhale, what moves?

   A. My shoulders move up and my chest rises. My stomach caves in.

   B. My stomach expands, and my chest sinks slightly. My shoulders don't move.

2. Now, exhale. What moves?

   A. My shoulders sink back down, and my chest falls.

   B. My stomach sinks back in. My shoulders and chest don't move.

3. Take another deep breath, both inhalation and exhalation. What sounds do you hear?

   A. Louder inhale than exhale.

   B. Louder exhale than inhale.

4. Take another deep breath and concentrate on the muscles in your chest. Are you exerting more effort:

   A. On the inhale than the exhale?

   B. On the exhale than the inhale?

5. Turn so you can see your profile in the mirror. Stand normally and look at your stomach. What do you see?

   A. Tightly contracted stomach muscles.

   B. A stomach just hangin' out.

6. Still in profile, take a deep breath. What moves?

   A. My chest.

   B. My stomach.

7. Place one hand on your chest and the other hand on your abdomen. Breathe 10 normal breaths. Which hand moves more?

   A. The chest hand.

   B. The abdomen hand.

8. Still in profile, look at your back. What do you see?

   A. I look pretty slumped. I should probably stand up straighter!

   B. A nice straight line from the crown of my head to my heels.

9. Pretend you are hyperventilating by breathing quickly with shallow breaths. (Don't do it for more than 10 seconds.) How does it feel?

   A. Not so bad—kind of natural.

   B. Unnatural and uncomfortable.

10. Without changing your breath rate, count how many total breaths (inhalation and exhalation) you make in one minute. How many did you count?

    A. More than 15 breaths.

    B. Fewer than 15 breaths.

Now, count how many A and B answers you have.

If you have more than five A answers: You definitely have some serious restricted breathing habits. Consider making breathwork a priority during your meditation sessions, as well as any time you need to relax. Becoming conscious of your breathing and practicing good breathing are the two most important keys to retraining yourself. Once you learn to breathe the way your body is meant to breathe, you'll probably be astounded by the changes you will experience. You'll feel better, have more energy, and your thinking will be sharper.

If you have more than five B answers: You have either relearned or never forgotten how to breathe deeply and fully. Of course, if you have even one A, you've got room for improvement. Who doesn't? Make breathwork a priority, especially since deep breathing comes easily to you. Capitalize on those good breathing habits to maximize your physical and mental well-being.

Sutra on the Full Awareness of Breathing

Learning how to breathe well is by no means something new. Breathing has been the cornerstone of meditation for centuries, and an ancient Buddhist text, called the *Sutra on the Full Awareness of Breathing*, or the *Anapanasati Sutta*, is considered by many to be among the most important meditation texts in existence.

CAUTION

Relax

Asthma, a condition in which the tubes in the lungs spasm, contracting and making breathing difficult, affects 1 in 20 adults in the United States, and the numbers are increasing. If you have asthma, regular deep-breathing exercises are particularly important. Deep breathing improves the tone of all your breathing mechanisms and also has a relaxing effect that can help to lessen the severity of an asthma attack.

In this sutra, the Buddha instructs his disciples on the importance of breathing in full awareness, which will eventually "lead to the perfect accomplishment of true under-standing and complete liberation." According to the Buddha, full awareness breathing is the first step toward perfection (translation by Thich Nhat Hahn):

> When the practitioner can maintain, without distraction, the practice of observ-ing the body in the body, the feelings in the feelings, the mind in the mind, and the objects of mind in the objects of mind, persevering, fully awake, clearly understanding his state, gone beyond all attachment and aversion to this life, with unwavering, steadfast, imperturbable meditative stability, he will attain the first Factor of Awakening, namely mindfulness. When this factor is developed, it will come to perfection.

Breathing Exercises

Breathing exercises make a wonderful warm-up for meditation, as well as becoming a point of focus during meditation. Following are some breathing exercises to try, adapted from many traditions.

Exhalation of Peace

This exercise calms and quiets the mind and invokes a feeling of oneness with the universe. Try doing this with several people. Each person can go at his or her own pace.

◆ Sit in your favorite meditative pose and close your eyes.

◆ Inhale deeply and slowly through your nose, feeling the breath filling you from your lower abdomen upward.

◆ Open your lips and softly begin to make the sound *om*.

◆ Allow the sound of *om* to encompass your entire awareness.

◆ Draw out the *o* sound, then let the *m* sound vibrate.

◆ Listen to the sounds of others around you. Listen to the sound of *om* within.

Wave Breath

This exercise helps you understand how to use and control your breathing by filling up your body with breath in stages, like a wave moving through the sea to the shore.

◆ Lie on your back. Place your hands along your lowest ribs, the floating ribs. As you inhale one full long breath, feel these ribs expand as the lower lungs expand.

◆ Continue this inhalation, keep this expansion, and bring the breath slowly into the middle of the lungs. Watch this area expand.

◆ Keep this expansion and finally bring the air to the top of the lungs, near the collar bone. Watch this area expand.

◆ All three areas of the lung are now fully expanded with this one full inhalation. The wave has crested, now it begins releasing with one long, slow exhale ….

◆ First release the collar bone area, and let it come down.

◆ Continuing the exhalation, release the middle of the chest. Let it come down.

◆ Continuing the exhalation, release the floating ribs. Let them come down.

◆ Full inhale and exhale completed. Here comes another wave. Let's ride it with our breath!

The Big Pause

Between inhalations and exhalations, we naturally pause for a second or two. In this exercise, consciously expand that pause and use those seconds as a meditative moment to contemplate the space within breath as a space for enlightenment and greater knowledge to enter into your consciousness.

- Sit comfortably with your back straight. Inhale deeply and slowly through your nose to a count of 10.

- When your lungs feel completely full, hold your breath to a count of five.

- Exhale through pursed lips to a count of 20. Imagine you are imitating the sound of the wind. On the count of 20, quickly and sharply blow out the last of your breath.

- When all the breath is blown out, wait five seconds before inhaling.

- Repeat.

To make breathing a conscious and purposeful part of your life is to fill your life with vitality, energy, and peace. Don't let another breath go by without knowing it and living it. Then, cultivate your breath so it becomes a tool for greater awareness and self-knowledge.

The Least You Need to Know

- Breath is life, and learning to breathe well might be the most important thing you can do for your mind-body.

- We are born knowing how to breathe well, but many of us lose the skill after years of bad habits and stress.

- The diaphragm muscle should move downward with the inhalation and upward with the exhalation.

- You can retrain your breath.

Part 4

Ommmmmm: How to Meditate

Now we're meditating! In this part, we'll introduce you to different techniques for sitting meditation, including the Zen technique of *zazen*, various yoga meditative positions, and what to do with your hands (positions called *mudras*). Next, we'll walk you through walking meditation, including a technique called *kinhin*, which is Zen meditation on the move, and labyrinth walking, a newly revived form of walking meditation that involves following a mazelike pattern into a center and back out again, plus other forms of moving meditation, from the ancient forms of tai chi chuan, and yoga, and to the more modern forms of dynamic meditation and ecstatic dancing. Lie back and relax with us in *shavasana*, the lying-down yoga "corpse pose" that embodies relaxation in its most supreme form. Last, we'll show you how to use sounds, including chanting and the repetition of *mantras*, to further enhance your meditations. And you thought meditation was going to be boring!

HI, I'M MEDITATING RIGHT NOW AND CAN'T COME TO THE PHONE. LEAVE YOUR NAME AND NUMBER AT THE SOUND OF THE MANTRA--**OMMMMMM**...

Seated Meditation: Finding Center

In This Chapter

- How to sit during meditation
- Flexibility: from easy pose to lotus pose
- Chair meditations
- Bandhas: intensify prana, the life-force energy
- Mudras: what to do with your hands

Although types, forms, and positions of meditation vary widely, most people probably think that one sits while meditating.

Indeed, sitting is the most widely practiced meditation position and the position the Buddha was said to be in when he attained enlightenment. If sitting meditation is good enough for the Buddha, it's certainly good enough for us!

Within the realm of sitting meditation, however, you still have a lot of options, which we'll explain in this chapter. Try them all, pick your favorites, then *om* away to your heart's content.

Zazen: Seated Meditation

The type of meditation employed by Zen Buddhists and Western "Zennists" (people who practice a nonreligious form of Zen separated from its Buddhist roots) is called *zazen*. Zazen involves the entire ritual of seated meditation. The actual meditation technique employed in zazen varies according to the teacher. Many agree that for true zazen, techniques like counting, following the breath, or focusing on a mantra are only techniques to train the mind to focus. Zazen is the experience beyond the techniques. It takes a focused mind to experience zazen.

For zazen, total uninvolved awareness of your thoughts, feelings, emotions, and sensations is the key. It is sitting and being, plain and simple. At least, this is so in the *Soto* style or sect of Zen meditation. In the *Rinzai* sect of Zen meditation, the consideration of those Zen puzzles called koans is the primary method for meditation. You sit and ponder the koan until you think you have the answer. You then present your answer to the Zen master, who tells you if you are right or if it's back to the ole' drawing board. If you have a local Zen center, inquire as to which method they follow, Soto or Rinzai.

You don't have to live in a Zen monastery to practice zazen—it can be practiced anywhere. In fact, part of the very nature of the Zen way is to strike out and find your own way, just like the Buddha did. He tried the ways of others and finally succeeded when he did it his own way.

However, many people enjoy practicing zazen in the company of others, and meditation halls or *zendos* for practicing Zen meditation are popular gathering spots. Even if you aren't an "official" Zen Buddhist, you might find meditating in a zendo with other people helps you be more disciplined and regular in your practice. Excellent! However, that first visit to

> **From A to Om**
>
> **Zazen** is the word for the practice of sitting meditation in Zen Buddhism, which can employ different techniques such as the consideration of a koan (a Zen riddle that defies logic, meant to lead the mind out of ordinary thinking and into enlightenment), quiet mindfulness, or other preparatory exercises like counting the breath.

> **From A to Om**
>
> Zen Buddhism consists of two main sects, **Soto** and **Rinzai**. In Soto Zen, "just sitting" is the primary method of zazen, based on the idea that sitting like the Buddha when he attained enlightenment will eventually bring enlightenment. In the Rinzai sect, the primary mode of meditation is the consideration of the koan during zazen.

> **From A to Om**
>
> A **zendo** is a Zen meditation hall.

a zendo can be a bit intimidating for the uninitiated, so we're going to give you a sneak peek at proper zendo etiquette, just in case you should need it.

The Rules of the Zendo

Every zendo has its own rules, but in general, most zendos operate something like we describe here. Follow these steps for a smooth transition into the world of the Zen meditation hall … and don't forget to be mindful. Despite the distracting presence of others, Zen meditation is still about mindfulness and pure being, so … let it be!

While the very nature of Zen may seem to preclude rules, zendos have rules designed to cause the least possible interference to the meditation process of others. Also, because self-discipline is so important for mastering the meditation habit, rules help the Zennist to cultivate self-discipline. Of course, if you don't like the rules, you can always meditate in the comfort of your own home. Also, some zendos are less formal than others.

- Before entering the zendo, remove your shoes and place them in the specified spot.

- Always enter the zendo with your left foot first.

- Before you sit to meditate, place your hands, palms together as if praying, a few inches in front of your chest with your arms parallel to the ground—a hand position called *gassho* in Zen Buddhism— and bow to the altar, which may be as simple as a burning incense stick on a small table in the room. Gassho is often used in conjunction with a bow to greet others and to show respect. The position is similar to the namaste mudra in yoga meditation.

  > **From A to Om**
  > **Gassho** is a hand position similar to the yoga's prayer position, the mudra called *namaste*. (See later in this chapter for an illustration of namaste.)

- When you walk across the room to get to your sitting spot, turn corners squarely. Don't meander, don't cross directly in front of the altar, and don't cut across the room diagonally. When in the zendo, always move and turn clockwise. Of course, don't bother anybody who is meditating.

- Place your hands in the gassho position again and bow toward your seat and to the people meditating on either side of you, who will respond with the gassho bow.

- Turn clockwise and face the people across the room, bowing in gassho to them. They also will respond.

◆ Sit down on your *zafu* (a special cushion to sit on while meditating) or small wooden meditation bench. Either of these may be placed on top of a thick mat or small futon called a *zabuton*.

From A to Om

A **zafu** is a small pillow for sitting during Zen meditation. A **zabuton** is a thick meditation mat or small futon placed under the zafu. These items make meditation more comfortable.

◆ Turn clockwise toward the wall to meditate in the Soto style. Turn away from the wall and meditate facing the center of the room in the Rinzai style.

◆ Sit down and start meditating!

◆ When you are finished, get up, bow again, and leave the room, following the same procedure as you used to enter it.

Zazen typically uses a three-point or tripod position of the body for greatest stability. The practitioner sits in the lotus position or kneeling position with both knees touching the ground or the zabuton (see the following figure). The third point is the zafu or small pillow the practitioner sits on. Small meditation benches can also be used and might be more comfortable for some.

At home, you can use a small pillow to achieve the zazen position of seated meditation. The position should be comfortable, not forced, so cross your legs in whatever manner is most natural for you at this time.

How to Do It

Once you've seated yourself in the proper position—which could be with legs crossed, or kneeling with a pillow or bench over your heels to sit on—here's what to do:

◆ Rock back and forth a bit to find the most stable position. You're looking for a center position that takes the least effort to maintain, one that feels balanced.

- Lift from the crown of your head as if a silk thread were pulling it up to the ceiling. Straighten your back and breathe easily.

- Lift your heart and feel your shoulders relax downward.

- Place your tongue behind your upper teeth to keep it out of the way. Keep your mouth closed on the inhale, breathing through your nose. On the exhale, open your mouth slightly or exhale through your nose. Inhaling through your nose is more relaxing and conducive to meditation. Your nasal passages also filter the air, making the air that enters your lungs cleaner.

- For zazen, keep your eyes slightly open but unfocused, angled about halfway between straight ahead and down. Don't actually look at anything. Let your focus blur.

- Take a few deep breaths to prepare yourself, then breathe normally.

- Place your hands together, palms upturned, your left hand cradling your right in your lap against your abdomen. The second joints of your middle fingers should touch, and your fingers should face each other and be parallel to your abdomen.

- Lift both thumbs and join them at the tips to form an oval. This hand position, or *mudra*, is sometimes called the cosmic mudra.

- The rest is simple (and incredibly difficult): Start being. Don't concentrate. Observe your breath, your body feeling, your emotions, your thoughts, and whatever comes into your mind, but don't concentrate on any one thing. If something captures your attention, acknowledge it, but stay emotionally disengaged from it. Let your emotions and thoughts be things separate from you. Watch them like balloons or dandelion fluff floating by you—with interest and appreciation, but without becoming them. Don't let them capture you. Watch them, and your body will gradually relax.

Zazen is, by its very nature, essentially techniqueless, so we can't really give you any zazen "tricks" or "rules." It is simply pure awareness. It is easy, yet it is also supremely difficult and takes years of practice to perfect. To explain it in the form of a koan: You don't have to do anything—but yet, you are doing nothing.

Now you're zazen-ing!

> **From A to Om**
>
> A **mudra** is a hand position that redirects energy emitted from the fingertips back into the mind-body by connecting the fingers and hands to each other in a "circuit." There are several different mudras, differentiated by which fingers and parts of the hands are joined in which shapes.

Chair Meditations for Home, School, or Office

We realize sitting on the floor to meditate isn't always practical in every situation—you might not want your boss walking into your office and stumbling over you on your zafu—but that doesn't mean you can't meditate at the office. You'll probably enjoy your job better (and perform it better, too) if you find a few minutes here and there for meditation.

A quick five-minute session in lieu of a coffee break will do wonders for your workday. If you smoke, a mini-meditation break is a great, healthy substitute for a cigarette break!

Your desk chair is a fine place for meditation as is any comfortable chair at home that has a firm seat for support. Learning a few quick steps for chair meditation will make meditation even more accessible because you can practice it daily at work, at school, or even at your own kitchen table or home office desk chair.

♦ Remove your shoes. (Removing your shoes is a way to humble yourself to your surroundings and is also symbolic of removing your Earth worries and concerns.) Sit up straight in your chair. Depending on the shape of the chair, you might not be able to use the backrest. Shift around until you find a steady, stable position centered over the hips that feels comfortable. Lift your heart and relax your shoulders down. Keep your feet flat on the floor to stay grounded. Or if your chair seat is roomy enough, cross your legs. Rest your hands on your knees.

♦ Take a cue from zazen and close your eyes only partially. That way, if something demands your immediate attention, you'll be able to adjust more quickly than if your eyes were closed. Of course, if you don't have to worry about distractions (which is ideal), you can close your eyes completely—as long as you aren't at risk for falling asleep! (We'd hate to see you fall out of your chair just as your boss walks by.)

♦ Take three very deep breaths originating in your lower abdomen. Breathe in through your nose and out through your mouth.

Bliss Byte

If the chair you choose has a reclining back, sit straight up on the edge of the chair and don't use the backrest. If your chair has a firm, straight back that can support you with your feet still planted on the floor, go ahead and make use of the extra support.

Mindful Minute

Today is a gift. That's why it's called the "present"!

Now choose your favorite meditation option from the following list. If varying techniques will keep you meditating more regularly, pick a different method each day:

◆ Focus on the feel of your breath as it moves in and out of your nostrils. Refuse to let other thoughts and feelings engage you, even as you notice their presence. Don't fight them. Acknowledge them, then go back to the breath.

◆ Focus on sound. What do you hear around you? Notice all the sounds of your office, your classroom, your kitchen, or wherever you are. Do you hear air coming out of the vents? Copy machines? Ringing phones? The low murmur of conversation? Focus on the pure sound, not the meaning of any of the sounds.

◆ Focus on an object on your desk. Whenever your mind wanders, bring it back to the contemplation of the object—say, a stapler. What does the stapler do? What parts does it have? How often does it need to be maintained? What is its purpose? What would the world be like without it? How have you used it in the past? And if you're really getting into it: What might the stapler represent in your life? Does it symbolize something for you? Does it have a cosmic meaning? Why did you choose it? What is your awareness trying to tell you about yourself? About the nature of reality?

◆ Focus on the mantra "Now." If you can't say it out loud (say you're meditating in a doctor's waiting room), repeat it in your mind. *Now. Now. Now.* Become the present moment. There is no past. There is no future. There is only now, and you are completely present in the now.

◆ Do a quick sitting body scan. Move your awareness from your toes slowly up your legs, your body and arms, your neck, and your head. Imagine your awareness is a warm, rose-colored ring of light moving upward, then moving back down again. As it moves up, it warms and relaxes your body, concentrating its heat in your body at the place where you hold the most tension. As it moves back down, from the crown of your head to your toes, imagine the sensation that your body is melting into total relaxation.

Seated Meditative Poses

If you're going to sit while you meditate, it helps to know how to sit. The position you choose can mean the difference between sticking to it and giving up after a few uncomfortable minutes.

We've already explained the traditional sitting position for zazen (sitting on a zafu in a cross-legged position or sitting with the knees touching the floor for a tripodlike stability). Meditating yogis, Zennists, and lots of other meditators use several other positions. We'll show you a few of the most common yoga poses practiced for seated meditation.

Comfort and good posture are keys to seated meditation. A slumped back constricts your breathing and keeps energy from flowing through your body to stimulate and open your chakras. If possible, try your seated meditation pose in front of a mirror to check your posture and correct it, if necessary. Seeing is believing! If your legs and lower back are not comfortable, use a small pillow to support your back and rest your knees on the floor, as is done in zazen.

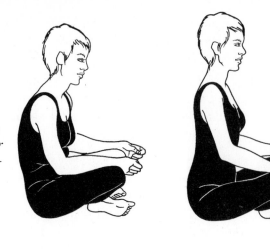

Easy Pose

This pose is perfect for the beginning meditator. This pose is called *sukhasana* in Sanskrit, which literally means "joy pose," and joyful is just how you'll feel when you sit in this stable yet simple pose. The easy pose helps quiet your mind and bring your body to stillness. It requires far less flexibility than some of the more advanced poses.

Joan demonstrates easy pose. Sit in a simple cross-legged position with either leg on top. Lift the crown of your head and feel your spine straighten. Rest your hands on your knees, palms down, and relax into the pose, rocking back and forth slightly to find the perfect center of stability.

(Photo by Saeid Lahouti)

But even though this is called "easy pose," it's not easy for many Westerners to do. If your spine is not comfortably straight in this pose, you should sit higher—on several folded firm blankets or a bolster—and even give your knees support if necessary. If this makes the pose a bit "easier" for you, go ahead and try it.

Kneeling Pose

The kneeling pose is one of the most common poses held by Zen Buddhist monks. It can be uncomfortable for the beginning meditator, especially on the knees, but sitting on a pillow or zafu (as shown Joan does in the following photo) eases the discomfort considerably. This is also the pose to use with a meditation bench.

In Sanskrit, this pose is called *vajrasana*, which literally means "thunderbolt pose" or "diamond pose." These names suggest the pose's power. The pressure from sitting on the feet helps stimulate circulation to the feet. This pose also opens the chest and relieves pressure on the diaphragm, making for more breathing room.

Joan demonstrates kneeling pose. Sit back on your heels, keeping your knees and heels together. Or place a pillow or small meditation bench (or even a thick, sturdy book) between your ankles and sit on it. Or place a larger firm pillow across your ankles and sit on that. Keep your spine straight, lifting the crown of your head. If you feel uncomfortable pressure on your knees, go back to the easy pose for a while.

(Photo by Saeid Lahouti)

Regular yoga practice will help make you more flexible, and eventually, this kneeling pose will feel great. Don't rush it! Meditative poses must feel good so your body isn't a distraction during meditation.

Hero Pose

The hero pose, or *virasana* in Sanskrit, is a more advanced version of the kneeling pose. This pose can also be hard on your knees, so don't force it or do anything that hurts. With time, stretching, and regular yoga practice, you'll relax into it eventually. Again, you can sit on a firm pillow, zafu, bench, or book to ease the knees.

Sit back on your heels, then gradually separate your feet until you are sitting on the floor between your ankles. Feel your breath move in and out of your body. Then, place your hands on your knees.

Lotus's Many Petals

The most classic meditation pose, and the pose most people envision when they picture someone meditating, is the lotus pose. In Sanskrit, this pose is called *padmasana*, which means "lotus pose," and the posture represents the lotus flower open to the light. This posture keeps the spine straight and is the most stable of the poses. It keeps the body still, and when the body is still, the mind eventually stills, too. In fact, you can even fall asleep in this position and not fall over! This posture keeps your chest open, gives you lots of breathing room, and opens your Venus chakra (heart chakra).

Mindful Minute

In 1983, a Detroit chemical manufacturing firm instituted a meditation program for their workers. According to owner Buck Montgomery, after three years, 52 of the 100 employees at all levels were meditating for 20 minutes before work and 20 minutes in the afternoon during work (yes, they were paid for the time). Productivity rose 120 percent, absenteeism fell by 85 percent, quality control rose 240 percent, injuries dropped by 70 percent, sick days fell by 16 percent, and profits soared 520 percent.

Full Lotus

For full lotus pose (*padmasana* in Sanskrit), sit and take a few deep breaths. Bring one ankle up over the opposite thigh, then bring the other ankle over the opposite thigh. For some people, putting the right leg on top is easier; for others, putting the left leg on top is easier. Your right leg is linked with your left brain and represents yang, solar energy, and male energy. Your left leg is linked with your right brain and represents yin, lunar energy, and female energy. Whichever leg feels more comfortable on top represents which energy force is stronger in you. If you feel pain in your hips or knees, return to a simple cross-legged position until your flexibility increases (regular yoga practice can help).

Joan demonstrates yoga's lotus pose. Remember, first and foremost, it is always important to be comfortable. Return to easy pose if lotus proves too demanding for this meditation session. Try again tomorrow!

(Photo by Saeid Lahouti)

Bliss Byte

The lotus pose is meant to evoke the symbolism of the lotus flower, which grows in muddy water, has its roots in slime, but ascends to the top of the water where it opens its beautiful and untainted flower. This symbolizes enlightenment, wherein the enlightened one is unaffected by the imperfect world, remaining pure and perfect. You, too, can have your feet firmly planted in the real world, but your mind can bloom like the lotus flower with pure awareness and enlightenment! The lotus flower shifts across the surface of a pond with the wind, yet stays rooted, symbolizing stability in an unpredictable world.

Half Lotus

The half lotus (*ardha padmasana*) has similar benefits to the lotus pose. In the half lotus, one foot is placed on the opposite thigh, but the opposite foot stays on the floor.

> **CAUTION**
>
> **Relax** _____
>
> Many meditation teachers recommend that a meditation pose not be held for longer than three hours.

If your sitting bones are stable and moving down into the floor, your body shouldn't lean but will remain straight. Half lotus pose is easier than the lotus pose and is a good way to work up to the full lotus if you periodically switch the foot that rests on top of the opposite thigh. Although this is called Half lotus, it is not half a pose. It is a full meditation pose that the Buddha often sat in to meditate.

Bound Lotus

Once you've mastered the full lotus, you can move on to the bound lotus pose, or *baddha padmasana*. This pose requires good arm and shoulder flexibility, as well as good leg and hip flexibility, but it offers an incredibly solid base and opens the chest even further, facilitating breathing and a deeply relaxed peacefulness.

Sit in a full lotus position. Cross your arms behind your back and hold your right foot with your left hand and your left foot with your right hand. With enough practice, you'll be as relaxed in this pose as Joan is! Take it one day at a time.

(Photo by Saeid Lahouti)

Lock in the Energy: Bandhas

Yoga postures fill the body with prana and activate the internal life-force energy. Yoga literature stresses the importance of holding prana in the body to keep the body healthy and balanced. How can you keep prana from escaping once you've activated it? And can you intensify it as it meanders through its channels, or *nadis?* Yoga has the answer: Heat it up and lock it in with specific movements called *bandhas.*

Bandhas aren't drastic movements. They are little movements, but they can be incorporated into your meditation program. The three bandhas are best used in conjunction with *pranayama,* or deep-breathing exercises. As prana infuses the body, bandhas lock it in, intensify it, even reverse its subtle direction along the internal channels in ways that make it merge with itself, heat up, and strengthen (to simplify an advanced yoga theory).

Try using bandhas during your next deep-breathing session, as preparation for meditation, or during meditation itself. You might find your meditation experience intensified. Practice the following bandhas in order, as specified, over a two-breath cycle, or work on one at a time.

From A to Om

Bandhas, literally "to bind" or "to lock," are muscular locks used during yoga postures and breathing exercises to intensify the energy of prana in the body. The three primary bandhas are *mula bandha* (at the perineum), *uddiyani bandha* (at the naval), and *jalandhara bandha* (behind the chin). **Nadis** are the internal channels or pathways—like power lines!—through which prana flows in the body.

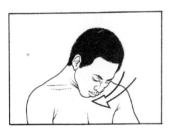

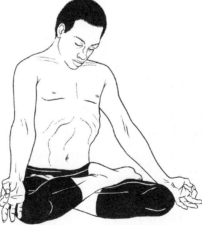

Practicing the three bandhas together is a powerful, advanced yoga technique for optimizing the positive affect of prana in the mind-body. Try it—gently. If lotus pose is too uncomfortable, relax into easy pose.

◆ **Jalandhara bandha.** Inhale deeply, slightly raising your chest; then, as you hold the breath in, place your chin gently into your chest to prevent the escape of prana from your upper body. Hold for a few seconds (be sure not to strain your neck—the hold is firm but gentle), release, and lift your head before exhalation.

- **Uddiyana bandha.** After you have exhaled completely, pull your navel up and back toward your spine. This action works the diaphragm muscle and forces prana up one of the nadis, when it would naturally be moving down, intensifying its energy. Release.

- **Mula bandha.** Inhale deeply, then contract the perineal muscle (the muscle you sit on, in the area between your rectum and your genitals). This lock prevents the escape of life-force energy from the lower body, pushing it back up. If you can't isolate your perineal muscle, contract your anal sphincter and the whole general area down there. Eventually, you'll be able to tell the difference between the different muscles (no hurry—that kind of muscle isolation is quite advanced).

Bliss Byte

Although advanced yogis practice the bandhas to a more intense degree, your bandha contractions should be light. Don't wrench your muscles into unnatural contractions. Place your chin gently on your chest, pull your navel back lightly, contract your perineal muscle with about the same effort you would make to close your eyes. Bandhas aren't meant to be strenuous or severe. It doesn't take massive physical action to internally redirect prana—just a little nudge from the mind-body.

Don't expect to feel anything dramatic at first. The effect of bandhas is subtle but real. Eventually, as you become more internally sensitive and self-aware (the inevitable result of meditation!), you will be able to detect the energizing effect of bandhas. Bandhas can also be brought into practice within other yoga postures. Practicing the bandhas can help to deepen the effects of yoga poses.

Bliss Byte

Placing your hands palms-down on your knees during meditation helps center and ground your energy. Placing your hands palms-up on your knees helps open you to the energies around you.

Mudras to Channel Chakra Energy

Once you've got your sitting position mastered, consider your hands. In the previous section on zazen, we described one hand position (the cosmic mudra), but there are actually many. These hand positions are called mudras, and their purpose is to rechannel energy, which is thought to emanate from the fingertips, back into the body.

Yoga practitioners developed many different hand positions to be used during meditation, but here are a few of our favorites.

- **Namaste mudra:** The namaste mudra indicates respect and humility.

- **Om mudra:** The om mudra joins divine energy and the self.

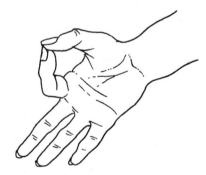

- **Gnana mudra:** The gnana mudra symbolizes enlightened individuality.

◆ **Buddhi mudra:** The buddhi mudra reminds us of the divinity within.

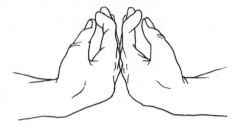

◆ **Chalice mudra:** The chalice mudra is a mudra of blissful energy.

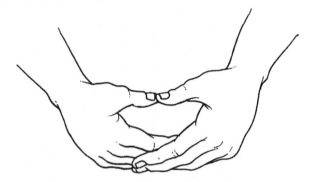

◆ **Shanti mudra:** The shanti mudra is a gesture of blessing.

◆ **Gomukha mudra:** The gomukha mudra symbolizes the unification of body and mind.

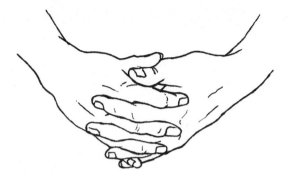

◆ **Prithvi mudra:** The prithvi mudra represents oneness with the earth.

You needn't practice the same sitting position or mudra each time, although some people have their favorites. Matching your meditation positions and gestures to your flexibility level, your moods, and your individual needs for the day will add a degree of flavor to your routine and customize your meditation sessions to be most effective.

You've assumed the position. You've got the gestures. You're ready to go. Have a wonderful 20 minutes (or more!).

The Least You Need to Know

◆ Zazen is the form of seated meditation practiced in Zen meditation.

◆ Chair meditation is also great for work breaks, school breaks, or short breaks at home. No flexibility is necessary!

◆ Yoga has developed many other meditative positions, each requiring different degrees of flexibility and with different effects, including the venerable lotus pose.

◆ Bandhas can be used in seated meditation to energize the life force, or prana, within you.

◆ Mudras are hand positions held during meditation and used for greetings and blessings. Mudras rechannel energy released through the fingertips back into the body.

Movement Meditation: Go in Peace

In This Chapter

- ◆ Can you meditate if you're busy walking?
- ◆ How, when, and where to walk mindfully
- ◆ Labyrinths and pilgrimages: sacred walks for everyday people
- ◆ Yoga, tai chi, and QiGong
- ◆ Dynamic meditation

Sitting isn't the only way to meditate! It is a good way to meditate, make no mistake, but you can also meditate on the move in a host of different ways. Simple walking can be an incredibly powerful and enlightening technique for meditation. So can a yoga or tai chi practice or even your own individualized form of ecstatic dancing. Movement and meditation go well together because meditation teaches you mindful awareness as you move through life, and that's a great skill to have.

On the Move with Walking Meditation

Walking meditation is probably about as old as the first person who ever had to walk somewhere by him- or herself. Solitary walking seems to encourage a meditative state. Many artists claim they get their best and most inspired ideas while walking. Walking through nature can be awe-inspiring and can invoke an appropriately meditative sense of wonder. Walking needn't be for the purpose of just getting somewhere.

In many traditions, walking takes a more formal turn, following specific patterns or directions. Whether walking the path of a labyrinth while engaging in meditative prayer or following the clockwise path around the zendo altar in walking zazen (called *kinhin*), walking can be accomplished solely for the purpose of being in the moment while walking.

All About Kinhin

Kinhin is just moving zazen. While the top half of your body retains the posture of sitting meditation, the bottom half is in motion. In Buddhist zendos (meditation halls), while some sit in meditation, others walk, always clockwise, around the altar in the practice of kinhin. (That way, nobody bumps into anybody!)

From A to Om

Kinhin is zazen (Zen seated meditation) performed while walking. While the upper body is held in the position used for sitting meditation, the lower body moves, very slowly, with complete and total awareness of the movement.

Sometimes walking and sitting meditations are practiced in alternation. Kinhin is typically performed very slowly, at the rate of one step per full breath (inhale and exhale—yes, that slowly), although in some traditions, it's slightly faster than this.

Slow walking allows for complete awareness of every movement and every motion. The awareness continues to move, too, but experiences every aspect of the movement. Kinhin can also be performed outside in a circle or in a straight line, back and forth.

Where Are You Going and How Do You Get There?

But you needn't call it kinhin to enjoy walking meditation. Many traditions have practiced and contemplated walking as a meditative form. One thing they all have in common is to abolish the thought of destination from the process of walking so only the walking remains. That doesn't mean you can't have a destination when you practice walking meditation. But if you do have a destination, it doesn't concern you during your meditation because you are living wholly in the present moment, and that moment is all of your awareness.

Ideally, meditative walking should be undertaken solely for the purpose of the walk. Where can you walk? Anywhere—but some environments are more conducive to meditation than others. Why not try the following:

- A hike through a national, state, or city park

- Walking around a beautiful flower bed, whether in your own yard or in a park

- A circle around the block of your own (or someone else's) residential neighborhood

- Walking the perimeter of a peaceful room in your home

- Walking slowly back and forth down the length of a long hallway in your home

- Organizing a nature walk or labyrinth walk (walking along a mazelike labyrinth path as a metaphor for traveling into the inner self—read more about labyrinths later in this chapter) with friends, or if you practice an organized religion, with other members of your faith

Bliss Byte

If appropriate, perform your kinhin barefoot. Even more ideally, walk barefoot outside. The closer your foot comes to making contact with the earth, the more vivid will be your experience and the earth energy you can utilize.

Bliss Byte

Do meditative walks work in groups? Walking with a friend can make meditation difficult because you will likely be distracted by conversation unless you both agree to make the walk a meditative one. Walking in groups can be a wonderful way to practice communal meditation, with everyone walking in his or her own meditative manner.

Wherever you decide to walk during meditation, in beautiful surroundings or in ordinary ones, outside or inside, in a sacred space or a living space, the most important thing is to be in the moment and experience the walking with full awareness. Where are you going during meditation? Right where you are. And how do you get there? You are there.

If you've got access to a safe natural body of water, take a meditative water walk for a change of pace. Put on your bathing suit and walk parallel to the bank of a lake or the beach of the ocean, hip- to waist-deep in the water. Really soak in the natural surroundings and feel how different it is to walk in water. An added benefit for meditation: The water will force you to slow your pace.

Mindful walking is a great way to ease into a practice of meditation. Stressful thoughts melt away as you concentrate on your movement, breathing, and the beauty of the world around you. Where you are going, and where you have been, fade in importance. What matters now is where you are!

How to Do It

Not sure how to begin your walking meditation as you step out into the natural world? Follow these steps (literally!) for a tranquil country meditation walk:

♦ Begin by matching your steps with your breath. Don't force a rhythm that doesn't feel right. For a slow pace, try one to four steps for every deep inhalation and one to four (or two to eight) steps for every long, full exhalation.

♦ Bring your awareness to your feet. Feel them as they make contact with the earth. Do they touch the ground heel to toe? How does it feel to touch the earth? Can you feel the movement of your weight shifting along the length of your foot as it touches the ground from heel to toe? Are you slamming your heel into the ground instead of placing it softly? (If the weather and environment permit, it helps to go barefoot or wear very soft shoes, such as moccasins, to better feel the contact.)

♦ Now, in your mind, tell yourself what you are doing, for example: *I am walking on this country road. I am walking down this mountain path. I am walking along this beach.* Repeat this phrase in your mind again and again, not automatically, but to remind yourself to experience the present moment. Whenever your mind starts to wander

> **Bliss Byte**
>
> Are you strapped for nature in your neighborhood? Take a stroll through a local upscale garden center. Sure, the nature may be in pots, but it is still beautiful. You may have to tell a salesperson you are "just browsing," but other than that, you probably won't be disturbed.

away from your actual walking experience, bring it back to you
ment. Pay attention. Pay attention. Pay attention.

◆ What do you see? Notice the colors, the textures, the pattern
ments of nature. What do you hear? Notice the sounds of natu
smell? Notice the aromas of nature.

◆ What do you feel? Stop occasionally to
put your hand on a tree, feel a beautiful
flower petal, brush your fingers through
the grass, examine a lovely seashell, or take
in an incredible view. Then continue on.

◆ The point of meditative walking in nature
isn't to completely internalize your awareness. It is, instead, to completely experience
your awareness and make contact with
nature again, to reenergize and replenish
your soul. We are all nature-hungry to
some degree. Feed yourself!

◆ Walk for at least 20 minutes. An hour is
better. An hour every day is best!

Mindful Minute

"Me? Hug a tree? I'm no
tree hugger!" Why not? Put
your arms around a tree—the
bigger and older the better—and
give it a solid, long, firm hug.
The tree breathes in the carbon
dioxide you exhale. You breathe
in the oxygen the tree exhales.
You are joined in a lovely symbi-
otic relationship symbolized by
your hug. You might be surprised
how reassuring it feels to hug a
tree!

Sacred Walks

Sometimes, meditative walking has a more internalized flavor and isn't meant so much for experiencing the present moment as for symbolizing
a journey into the self. Not surprisingly, many
formalized sacred walks are associated with particular religions or religious institutions, but
sacred walks don't "belong" to any creed. They
are universal, spiritual tools that anyone of any
belief can use for self-discovery.

Relax

Although night can be
a beautiful and peaceful time for
a meditative walk, these days,
we can't recommend walking
alone at night, especially in
larger cities. Unfortunately, the
world isn't always a safe place.
If you do want to walk at night,
make sure you walk in a safe
place and take a buddy along
with you.

The Labyrinth

One type of sacred walk that has become popular in recent years is the *labyrinth*.
Labyrinths have been around for thousands of years, but they've never been as

portable and well traversed as they are today. Labyrinth patterns are in evidence on artifacts up to 4,000 years old, from all over the world, including India, Egypt, Sumatra, Peru, Afghanistan, England, and the American Southwest.

From A to Om

A **labyrinth** is a maze-like pattern or structure consisting of a single or **unicursal** path leading to the center. Typically, the pattern consists of seven interconnected concentric circles.

Labyrinths are somewhat like mazes, and mazes are sometimes called labyrinths. However, a classic *unicursal* labyrinth has only one path, as opposed to a maze, which has many paths and is designed to challenge the intellect to find the center. The labyrinth is meant to represent the spiritual journey into the interior self.

Labyrinths typically consist of 7 or 11 concentric circles containing a winding path that leads, quite indirectly, to the center. Walkers step into the labyrinth and slowly follow the circuitous route to the center while meditating, praying, reading scriptures, breathing consciously, or simply walking with slow deliberation. Frequently, evocative music plays in the background—classical music or Gregorian chants, for example. How transforming could the experience be? Incredibly, many who walk labyrinths claim they experienced incredible emotional or spiritual upheavals.

According to Reverend Lauren Artress of Grace Cathedral in San Francisco in her book *Walking a Sacred Path: Rediscovering the Labyrinth as a Spiritual Tool,* "To walk a sacred path is to discover our inner sacred space: that core of feeling that is waiting to have life breathed back into it through symbols, archetypal forms like the labyrinth, rituals, stories, and myths."

Dr. Artress is largely responsible for the recent popularity of labyrinth walking. In 1991, she walked the 11-circle labyrinth at the Chartres Cathedral in France and understood the process as a spiritual tool and a universal archetype of our culture. Soon after, she constructed a 35-foot replica of the Chartres labyrinth, painted with purple paint on a portable canvas, for her San Francisco church. Since first making that portable labyrinth available, Grace Cathedral has constructed a 36-foot-wide wool tapestry labyrinth in its nave and a 40-foot-wide terrazzo labyrinth on its grounds. More than a million people have walked the labyrinths at Grace Cathedral.

Today, many cathedrals and other places of worship feature portable labyrinths. Check your local religious organizations to see if one is available in your area.

The experience of walking the labyrinth might surprise you—what starts out as pure fun and discovery transforms into a profound exploration of the self; one that you share with the other labyrinth walkers as they wind in and out of your ritual path.

Graduations

Life is full of opportunities for walking. Some are the *big* walks that symbolize a life transition. For these moments, mindful walking is especially important. These are the moments you'll want to remember for as long as you can, but they also tend to be the moments in which we don't focus because we are so overwhelmed with stress, emotion, or organizational details. Once your life-transition walk has begun, however, let everything past and future disappear. Live fully and wholly in the now when you …

- ◆ Walk across the stage to receive your diploma.
- ◆ Walk down the aisle to get married.
- ◆ Walk to the podium to give a speech or presentation.
- ◆ Walk out of an old home for the last time.
- ◆ Walk into a new home for the first time.
- ◆ Walk into or away from any life-changing situation: a birth, a death, walking toward someone you love, physically being apart from someone you love, walking into a new job or away from an old job, waking up on your birthday.

Walking seems like such a mundane act, yet it can be a spiritually intense or profoundly relaxing experience. Learn to walk just for the sake of the walk, and your journey will become your destination.

Live your defining moments, and gradually you'll learn to live all your moments—because really, the only moment that truly defines you is *this* moment.

Students at Washington College in Chestertown, Maryland, begin the ritual walk marking their graduation. It's all in the feet!

(Courtesy Washington College; photograph by Trisha McGee)

The Many Modes of Moving Meditation

If sitting can be meditation and walking can be meditation, can anything be meditation? Yes, anything *can* be meditation. With practice, you can maintain a state of mindful awareness 24 hours a day. So once you've learned to meditate while sitting and meditate while walking, expand your meditation practice to other areas of movement. If movement is more your style, get out your energy with dynamic meditation *before* you attempt sitting meditation.

For centuries, various cultures have attempted to extend the meditative state into other areas of physical activity, resulting in many forms of mind-body-spirit fitness programs, from yoga to whirling. Each of these systems is designed to nurture, maintain, strengthen, and actualize the entire self. To reap the maximum benefit, they are best practiced in a state of mindfulness.

Whether you're looking for an interesting variation to your regular fitness program or want to immerse yourself in the spiritual dimension of your favorite tradition, consider adding moving meditations to your meditation repertoire.

Yoga Is More Than Exercise

These days, yoga is big news. Yoga classes of all types are popping up everywhere. Some of the more high-profile yoga teachers have become minor celebrities, while major celebrities are turning to yoga more often as their favorite fitness method. Just ask Sting, Madonna, or Gwyneth Paltrow about their yoga practice. (What? Gwyneth isn't returning your call? She must be busy meditating.)

Of course, popularity isn't a reason to engage in anything, but yoga is no passing fad. It has been around for thousands of years, and we're betting it will be around for thousands more. Yoga is a complete program of mind-body maintenance, including physical exercises, breathing exercises, and an important relaxation technique called *shavasana* (see Chapter 15 for more on shavasana).

Yoga doesn't have to be static, either. Although many of the yoga poses are held for minutes at a time, yoga also contains *vinyasas*, or flowing, dancelike sequences of postures. To practice yoga well and in the true spirit of meditation, find a qualified yoga teacher and try a class. Once you find a teacher you can connect with, you're in for a delightful experience and a form of meditation that can open up new mind-body channels you never knew existed. You'll gain flexibility, energy, strength, and who knows ... maybe even enlightenment!

Probably the most well-known vinyasa is the sun salutation. Our solar system revolves around the sun, and the sun powers our planet. This yoga vinyasa offers thanks to the sun for all it gives us and is most appropriately performed outdoors at sunrise, facing east (although you can, of course, perform it any time, anywhere). Feel the sun's energy flowing through you as you move meditatively through this vinyasa, filling you with vitality.

> **From A to Om**
>
> **Yoga** means "union" and comes from the Sanskrit root *yuj*, meaning "to yoke or join together." It is a centuries-old system for mind-body health designed to gain control over the body, breath, and mind so enlightenment can be attained. **Vinyasa** is a steady flow of connected yoga postures linked with breathing exercises in a continuous movement.

◆ *Stand with your feet together, back straight, hands together in front of your chest as if in prayer.*

◆ *Inhale and raise your arms up and slightly behind your head, leaning back slightly to look toward the sun.*

◆ *Exhale and bend forward, dropping your hands toward the floor.*

◆ *Inhale, place your hands on the floor, and step back with your left foot so your left leg is extended behind you.*

◆ *Exhale as you bring your right leg behind you and hold your body up as if about to do a push-up.*

◆ *Exhale further and touch your knees, chest, and chin to the floor.*

- Inhale and lift the front part of your torso off the ground. Look up.

- Exhale, lifting your hips so your body forms an upside-down V.

- Inhale and bring your left leg forward, leaving your right leg extended behind you.

- Exhale and stand up but leave the front part of your torso hanging forward.

- Inhale as you bring your torso up to stretch slightly back, arms up, looking again toward the sun.

- Exhale and stand straight and tall with your hands to your sides.

- Repeat.

QiGong: Live Long and Prosper

QiGong (also known as *chi kung*) is another centuries-old system of mind-body maintenance originating in China and based on many of the principles of Taoism. QiGong is sitting or standing meditation; exercises for stretching, releasing energy, and purifying the body; massage; breathwork; and certain targeted movements to correct imbalances or disease.

QiGong is based around the concept of chi (or Qi) and the meridians through which it flows. It also deals with the energy field around the body. QiGong exercises are designed to purify and open the meridians so energy can flow freely through them to heal the body. Its exercises are simple and many are designed for people who are ill or injured. Meditation is an important part of QiGong, but many QiGong practitioners meditate standing up. The mind should remain in a meditative state during the exercises. QiGong also has a form of walking meditation.

From A to Om

QiGong means "energy skill" and is sometimes translated as "empowerment." It is a 5,000-year-old system of health and life-force energy maintenance and also a healing art. It is the forerunner of tai chi and the other martial arts systems from China. QiGong typically exists in three forms: martial, medical, and spiritual.

From A to Om

Tai chi means "way of the fist" and is an ancient martial arts system. Today, tai chi has evolved from its martial arts origins into a practice of movement meditation and fitness for peaceful purposes.

One specialized breathing technique sometimes used in QiGong is "reverse breathing." Unlike incorrect reverse breathing, this type of breathing is conscious and mindful, engaging and strengthening the lymph glands, the descending aorta, and the sacral lumbar area, as well as the diaphragm muscle.

Place your hands on the lower abdomen. As you inhale, press your hands in and contract the abdomen. As you exhale, push your abdomen out and relax. Repeat for 50 breaths.

Tai Chi: The Restorative Power of Slow Motion

Tai chi is an ancient martial arts form practiced today all over the world—especially in public parks and homes all over China—as a form of relaxation and fitness. Tai chi involves slow, flowing movements designed to free the passage of life-force energy, or *chi*, through the body's meridians. In the West, tai chi is gaining popularity as a gentle, slow, yet exhilarating form of physical and spiritual exercise, and tai chi classes are widely available. Tai chi isn't strenuous and anyone can do it, but look for a qualified teacher, preferably one who can talk to you about the meditative aspects of tai chi.

Joan demonstrates the QiGong exercise, Tiger Plays with Ball. Imagine a great ball of bright energy in front of you. Grasp the ball with your arms and hands. Feel its radiating electricity and heat. This is your energy! Explore it with confidence and love.

And You Thought You Wouldn't Sweat!

Many other systems for moving meditation exist as well. Some of them, including dynamic meditation, ecstatic dancing, and whirling, are incredibly intense, both physically and emotionally. The point of these high-intensity moving meditations is to shake the holds on the mind by shaking and completely exhausting the body. When the physical barriers have been dissolved, the mental barriers fall away and the mind is free. These moving meditations, which are actually more like meditation preparations, aren't for everyone. But if you want a good workout that is emotionally intense and will facilitate sitting meditation, give them a try. Ask your local meditation center, yoga center, or other holistic or spiritual resource center about the availability of instruction in other forms of movement meditation.

Dynamic Meditation

Dynamic meditation is meditation with movement. Yoga vinyasas, QiGong, and tai chi are meditation with movement, too, but dynamic meditation has no other purpose than to facilitate meditation. What is it, exactly? Dynamic meditation can mean seated meditation during which the meditator simply moves his or her hands and arms slowly and mindfully, remaining aware of the movement. On the opposite end of the scale, it can mean rapid breathing, frantic crazed thrashing dance movements, and total collapse to the floor after the body has become completely exhausted. Different teachers have developed different methods, but if you are a mover and a shaker and find it impossible to sit still, consider trying dynamic meditation.

> ### Bliss Byte
>
> Movement can be meditation, but it can also be preparation for meditation, getting rid of excess energy and excess thought before attempting meditation. If you are feeling too "wound up" to meditate, try some high-energy dancing, whirling, jumping up and down, shaking out your body parts, or even taking a quick sprint around the block first. If you tire out your muscles before, meditation may be easier, especially if you are used to a lot of activity and find it difficult to sit still.

The point of exhaustive movements is actually to prepare the body for stillness. When past traumas, present stress, and dread of the future armor the body with tension, it can be extremely difficult to let the body relax, let alone be open to enlightenment. Dynamic meditation shakes loose this armoring, stirs up the internalized emotions, and rattles them around until they come loose. After the movement session, dynamic meditation usually involves a period of complete stillness, allowing the mind to discover what is happening in the body.

Sound interesting? Try the following dynamic meditation exercise:

♦ If you desire, put on music, preferably instrumental-only and high-energy.

♦ Stand with your feet about shoulder width apart, arms loose. Roll your head from side to side, shake out your arms and legs, and breathe easily.

> ### Relax
>
> Shallow, rapid breaths could cause hyperventilation. When trying rapid breathing as preparation for dynamic meditation, keep your breath deep and full. If you become dizzy, breathe normally for 30 seconds, then continue.

♦ Now increase your breath rate so it is rapid but inhalations remain very deep. Don't make any attempt to regulate the breath to any rhythm. Just suck it in, then blow it out. Continue for two minutes.

♦ Next, let your body begin to move. Don't follow any patterns or move in a way that you think would "look right." Feel the movement. Let your body move the way it wants to move. Let the movement be organic, originating from inside your body, not from your brain. You might want to close your eyes so you aren't as conscious about how you look.

♦ Allow your body to pick up the pace if it wants to. Really go crazy. Thrash your arms around, jump up and down, let out any sound that comes to you. A hearty "Ha!" or "Hoo!" or "Ho!" is good, but whatever comes out of you is fine, too. Be mindful of what your body is doing, don't just let your mind drift away. But do let everything go. Don't hold back anything. Continue dancing in this way for 20 to 30 minutes or until you are too exhausted to continue (the amount of time depends on your level of exertion and your fitness—a shorter time doesn't mean you did it wrong).

♦ Now, let your entire body collapse to the floor and lie there in whatever position you landed, utterly still. Be completely present in your body. Feel what has happened to it. Notice all the sensations. Feel whether any emotions have released, whether you feel good, upset, cleansed, or angry. All are possible. Just stay in stillness and mindfulness for 10 minutes.

Dynamic meditation can be an intense experience, but it can also be darned fun! And it really does make sitting meditation a lot easier.

Ecstatic Dancing

Ecstatic dancing is similar in theory to dynamic meditation. It exists in various forms in many indigenous cultures, but you can practice it in your own living room. Put on music and let yourself go. Really dance. Dance up a storm. Cut that rug in two. Dance nonstop with everything you've got for 20 minutes, then relax into a seated meditation in easy pose. *Ahhhhhhhhhhhhooooommmmm.*

Whirling

Whirling is most often associated with the Sufis and a related sect, the dervishes. (You've probably heard of whirling dervishes.) Sufism is a mystical version of Islam, and meditation is an important part of the Sufi way. Whirling is a way to spin off negative energy and exhaust the body so it doesn't interfere with the spiritual journey. It also puts your body into a transformed state. You can do it, too—just make sure you don't try it in a room where you could knock anything over or get hurt! Outside in a big yard (with no trees) is a good option.

♦ Stand relaxed with your arms down and knees slightly bent. Slowly begin to spin in a circle, counterclockwise (or clockwise if counterclockwise seems unnatural).

◆ Spin faster and faster, to music if it helps, with your eyes unfocused to prevent dizziness. Don't try to see anything.

Relax _____

Whirling can be fun and a great meditation technique, but if you have a medical condition that involves dizziness, suffer from vertigo (dizziness) or tinnitus (ringing in the ears), whether associated with another condition or not, or if you are taking any medication for which dizziness is a side effect, leave the whirling for the dervishes and practice a different form of dynamic meditation instead.

◆ Remain mindful. Notice every sensation and how your body feels as you whirl.

◆ Keep spinning until you are going as fast as you can, and go as fast as you can until your body naturally falls over. (Remember, do it in a room where you can fall over and not get hurt.)

◆ Once you've collapsed to the floor, lie in perfect stillness and feel the earth moving below you. Notice how you feel and whether your awareness has changed in any way. Is it sharper? Duller? How is it different?

◆ Eventually work up to about 20 minutes or so of whirling.

Moving meditation might not always seem like meditation, but if it is always mindful, it will be meditation. It will also help to calm, strengthen, control, and quiet your body and make sitting meditation easier. So get moving!

The Least You Need to Know

◆ Kinhin is the walking form of zazen (the Zen form of seated meditation) in which the meditator walks in a slow circle around an altar in a meditation hall while letting the mind be open in pure awareness.

◆ Mindful walking means walking for the sake of walking—with one-pointed focus and concentration on the walk itself—not for the sake of a destination.

◆ Walking the ritual path of a labyrinth to reach the center is symbolic of journeying to the center of the self for greater self-knowledge.

◆ Many cultures have developed forms of moving meditation such as yoga, QiGong, tai chi, ecstatic dancing, and whirling.

◆ Dynamic meditation, ecstatic dancing, and whirling can exhaust the body so it doesn't interfere with meditation.

15

Shavasana: It's Not Just Lying Around!

In This Chapter

◆ Shavasana: yoga's ultimate relaxation meditation

◆ It's not as easy as it looks

◆ The importance of relaxation

◆ Being and nothingness

Despite what you think about the complexities of—and flexibility and/or strength required for—advanced yoga poses, the most difficult yoga pose of all doesn't take any flexibility or boundless physical strength. It's the most important of all the yoga poses, the perfect preparation for meditation, yet it entails only lying on your back on the floor and … that's it!

Actually, *shavasana* is more complicated than just lying down. While lying on your back on the floor, you actually have to (are you ready for this?) *relax*. (It's tough.) You have to slow your thinking through meditation. (Tougher still.) And at last, you become able to transcend your body

From A to Om

Shavasana literally means "corpse pose" and is the most important of all yoga postures, designed to bring the body into total, conscious relaxation using meditation to remove both physical and mental distractions.

and your mind to commune with your true self. (Now that's challenging!) See, we told you it wasn't easy. But it's definitely worth the effort, for many reasons.

Concentrate on Relaxing

You could probably spend a lifetime working on the first step of shavasana: relaxation. Relaxation is a fine art, and shavasana is the perfect canvas.

In the 1970s, research was first seriously applied in this country to the physiological benefits of relaxation, specifically as it occurs during meditation. Almost half a century later, the notion that relaxation is good for the body and the mind is almost instinctual. We all know it's healthy to relax. As Herbert Benson, M.D., documented in the 1970s when studying the physiological responses of meditators (he subsequently authored the best-seller called *The Relaxation Response* (Avon Books, 1976; the book was updated and expanded and republished in 2000), meditation results in the following:

- Lowered heart rate

- Lowered metabolic rate

- Lowered respiratory rate

- Lowered blood pressure, a condition that persisted with regular meditation

This "relaxation response" was, and remains, exceptionally beneficial for the physical body, especially for those subjected to frequent stress (and these days, who isn't?). Because stress has the exact opposite effect—increased heart rate, metabolic rate, respiratory rate—and because chronic stress might result in elevated blood pressure, meditation—and the subsequent changes it elicits in the body—is like a stress antidote. It balances the body, helping restore the equilibrium that chronic stress has disturbed.

Dr. Benson also demonstrated the keen mental benefits of the relaxation response but focuses primarily on the affect this mental relaxation has on the physical body. Of course, it's all tied together. Stress due to mental anguish or physical circumstances results in a physiologically heightened state and a quick, frantic mental pace. Relaxation through meditation stems the reaction of stress by quieting both body and mind. Eventually, the spirit has space to flourish and find its own equilibrium in the context of the mind-body.

That's quite a bit of power you can get from lying on the floor! In Dr. Benson's research, the procedure for inducing the relaxation response was to sit quietly, relax completely, breathe through the nose, and focus on a single mentally repeated word such as *one*. Sounds something like yoga meditation or zazen, doesn't it? Yet the relaxation response is just as easily invoked in a prone position, and that's what shavasana is all about: prone, profound relaxation.

Where and When to Do It

Lying on the floor in a way that facilitates relaxation takes a little forethought.

First, find a place where you won't be disturbed for the duration of your shavasana meditation session (20 to 30 minutes is nice). Second, you'll want a comfortable but firm surface. A clean, carpeted floor, the floor with a mat, or the earth itself is perfect. Third, you'll want to choose the right time for shavasana.

Unless you have a very understanding boss, you probably can't do shavasana on the job. ("What happened to Mary? Why is she lying on the floor? Oh, Mary? Are you awake?") To keep from falling asleep, you probably shouldn't practice shavasana on your bed. You associate that spot with relaxation, yes, but also with sleep, and shavasana is distinctly *not* about napping. Plus, a bed doesn't offer the firm support that's optimal for performing the pose (although shavasana in bed is a good way to cure insomnia and to fall asleep in a slow and relaxed fashion, if that's your intention). The kitchen floor isn't the best place, either, unless you don't mind looking at that dirty refrigerator vent close-up (even if you close your eyes, you'll *know* it's there). So where is the best place to practice this all-important yoga pose? How about …

- Your living room floor when no one else is home.
- Your bedroom floor, with a Do Not Disturb sign hung from the outside doorknob.
- On a soft blanket on the grass in your backyard or out on your deck (the neighbors will think you are sunbathing).

As long as your chosen location is comfortable, supports your body firmly, and is free from distractions, you've got your spot!

Bliss Byte

Shavasana is the perfect meditation pose for people who, due to health reasons, find it painful to sit upright for long periods of time without back support. The elderly and chronically ill might find the benefits of a steady practice of this pose relaxing and stress-reducing. However, shavasana shouldn't be practiced to the exclusion of any movement exercises or physical therapy regimen recommended by your physician or physical therapist.

When you do shavasana largely depends on you. Shavasana in the evening after an exhausting day might catapult you straight into dreamland. On the other hand, it might be just the pick-me-up you need to get dinner ready and the kids to bed. Same thing with early morning shavasana. The only way to know when your body will respond best to shavasana is to try it at different times of the day to see what works best for you.

Try the following to help determine when shavasana is right for you:

◆ As soon as you wake up in the morning, yawn, stretch, get out of bed, and lie down on the floor. If you tend to fall right back to sleep, this is not a good time for you to practice shavasana.

◆ After your morning exercise and a shower but before breakfast (shavasana is best performed on an empty stomach). Still falling asleep? Morning probably isn't your best time. (Or you're not getting enough sleep. If you always *thought* you were a morning person, try going to bed an hour earlier and give it another go.)

◆ Mid-morning, about an hour or two after breakfast. This is a high-energy time for many people and a good time to practice shavasana if you have a stressful day ahead of you.

◆ Lunch break. If you go home for lunch (or are already home for lunch), try shavasana for 20 minutes before you eat. You'll probably find you can eat your lunch more slowly and with greater mindfulness after a satisfying shavasana session.

◆ Mid-afternoon is sleepy time for most people and not the best time for shavasana (although a great time for a cat nap). And if your nap and shavasana practice blend together, so much the better. Eventually, with practice, you'll learn to stay alert in shavasana.

◆ Late afternoon, right after school or work, is a great time for shavasana if you aren't too tired. It can calm you and ease the tensions from your workday, helping you make the transition from work to home. After shavasana, you can concentrate fully on your home life without suffering what the Chinese call "monkey brain" (in other words, incessant mental chatter).

◆ Early evening is another high-energy time. A few hours after dinner when you are feeling calm and relaxed, take a 20-minute shavasana break. Later, you'll sleep like a baby.

◆ If you're a night owl, late night might be the best time for you to practice shavasana. If your awareness is sharpest when the moon is highest, falling asleep might not be a problem.

Whenever you practice shavasana, don't feel too bad if you do fall asleep. You probably needed the catnap. Try again at a different time.

The Mind-Body Scan Becomes Your Meditation

Remember the various mind-body scans we've included in this book? Here's how to use the mind-body scan in conjunction with shavasana. This time, the sole purpose of the mind-body scan is to relax your body.

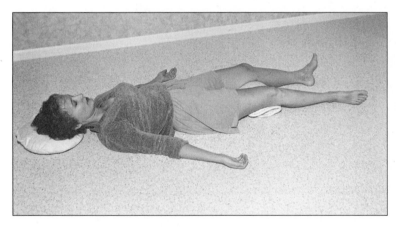

Joan takes a break to prepare for meditation at home in supported shavasana. People with lower-back problems will find it uncomfortable to lie flat on the floor. Place a pillow or rolled blanket under your knees to take pressure off that sensitive lower back. You can also support your head and neck with a small pillow.

First, lie in the shavasana position, flat on your back on the floor, arms slightly out, legs slightly apart and relaxed. Try not to "hold" anywhere. Breathe and feel your spine sinking into the floor. On each of the following contractions, hold for a slow count of three. Now …

◆ Bring your awareness to your left foot. Flex your ankle and fill your foot with tension. Hold, then release, letting all the tension flow from your foot.

Relax _____

If you are worried you'll fall asleep during shavasana, set a soft-sounding timer! Try to focus completely on relaxation, even if only for a few brief moments. If you know the timer is set, you won't have to worry about the time in the back of your mind.

◆ Flex your left calf muscle and hold, then release, letting tension flow out your lower leg, through your toes.

◆ Bend your left knee just slightly and contract your thigh muscle tightly. Imagine all the tensions and negative or stagnant energy in your left leg gathering in the thigh muscle. Then, release and visualize this negative energy and tension flowing down your leg and out your toes, transformed as positive, life-affirming energy. Notice the relaxed feeling in your left leg. Does it feel more relaxed than your right leg?

◆ Repeat with your right leg, then note whether both legs feel equally relaxed. Stay mindful!

◆ Squeeze your buttocks together as tightly as you can. Release, and feel the tension flowing away.

◆ Squeeze your abdominal muscles as tightly as you can. Release, and feel the tension flowing away.

◆ Bring your awareness to your spine. Imagine the tension trickling down your spine and flowing out your tailbone. Feel each vertebrae becoming heavier and looser, sinking into the floor.

◆ Contract your upper abdominals, under your rib cage, drawing your navel back toward your spine as far as you can, then release, allowing all the tension in your torso to flow out your tailbone.

◆ Contract your chest muscles as tightly as you can, then release, feeling the energy flow down your spine and out your tailbone.

◆ Now, bring your awareness to your left shoulder. Tighten your shoulder muscle, lifting it slightly off the floor with the effort. Then release, letting the shoulder sink into the floor. Imagine the negative energy and tension flowing down your arm and out your fingertips, again, transformed as pure joy.

◆ Tense your upper arm muscles (biceps and triceps) as tightly as you can, lifting your upper arm slightly off the floor. Then release, and feel the tension flowing down and out your fingertips transformed as joy.

◆ Tense your lower arm, lifting it slightly off the floor. Release, and feel the tension flowing down and out your fingertips transformed as joy.

♦ Make a tight fist with your left hand. Squeeze, then release, letting the tensions flow away.

♦ Now, spread the fingers of your left hand wide and hold. Release, then feel all the remaining tension in your left arm flowing away out the ends of your fingers. Notice the feeling of relaxation in your left arm. Does it feel more relaxed than your right arm?

Mindful Minute

Shavasana has measurable physical benefits on the body. It calms the nerves, lowers blood pressure, improves blood flow to the heart, and lessens fatigue. Shavasana is a great pose for opening the chakras to free the flow of prana through the body.

♦ Repeat with your right arm. Then notice whether both arms feel equally relaxed. Stay mindful!

♦ Pull your chin back toward your neck, tensing the muscles of your neck and throat. Release, and imagine the negative energy and tension flowing down your spine and out your tailbone, transformed as pure, positive joy.

♦ Clench your jaw tightly and scrunch up your whole face, then release. Feel the negative energy flowing out the crown of your head, transformed as joy.

♦ Open your eyes and mouth as wide as you possibly can, hold, and release, feeling the negative energy flowing out the crown of your head, released as pure, positive energy your body has gathered and transformed.

♦ Now imagine your awareness is a warm, glowing ring of light. It begins around your toes and moves slowly, slowly up your body from your toes to your crown, searching for tension. Whenever it senses tension, it glows red, alerting you to tense areas. Let this "scanner" move up and down your body several times. Whenever it senses tension, tense the area again, then release, until all tension is gone. Imagine the ring of light gradually turning a calm, tranquil blue as you progressively relax.

♦ At last you should be feeling completely relaxed. Imagine your body melting into the floor or ground. Breathe deeply, and with each breath, feel your muscle fibers dissolving and loosening. Remain completely mindful and aware. Try not to let your mind drift away into sleep. Notice everything. Let your consciousness vibrate with the intensity of your awareness.

♦ Remain in that still, relaxed position for 10 minutes or so, then slowly imagine your body separating from the earth and becoming itself again, lighter, easier, and freer.

♦ Sit up slowly, stand up slowly, and voilà! No more stress.

The mind-body scan moving into shavasana is a way to help you relax, but it is more a shavasana prelude than the actual practice. The real shavasana comes when your body is able to fully release, relax, dissolve—when you feel as if your body is, well … a corpse.

> **Bliss Byte** _____
>
> Did your parents ever tell you that patience is a virtue? It is certainly a virtue in shavasana, and one that can be cultivated. If you find your mind racing, try counting very slowly to 10, then starting back at 1 again. Repeat until you feel better able to relax. You can also visualize your body slowly sinking into the floor or your muscles relaxing and melting. If you get an unbearable itch, give it some time, but don't torture yourself. If it won't go away, scratch it, then relax again. You can do this! And with practice, shavasana really does become easier.

Shavasana: How to Do It

Shavasana is the Sanskrit term for "corpse pose." Doesn't sound like a nice way to spend your afternoon? Oh, but it is! The corpse pose is so named for more reasons than the fact that you lie as still as a corpse. In shavasana, you certainly aren't dead, but in many ways, you can be like the dead. Your body should become very still. Then your mind should become still. At last, only your awareness is left, the essential you, unencumbered by the fetters of body and mind. Who knows … that might be just what death is like!

According to yoga theory (and many other theories like those inherent in Tibetan and other forms of Buddhism), that's exactly right. This is exactly what happens at death—your soul is released from the trappings of body and mind and is free to be itself—at least until it moves into another body to be reborn. Shavasana allows your soul to get a little taste of that freedom and a short break from that sometimes-troublesome body armor and worrisome brain.

Being and Nothingness

To borrow the title of a work by the famous French existentialist playwright and author Jean-Paul Sartre, shavasana is a little like "being and nothingness." You *are*, yet you are nothing. And you are everything. Your body lies there, yet it does nothing. Your mind is there, but it is still. Your true being—your soul—is set free by the temporary nothingness/everythingness of your body and mind. It's not a scary thing, it's a liberating thing. And of course, when you are done, you come back to your "old self."

Well, maybe not exactly. If your "old self" was pretty stressed out, you might feel a lot different: more relaxed, calmer, and more at peace with exactly who you are. Oh, and that nasty kink in your back? Could it be gone?

To get to this stage of shavasana wherein body and mind dissolve into each other and into the world around them—stepping out of the soul's way to allow for full commune with the universe—isn't easy. We're not saying you'll be able to do it the first time around. But that is what you can move toward as you practice shavasana.

Taking Root in the Earth

During pure shavasana, your thought slows and, ultimately, thought will be suspended. But to get to that point, it sometimes helps to engage in thought that moves you in the right direction. Shavasana can be effectively visualized in many ways, but we'd like to suggest two: as the body merging with earth, and as the body merging with sky. The total suspension of thought for any length of time only occurs in the advanced stages of samadhi, but you might experience a slowing down or momentary suspension of thought early on in your meditation practice.

Bliss Byte

Especially for children and teenagers, some pre-meditation energetic activity like running, aerobic dance, or Hatha Yoga postures can make the shavasana pose easier to maintain. Shavasana is an excellent activity for children and teens. It teaches focus, concentration, balance, centering, patience, and stress management—qualities many children no longer possess (or never learned) in our fast-paced world. Practice shavasana with your kids and teach your teenager, too. Shavasana can be a way for your children to gain a sense of control over their bodies and minds, which will cultivate self-esteem—and everyone can use more of that!

For the first option, try the following visualization to ease you into shavasana:

Lie down on your back on the floor, arms slightly out from your body, legs slightly apart. Shift your body until you find a comfortable position. Close your eyes and breathe deeply.

With each breath, imagine you are inhaling peace, which feels cool, soft, and light. This peace gathers up the body's chaos, chatter, and distraction. On the exhalation, all is exhaled as peaceful, positive energy. In with peace, chaos transformed, out with joy. In with peace, chatter transformed, out with calm.

With each inhalation, feel your muscles relaxing and your bones becoming heavier. Imagine your spine is falling with the weight of gravity. Feel your foot bones, leg bones, hip bones, shoulders, neck, and head growing heavier, melting, joining with and rooting into the earth. Relax into the arms of Mother Earth. Breathe in peace; breathe out peace.

Soon, your muscles, bones, and entire body have sunk gently into the earth and you feel cool and relaxed. Your breath is easy and soothing. You are completely supported, nurtured, and rocked by the planet. You feel complete comfort and ease. All your thoughts have given way to the flow of your exhalations. Stay in this position for 10 to 20 minutes, then slowly offer a blessing to the earth. Feel yourself becoming lighter. Feel your thoughts returning, relaxed and easy now. Slowly sit, then stand. Carry your awareness of your communion with the earth throughout the rest of your day.

Floating Like a Cloud in the Sky

This second visualization option can help you to ease into shavasana by imagining your body going up instead of down. Try this one:

Lie down on your back on the floor, arms slightly out from your body, legs slightly apart. Shift your body until you find a comfortable position. Close your eyes and breathe deeply.

Mindful Minute

Some physicians claim stress is the original source of all illness. Even in cases where illness or the source of pain isn't caused by stress, stress-reduction techniques can promote healing and reduce the experience of pain. In one study conducted by the Stress Reduction Clinic at the University of Massachusetts Medical Center, after an eight-week training period in the clinic during which patients were taught a variety of stress-management relaxation techniques, 75 percent of patients with chronic pain achieved a 33 percent reduction in their pain (according to how they rated their pain on a questionnaire), and 61 percent of pain patients achieved at least a 50 percent reduction in their pain. In addition, most showed an improvement in their ability to engage in normal activities and a drop in negative mood states.

With each inhalation, imagine you are breathing in pure, white, playful light. Imagine the light gathers up and soothes all the heaviness, stress, pain, negative emotions, and darkness lingering in your body and mind. With each exhalation, the transformed energy leaves your body as pure joy. In, white light. Out, heaviness and pain.

As you continue to inhale the light, imagine it filling your body as helium fills a balloon. First, the light fills your toes, your feet, and your legs. Imagine it cleansing your body, dancing inside you. Imagine it is airy, joyful, laughing light as it fills your torso, your arms, your neck, and your head.

Imagine the last of the negativity purified to flow out with your breath as healing, positive energy. The white light is taking up all the space now, it begins to glow, and you begin to glow with it. Imagine the lightness radiating from your body, from around your head like a halo, from out of the tips of your fingers and toes, encircling your body so you feel safe, calm, happy, and completely at home.

Bliss Byte

Visualizing colors from nature can have a calming effect on the body. The blue of sky and the green of grass and trees are naturally relaxing colors that calm the nervous system. Consciously incorporate colors like blue and green into your visualizations.

Now, the light is becoming even lighter. It washes over your arms with a rush like a spring zephyr, and you feel your arms begin to lift. It rushes over your legs and feet, and your legs and feet feel as if they are rising in the breeze, too. The light wraps your body with its comforting arms and cradles your head. Gravity no longer has any effect on you. Up you go, floating, flying, hardly able to keep from laughing with joy.

Imagine floating up as the space in your ceiling opens. You drift into the open sky, surrounded by light. The blue of the sky surrounds you. Then you feel the cool mist of a cloud wrapping you in its airy mist. You realize you are resting in a cloud, and no place could be safer or more beautiful. The cloud sparkles with gold light and rocks you gently, softly. You recognize that you are pure spirit. Your old, clunky body is waiting for you far below, but for this moment you can fly. Rocked in light, embraced by peace, you are serenely safe in the sky.

Stay here for 10 to 20 minutes, basking in pure, unhindered awareness. Then, slowly offer a blessing to the cloud and feel gravity, bit by bit, slowly coax you downward. Float gently earthward through the heavens, through the roof of your home, and back into your waiting body. In your absence, you notice, your body has become relaxed. Your thoughts have stopped chattering around the ceiling and have floated back into you, slower, quieter, and relaxed. Open your eyes and slowly, mindfully aware of your body, sit up, then stand. Carry your awareness of your communion with the sky throughout the rest of your day.

Breathe to the Center of Peace and Tranquility

You might have noticed that most of the space in the preceding exercises has been taken up with the visualizations used to get into the state of shavasana, but not much space is spent describing the state of shavasana. That's because, for the most part, shavasana is an indescribable state. It is the soul communing with the universe, the true nature of the self revealed. These things can hardly be described in ordinary language.

Bliss Byte

Visualizing yourself surrounded by a beautiful white light might bring out your best, but it can help your relationships with others, too. The next time someone is troubling you, imagine they're surrounded by a white light. How does your perception of the person—and consequently, your actions toward that person—change?

But when you are in shavasana, it may not always match this ideal. Your thoughts will probably keep trying to infringe on your peace. What business does a thought about whether the pest-control guy is coming today have to do with the true nature of you? No business at all, but thoughts are notorious for going places that aren't any of their business! To keep them at bay, as well as the intrusive body sensations you'll probably also experience (the familiar itching, twitching, cramping, and aching), keep in mind one thought. Return to it whenever your mind or body behaves out of turn: *Breathe to the center*. (And if itches are a real problem, give yourself a break and scratch them, then return to your thought. If you think you can't scratch, you'll itch even more!)

Imagine that each breath comes and goes from the very center of your being, where only peace and tranquility live. Breathe in peace; breathe out peace. Your breath will be deep and long and full because each breath comes from so far inside you. Imagine that the center of yourself is a planet all its own, the planet *you*, and your body and mind are its galaxy. Come back to the image again and again, and breathe, breathe, breathe. Before long, your body and your thoughts will get the hint and learn to behave. Prana, or life-force energy, will move through you and in and out of you more freely, revitalizing your physical, astral, and causal bodies (see Chapter 9). You'll have more physical energy as you move through life, but you'll also have more energy on the other, more subtle levels that are also you.

You Are the Universe: Paint the Sky with Stars

Many ancient cultures believed (and many still believe) that we are more than just the world. We are microcosms of the universe. Our bodies are like mini universes, and the big universe around us is really just us in macro-scale.

If this is true—and let's just postulate for a moment that it is—then nothing true or real can threaten us, harm us, or destroy our lives. Sure, things can affect and drastically change the course of—or even spell the end of—the lives we experience in these physical bodies. But our true life (our soul life), and our true self (our soul self) can't be hurt by anything that happens. Even if our energy transforms into something else after our bodies are gone, even when our energy no longer takes the shape of "us," it still remains intact as an essential ingredient of the universe.

And what can hurt the universe? The universe is everything, and the earth is just a tiny, tiny portion of it. And it is us, so we are everything, and our physical bodies going through our daily lives are just a tiny, tiny portion of who we are. That's power. And that's also a fantastic opportunity.

You have the opportunity to make the most of your personal universe. You can ignore it, pretend it isn't there, even deny it or get angry at it. Or you can live in it, watch it, love it, nurture it, experience it, and paint it with stars. The choice is up to you. We suggest you grab your paintbrush, lie down on the floor, and relax into meditation.

The Least You Need to Know

- Shavasana is the easiest yoga pose, physically, but also the most challenging because it involves true and total relaxation and a dissolving of the body and mind.

- Visualizations and breathwork can help relax your body and mind to better facilitate meditating in shavasana.

- The quality of your existence is your own responsibility. You have the power to make it beautiful.

Chapter 16

Mantras: Sacred Formulas to Live By

In This Chapter

- ◆ Chanting around the world
- ◆ The sound of silence
- ◆ How to hear, how to listen
- ◆ Healing with sound
- ◆ Chakra sounds
- ◆ Do-it-yourself mantras

"Ommmmm." We keep saying it, and you've probably heard it elsewhere, on television or in a movie or in a book. You probably know *om* is a word stereotypically repeated during meditation, and if you remember Chapter 1, you also know it is a word designed to imitate the sound of the universe's vibration.

But what's the deal? Is *om* some magic word? And why do you need to make sound while you are meditating, anyway? Does it have some benefit?

You bet it does.

The Meaning of Mantra

The sound *om* is what is called a *mantra* in meditation. Actually, mantras are much more than points of concentration, although they do serve that purpose during meditation, just as something you look at or think about can be a point of concentration. Mantras also use the power of sound, and sound can be a powerful ally to meditation. Many practitioners of the mantra form of meditation believe the vibration and sound of a mantra cleanses the body and mind of negative thoughts and energy, invokes spiritual power, and can even heal the body. Mantras can be chanted, spoken, sung, thought, and even written, but saying them out loud may have a particularly powerful effect because of the vibrations of the sound waves you create when chanting, speaking, or singing them. Mantras are potent meditative tools you can use in your own meditation practice.

> **From A to Om**
>
> **Mantra** comes from the root *man*, meaning "to think," and *trai*, meaning "to protect or free from the bondage of the phenomenal world." Mantra, then, can be interpreted as "the thought that liberates and protects." It is a sacred sound or combination of sounds that embodies particular states of consciousness.

Chants: From Gregorian to Native American to Tibetan

Chanting is the most common way meditators use mantras, and it is common to virtually every world culture in one form or another. Not all traditions use the word *mantra*, but repeating certain vowel sounds and an intense focus on the vibration of sound, called *harmonics*, and/or *overtones*, is a common thread in many of the mystical traditions around the world.

Gregorian chanting, part of the tradition of the Catholic Church, makes use of sound vibrations, and overtones are audible in Gregorian chants. Sufis chant vowel sounds for spiritual communion and for healing. Chanting the names of God is part of Kabbalah. Shamans in Mongolia practice a tradition called *hoomi* (also *choomig* and *xoomij*), which is a type of throat singing that produces overtones.

The Aborigines in Australia blow through an instrument to produce a sound with overtones similar to those made by chanting. Native American shamans chant using vowel sounds during their rituals. Tibetan Buddhist chanting is so advanced that some monks can produce a three-note chord with a single

> **From A to Om**
>
> **Harmonics**, also known as **overtones**, are a phenomenon connected with sound in which faint higher tones that are mathematical ratios of the tone can be heard when a tone is sounded.

voice. Even the original religion of Tibet, called Bon (prior to the arrival of Buddhism from India) was based around chanting, and the word *bon* actually means "to chant" in Tibetan.

In Hinduism, mantras are thought to have originated with ancient seers, the mantras given to them as gifts from the divine spirit. These mantras have been passed down for millennia from guru to student, and when a guru gives a student a mantra, they must both chant that mantra throughout their lives—linking them together and also to that mantra's aspect of God. Hindus believe that repeating the mantra in the exact way, with unaltered melody and notes from the original, will preserve the mantra's incredible vibrational power to cleanse negative energy and put the chanter in direct communion with God. Each person supposedly has a mantra that is just right for him or her, which can be found or, ideally, given by that person's guru.

Mindful Minute

When a mantra is spoken, it is known in Sanskrit as *Vaikhari Japa*. When it is whispered or hummed, it is known as *Upamsu Japa*. When the mantra is repeated mentally but not spoken out loud, it is known as *Manasika Japa*. When the mantra is written, it is called *Likhita Japa*. In Likhita Japa, the mantra is sometimes written again and again in very small letters so the words form a picture, making it an art form.

In Tibetan Buddhism, mantras are thought to be charged with spiritual power, and chanting them releases this power. The more times a mantra is chanted, the stronger the spiritual energy. Tibetan prayer wheels contain large numbers of mantras written in very small letters on pieces of paper. Each spin of the prayer wheel is thought to be the equivalent of chanting the mantra as many times as it is written. For example, if a prayer wheel contains a mantra written 1,000 times, 10 spins of the prayer wheel would offer the same benefits as chanting the mantra 10,000 times. Some modern Tibetan Buddhists put mantras on a computer and believe that each spin of the hard drive sends mantra power into the universe!

No matter what tradition you believe in, chanting helps prolong the exhalation of the breath, calm the mind, slow the heart, and after long periods, helps bring the meditator into an alternate state of consciousness. Whether this is due to the effect on breathing, the effect of one-pointed thinking, the effect of the repetition, the vibrations of the mantra itself, or (most likely) a combination of the four hasn't been proven, but chanting or reciting mantras does seem to be a highly effective form of meditation for people of many beliefs, traditions, and cultures. It might be just the technique for you.

Mantras Just for You

Many mantras are Sanskrit words (like *om*). Sanskrit is considered a sacred language because its sounds actually signify what they refer to—the vibration of the things represented by the sound. As we've mentioned, *om* is actually thought to *be* the sound of the universe.

But mantras don't have to be in a foreign language. Any word that contains spiritual meaning for you and feels right to you will work, especially if it is a word that has been repeated by many people throughout history (increasing, it is thought, the spiritual power of the word). Every word has its own meaning but also its own sound and its own vibrations. When meaning and vibration both resonate for you (something you might be able to sense intuitively), you've found your mantra! Some possibilities include the following:

- *Peace*
- *Love*
- *Joy*
- *Bliss*
- *One*
- *We are one*
- *One is all, all is one*
- *I am all*
- *Let it be*
- *Amen*
- *Spirit*
- *Sun, moon*
- *Shalom* ("peace" in Hebrew, pronounced *shah-loam*)
- *Om shanti shanti shanti* ("All is peace, peace, peace"; pronounced *aum shahn-tee shahn-tee shahn-tee*)
- *Hallelujah*
- *God, Yahweh* (a Hebrew name for God; pronounced *Yah-way*), or *Allah* (Islamic name for God; pronounced *Ah-la*)

> **Mindful Minute**
>
> According to the yoga of sound, called Nada Yoga, the mantra you choose is very important because there is a particular sound vibration that corresponds with your spiritual nature. Your body will respond better to that vibration than to other vibrations, so the wrong mantra won't affect you while the right mantra can have a profound spiritual impact. How do you find the right mantra? Stay open to the possibilities and for the mantra that "seems" or "feels" right for you. As you progress in your studies, a trusted teacher may be able to help you find the right mantra to work with.

Poetry and Music as Mantra

Although most people think of mantras as short words or phrases, longer songs, poems, and chants also work. It just depends on your preference. According to some practitioners of mantra meditation, longer chants are mantras, but according to others, a mantra shouldn't be more than you can keep in your mind at once.

If you like the idea of a longer chant, look for short poems, bits of songs, hymns, prayers, Zen koans, or other passages of writing or music that resonate for you. Sacred texts from various cultures are full of passages with mantra potential.

Or maybe you have a favorite song that makes you feel peaceful and centered. It doesn't matter if the song is popular, was written yesterday, and doesn't even mention spirituality. If it speaks to you, sing it while meditating. Let the sound fill you. Or just say the lyrics if you aren't comfortable singing. The same thing goes for poetry or other pieces of prose that have meaning to you. Let them work as your mantra. You can even use a mantra—a song, a poem, a fiction or nonfiction passage—you've written yourself.

> **Bliss Byte**
>
> Try using beads to keep track of the number of times you chant a mantra, as many meditators in a variety of traditions do. In Hinduism, the chanter moves the beads between the thumb and ring finger with each recitation of a mantra. A rosary is a string of beads divided into different groups, each representing different short prayers.

Silence vs. Sound

Don't forget the flip side of the mantra: silence. Silence can be just as powerful as the mantra itself and is indeed an integral part of practicing mantra meditation. Listening to the silence between mantras is like turning your awareness to the space between inhalations and exhalations of the breath. Silence has its own energy, and that energy can empower you if you tune in to it. If you've ever been alone in a soundproof room, you might have felt the energy of silence—surprising, strong, and capable of altering awareness. But how often are we truly present in silence? (And how often do we get to sit and meditate in a soundproof room?)

Try sitting in silence for a while before you begin reciting your mantra. Don't make a sound. Just listen. Chances are you can hear something. What do you hear? Listening is a fine art, far different from hearing. Hearing happens. Listening requires mindfulness.

Are You Listening?

When you aren't used to cultivating your listening skills, you might find listening difficult. But listening can be a great way to meditate, and good listening skills can improve other areas of your life, too. For example, how often do you listen when someone talks to you? How focused are you on what they are saying? Are you waiting for your turn to speak? Are you thinking about other things? Or are you really tuned in with complete mindfulness? When you learn to listen to what people say, you might be surprised by what you hear!

Bliss Byte

After repeating any mantra, spend time in silence. This silence is very important to allow the vibrational aspects of the mantra to settle within your stilled self where they will resonate through the chakras to stimulate and awaken them. Vibration and sound are intimately joined in the human body. To understand just how important vibration is, breathe in deeply and hum out one long consistent note. Feel the strong vibration in your throat at the Mercury chakra—the seat of communication. Consider how this sound is experienced by someone who is Deaf—the Deaf person will interpret and process the sound solely as vibration; they *feel* the sound. See how the quality and placement of the vibration changes as you hum different musical notes.

But even when no one is saying a word, you'll find much to hear. Try this meditative listening exercise to cultivate your listening skills before you try chanting a mantra:

1. Sit comfortably on the floor with your back straight, your legs crossed, and your hands open, palms down, on your knees. Breathe a few deep breaths, then allow your breathing to become normal. Shift your awareness away from your breathing. As you relax more, turn your palms upward, symbolizing openness and

willingness to listen. Close your eyes so visual impressions don't mingle with sound impressions. Listen.

2. Don't analyze what you hear, simply listen. As you hear sounds, list them in your mind. If you don't know what they are, describe them. Let your awareness move freely from sound to sound to sound, nonjudgmentally but mindfully. Don't preface the items on your list with "I hear," because that involves an act and the ego. Your mental list might go something like this:

   - Car driving by

   - Bird singing

   - Air from vents

   - Refrigerator compressor

   - Voices

   - Distant music

   - Heart beating

   - Buzzing

   - Whirring

   - Whispers

   - Computer hum

   - Running water

   - Breathing

> **Mindful Minute**
>
> According to French physician Alfred Tomatis, M.D., many of the cranial nerves lead to the ear, including a nerve that also affects the organs of speech and breathing, the heart, and the gastrointestinal tract. This suggests that a great many bodily functions could be affected by what we hear, including what sounds we are able to make.

3. Keep listening for 10 to 20 minutes, then open your eyes. Try to keep the sense of listening with you throughout your day. The more you practice this meditation, the keener and more sensitive your hearing will become. You'll hear sounds beneath sounds, layers of sounds, subtle sounds, and barely audible sounds. You'll hear mindfully, and what you hear will take on more meaning.

Are You Really Listening?

Some people believe you can train yourself to hear the harmonics, or overtones, of sounds. The more sensitive your hearing becomes and the more aware you become of layers and nuances of sound, the better you will be able to hear the sounds above sounds and the sounds above those sounds.

In some cases, overtones are easy to hear. In Gregorian chanting, for example, when musical instruments are played a certain way, or in other types of singing, overtones sometimes pop out quite evidently. But according to some who have studied the subject, overtones exist for every tone, and hearing them is merely a matter of training the ear. Conversely, the ability to produce harmonics and overtones is an art that supposedly can be taught. Monks of many faiths typically engage in chanting and singing, and some are able, through diligent practice and guidance, to produce audible harmonics with their voices (such as the one-voice chords produced by some Tibetan monks).

Healing Sounds

Mantras and other sound vibrations are also thought to have a healing effect on the body in two ways: Listening to harmonic tones and music induces a relaxed state and promotes healing, and chanting or singing harmonic tones produces a similar response.

One study showed that the repetition of a single word actually lowered blood pressure, slowed heart rate, reduced respiration rate, and calmed brain wave activity in the test subjects, increasing alpha waves (the brain waves associated with relaxed attention and meditation states).

An interesting anecdote about the power of chanting involves a Benedictine monastery. A new abbot had the monastery's monks stop their six to eight hours of daily chanting, thinking the chanting served no purpose. Soon afterward, the monks became fatigued and depressed. Various doctors had suggested the monks change their diets and made other recommendations, but nothing worked. Finally, the leaders of the monastery approached the French otolaryngologist, Alfred Tomatis, M.D., who specialized in the study of ear function and of listening. Dr. Tomatis, who believed that the cortex of the brain is charged with energy via sound waves, suggested the monks return to chanting.

The monks reinstituted chanting, and their symptoms soon disappeared. They easily resumed their schedules, which included only four hours of sleep. Many sound researchers believe that disease is simply the body being "out of tune" and that sound can be used to tune the body so it can heal. Some work with computers that produce specific sounds meant to heal and even to change the molecular structure of the human body. Some also believe that producing vocal sounds, especially using harmonics, combined with the intention to heal, will produce healing.

In Hinduism, the mantra *Hari Om* is the healing mantra. *Hari* (pronounced *ha-ree*) means "to take away" and *Om* (pronounced *ah-oh-m*, or *aum*) refers to the Hindu trinity of creation, preservation, and destruction. Hari Om calls on the preservation aspect of God to preserve health. Many traditions believe reciting a mantra for someone who is sick will send healing vibrations into them and that even chanting a mantra when you hear about someone who is sick or injured, even if you aren't with them or don't know them, will send healing energy their way. Perhaps the healing effects of intercessory prayer documented in so many studies are related to this effect.

> **Mindful Minute**
>
> In a study of the therapeutic effects of music for cancer patients conducted at the Bristol Cancer Help Centre in the United Kingdom, researchers found that listening to music enhanced patients' ability to relax, release tension, improve their sense of well-being, and boost energy. When participating in musical improvisations with instruments, patients experienced the same benefits.

Such is the power of the mantra!

Resonating the Chakras

Many traditions also associate different sounds with each of the chakras. Sound researchers in the West have been studying the effects of various mantras and vowel sounds on the chakras, for healing, energy, and spiritual well-being. Chanting the correct sound can resonate within the chakra, helping open it and free the energy.

Different traditions and researchers have associated different sounds with each of the chakras.

Chakra Sounds

According to both yoga philosophy and Tibetan Buddhism, each chakra contains a "seed sound" (or *biji*) associated with that chakra. These sounds can be used as mantras when meditating on the chakras. As you chant the sounds, allow them to vibrate into the chakra with which they are associated and feel the sound vibration activating the energy of the chakra.

Although several Western researchers have developed their own systems for chakra sounds, the traditional Sanskrit sounds are as follows:

 ◆ Saturn chakra (at the base of the spine): *LAM*

 ◆ Jupiter chakra (lower abdomen): *VAM*

- Mars chakra (behind the naval): *RAM*

- Venus chakra (behind the heart): *YAM*

- Mercury chakra (in the throat): *HAM*

- Sun chakra (the third eye, in the middle of the brow): *OM*

- Thousand-Petalled Lotus (the crown): *OM*

Mantra meditations on the chakras.

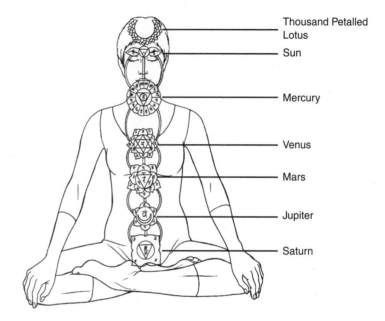

Thousand Petalled Lotus

Sun

Mercury

Venus

Mars

Jupiter

Saturn

Creating Your Own Mantras

Maybe none of the mantras we've mentioned appeal to you. That doesn't mean you can't create your own. The best way to know if a mantra is right for you is to use your intuition. Does it feel right? Do you like the sound of it? Do you like to say it? Does it energize you or put you in a spiritual or reverent frame of mind? Does it make you feel good?

Listen for mantras as you go through your life. Listen for words, songs, and sounds that "strike a chord," so to speak. Or simply experiment with sounds using your own voice. What resonates for you? Which vibrations feel good?

Try the vowel sounds—*A, E, I, O, U.* Try variations—*AH, AYE, EE, OH, OO.* Try vowel sounds from other languages, sing simple melodies using vowel sounds, or, as we've said before, pick words you love. String them together in combinations. There's no harm in trying lots of different mantras, both established and of your own making.

When you find one (or more) you love, write it down, memorize it, and keep it close to you.

Having trouble getting started? Try this create-your-own-mantra exercise. We don't use any "special" or "secret" formula here; this is just an opportunity for you to play with sound and, we hope, instigate an accidental discovery of sound that will be just perfect for you:

Write down one word that begins with each of the following letters. The word should have a pleasant connotation to you and make you feel relaxed or invoke a beautiful or soothing image, for example, A: air, B: bliss, C: crystalline, D: dune. If you can't think of a good word for one of the letters, just fill in the word *one*.

A: _____   N: _____

B: _____   O: _____

C: _____   P: _____

D: _____   Q: _____

E: _____   R: _____

F: _____   S: _____

G: _____   T: _____

H: _____   U: _____

I: _____   V: _____

J: _____   W: _____

K: _____   Y: _____

L: _____   Z: _____

M: _____

Now, make the following mantras by combining words on your list as follows:

_____	_____	_____	_____	_____
A word	C word	D word	T word	R word

_____	_____	_____	_____	_____
E word	B word	G word	L word	P word

_____	_____	_____	_____	_____
H word	I word	Z word	M word	O word

_____	_____	_____	_____	_____
N word	S word	U word	C word	U word

Now try your own combinations:

_____ _____ _____ _____ _____

_____ _____ _____ _____ _____

_____ _____ _____ _____ _____

_____ _____ _____ _____ _____

Some might come out sounding silly, some so-so, and some might be just right! We hope you find some mantra combinations that become permanent additions to your mantra repertoire.

> **Bliss Byte**
>
> Try focusing on the following sounds during meditation to help purify your mind of negative energy: waterfall, ocean waves, bells, the sound of the sea in a conch shell, thunder, echoes, bass drum, rainfall, whistling wind, or the sound of a flute. You say it isn't convenient to meditate by a waterfall, a beach, a rainforest, or in the vicinity of a talented musician? These sounds are widely available on CDs and tapes. (See Joan's CD offer at the back of this book.) Check your local enlightened bookstore or music store. Rolling meditation balls in your palm also makes a nice, cleansing sound for meditation—and releases extra tension, too.

Sounds of the World

A mantra doesn't have to be something you say yourself. Loosely interpreted, it can be any sound that helps you focus during meditation. Whether you purposefully ring a bell, put on a CD, or sit in meditation at a music concert, the world is filled with beautiful, meditative sound vibrations that can help you in your quest to be ever mindful.

Bells, Gongs, and Chimes

Using bells, gongs, and chimes in meditation is nothing new. Many ancient traditions employ these sound-producing instruments in meditation. The sounds of bells, gongs, and chimes can help dispel negative energy, both in your environment and in you. They can help clarify and purify your thoughts in preparation for meditation and can serve as a periodic reminder to bring your mind back to stillness during meditation. (In fact, Vietnamese Zen master Thich Nhat Hahn suggests that, as you go through life, whenever you hear any bell, you can consider it a reminder to be mindful.) Meditation balls, metal balls with chimes also used to exercise the hand muscles, make a soothing sound that dissolves tension.

Bells, gongs, and chimes can also be beautiful additions to your personal altar and can clear the energy in a room before you meditate. Look for quality instruments that will last. Better materials make for more resonant and purifying vibrations. For example, a cheap aluminum bell won't sound nearly as beautiful or powerful as a bell made from silver, brass, bronze, or high-quality metal combinations.

Music, Music, Everywhere

Music is a powerful force in our society and all over the world. Sometimes listening to music is a great way to use sound in meditation. Music stirs our souls, and its vibrations can quiet us, rouse us, energize us, or put us to sleep, depending on the quality of the music.

Many musicians have devoted their lives to the creation and production of meditative music in particular. Bookstores and music stores have many CDs designed for meditation, and many jazzy and New Age musicians have entire albums filled with the perfect "soundtrack" for a meditation session. Some combine the sounds of nature— ocean waves, waterfalls, wind, birdsong, whale song—with music. These CDs can really set the mood and help you stay focused during meditation.

Even if New Age music isn't your thing, many other types of music will work well for meditation. Try classical, soft jazz, opera arias, even meditative pop or rock music. Hard-core punk rock is more your style? Well … who knows. Maybe that's what will work for you. However, music with lyrics that talk about or suggest violence, subjugation of other people, or that have a negative energy about them aren't ideal for meditation. We're not saying this kind of music can't be technically skilled or even artistically inspired, only that it isn't conducive for peaceful focus and unengaged concentration.

Also, music that is beautiful but that invokes a strong emotional response in you might not be best for meditation. Remember, you are trying to disengage from your emotions, step back from them, and observe mindfully. That song that always makes you weep probably won't help you do that.

Whatever your favorite meditation technique—chanting, praying out loud, reciting poetry, or listening to Mozart—don't neglect the power of sound for healing and spiritual renewal.

Meditation makes use of visual and auditory sources of focus for the mind-body, from the steady flame of the candle to the sound of a bell or chime sounded before, during, or at the end of your meditation session.

Chinese meditation balls make a soothing sound but also stimulate your sense of touch during meditation.

The Least You Need to Know

◆ Chanting and the repetition of certain words and syllables are traditions utilized by most major and many minor world religions and cultures.

◆ Silence is as powerful as sound, and both can be used during meditation.

◆ Sound can resonate the chakras, releasing chakra energy.

◆ You can use an existing mantra or create your own. Mantras can be Sanskrit chants or American pop tunes!

◆ Ringing bells, gongs, or chimes or listening to music can also help you utilize the power of sound during meditation.

Part 5

More Ways to Meditate

As if you don't have enough options, in this next part we'll show you how to meditate with a visual focus. We'll introduce you to mandalas, those beautiful works of art traditional to Tibetan Buddhism and commonly used as meditation focal points. We'll show you how to find mandalas in the world around you, contemplate your own body as a mandala, even create your own mandala works of art. Next, we'll introduce you to guided imagery and creative visualization—techniques that use the power of your imagination to help you fulfill your dreams and change your life. We'll show you how drawing, writing, and the sports you love can be forms of meditation. And last, we'll introduce you to meditation techniques adapted from the great traditions of the world, from ancient Mexico to Africa, Europe to the Middle East, Asia to Native America, so you can learn about other cultures, broaden your mind, and enrich your own meditation experience.

Chapter 17

Seeing Is Believing: Guided Imagery, Mandalas, and Creative Visualization

In This Chapter

- What mandalas mean: the circle of life
- Make your own personalized mandala
- Reawaken your imagination
- Taking a tour of the inner you
- Fine-tuning your visualization power

Everyone learns differently and responds differently. For some people, mantra meditation may not be comfortable or meaningful, but mandala meditation, guided imagery, or creative visualization might be exactly right.

For the visually inclined, image-based meditation can become a powerful mind-body tool. What you see, either in front of you with your eyes open or in your mind's eye, can help you focus and concentrate—the purpose for a mandala—and can even help you expand the boundaries of your thinking and help you imagine and eventually make real the changes you want to make in your life. You can do it all through the power of your inner and outer vision.

What's a Mandala?

Mandalas are beautiful circular designs that can be used as a point of focus and for contemplation during meditation, but they are far more than pretty pictures. Mandalas are rich with symbolism and are an important part of the sacred rituals of many cultures.

Mandalas' circular designs represent the nature of both the universe (in macrocosm) and the body (in microcosm). Classic mandalas (such as the Cretan labyrinth) usually consist of seven or more concentric circles in quadrants aligned with the four directions and contain a square center, often with a representation of a God or other symbol of purity or perfection.

Other mandalas are based on 11 circles (such as the labyrinth at Chartres Cathedral in Paris and the elongated mandala of the Tree of Life from the Kabbalah). The Hopi medicine wheel is based on the number four, and Tibetan mandalas might have different numbers of circles, representing the chakras, for example, or the elements, or protective deities. Mandalas are archetypes. They appear in all cultures and all ages. The body itself is a sort of mandala, and so is the universe.

The culture most famous for its mandalas and one of the likely origins of the mandala as we know it today is Tibet. These days, Westerners are increasingly well versed in Tibetan culture, as Tibetan Buddhism gains in popularity. The mandala is perhaps the most characteristic symbol of Tibetan Buddhism, known for its colorful and decorative rituals.

> **Mindful Minute**
>
> Tibet is located in the upper elevations of southwest China. Since 1965, the Tibetan government has been under the rule of Communist China. Tibet's Dalai Lama lives in exile in Dharamsala, India, where he presides over Tibetan Buddhism, as well as the Tibetan nation-in-exile.

In Tibet, mandalas are often painted on paper or dyed into cloth. An important part of the Tibetan monk initiation ritual is the formation of highly intricate, amazingly beautiful mandalas made by pouring colored sand on a flat surface with very fine tools (this takes about eight days). The ritual presents the mandala, the meditators, and other offerings to the guru, to the deity, and to the Three Jewels (the Buddha, the Buddha's teaching, and the community of monks). The ritual also involves purification, protection, and other basic elements of Tantric Buddhism initiation (the foundation of Tibetan Buddhism). Then, these spectacular works of transitory art are swept up, put into a jug clothed as a deity, and poured into the river.

Of course, you don't need to be entering a monastery to use a mandala. Meditators use mandalas or figures like them all over the world as a way to focus the attention. They all serve as an inspiration and a source of contemplation. What does the mandala say about who you are?

Planet Mandala

Considered a sign of life, eternity, and/or divinity in many cultures, the circle of the mandala in both simple and complex forms is everywhere. Of course it is—because it's everywhere in nature—the sun; the moon; the earth; a tree trunk; a tree canopy; stones; the sky; ripples of water around any object dropped into the water; or spots on the leopard, on a butterfly, on a fish. We're sure you can think of more examples.

Many of the yoga mudras (hand positions; see Chapter 13) bring the fingers or hands into a circle to redirect energy back into the body. On a much grander scale, many cities throughout the world employ a circular design, even placing the city's most respected or sacred spot in the center, like a mandala: Rome, Jerusalem, and Baghdad, to name a few.

Bliss Byte

In addition to the human body itself as mandala, many circles exist within the body. The Circle of Willis at the base of the brain equalizes cerebral circulation. The eyes, the nostrils, the open mouth, and the face itself are all roughly circular. The passage of oxygen into the lungs, into the blood, through the heart, back into the lungs, and out again is circular. Sit in stillness and feel the circle of life at work in your own body.

Circles are integral parts of religious traditions around the world. Although links between circles and the sacred are too numerous to mention, here are a few significant ones:

◆ Aztec calendars

◆ Navajo creation paintings

◆ Halos around angels

◆ Tibetan prayer wheels

- Depictions of the four elements from many cultures

- Depictions of the four directions from many cultures

- Earth itself

The list goes on. Many cultures have many versions of the concept of the circle of life: We are born, we live, we die, we are reborn. Or we are born, we live, we die, we become part of the earth, which in turn provides nourishment for new life. Parents bring children into the world, then the children become parents, then their children become parents. We are spirit, then flesh, then spirit. Whatever your personal version, few can deny life has a distinctly cyclical nature.

Mindful Minute _____

The Native American medicine wheel is another sacred circle meant to represent the circle of life. In Native American culture, the word *medicine* refers not to pharmaceuticals, but to anything that helps grow the soul, leading to higher self-knowledge and awareness. Medicine wheels are circles made from stones or other natural materials that attract spiritual energy. They contain sacred points, such as the four directions or the four elements. To meditate inside a medicine wheel is to create a sacred space, a mandala for which you are the center.

The Inner Mandala: YOU

Just as the cosmos is shaped like a body, so the body is structured like the cosmos. The body itself is considered a mandala in the Tibetan tradition. In fact, the three-dimensional mandala can be overlaid on a picture of the human body to show the correspondence. The disks forming the base of the mandala ring the feet, lower legs, upper legs, and hips, forming the realms of air, fire, water, and earth. The torso represents the realm of the chakras and the energy that moves through them, containing the potential for enlightenment. The head is the center and uppermost point of the mandala, minutely centered around the third eye.

Mindful Minute _____

Buddhists place the human-inhabited earth along the margins of the cosmos. The center of the cosmos is occupied by the gods. The cosmos is structured like the human body, and through meditation, one attempts to return to the center of all things, where divinity lives.

This isn't the only way the body has been represented as a mandala. Another model demonstrates the movements of the different energies and bodily fluids through the body's meridians in a pattern that resembles a mandala. Also consider the layers of subtle bodies in yoga philosophy (see Chapter 7), or even your eyes, those mandalalike windows to your soul. The subject is interesting to study, but to consider yourself a mandala, all you need to know is that you are a sort of energy spiral and your deepest, truest, most spiritual self lies in your center. Through meditation, you can wind your way inside and discover that center.

Relax

If your head is spinning trying to understand the sacred history and theory behind mandalas, relax! Mandalas are meant to be visually grounding and calming. Go look at one for a while, and you'll see what we mean.

Creating Your Personalized Mandala

You don't have to be a talented painter or skilled with the intricate tools Tibetan monks use to create their sand mandalas to create your own personal mandala. Although you can probably find beautiful representations of mandalas in books, on posters, on tapestries, or from other sources, a mandala you make yourself can mean more and hold more spiritual power than the most intricate and artful construction in the world.

To make your own mandala, tape a blank sheet of paper on a flat, hard surface and trace or use a photocopy of our mandala template. Now, decorate your mandala. The center can contain a picture, symbol, or mantra that is sacred and meaningful to you and your personal quest. The rest of the mandala can be decorated in whatever way you like, whether you decide to fill it with ornamental concentric rings or simply fill it with a solid color. Give it a border, make designs or pictures at each outer corner … or don't. Don't worry about making it artistically impressive. This is a personal project, for your eyes only if that's the way you want it.

Bliss Byte

Remember the "Magic Eye" art, that huge fad from a few years back? First you see an evenly patterned design, but if you stare just right, your vision shifts and you see a three-dimensional picture. These works are a sort of pop-culture, modern mandala. They induce an intense state of focus and concentration, and some are surprisingly beautiful, too, in their own way (though they are computer-generated, quite unlike the painstaking sand art of Tibetan monks).

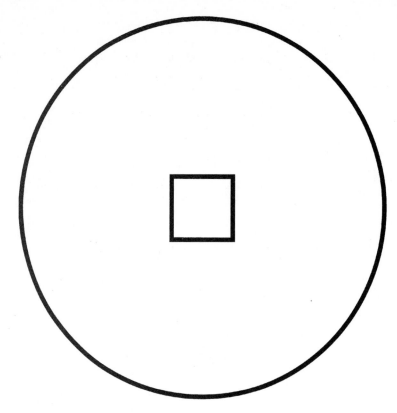

Photocopy this template and use it to create your own mandala. Simple or intricate, let your mandala creation reflect your own spiritual nature. You are the artist!

Meditating on the Circle

Meditating using a mandala can take several forms. You can contemplate the mandala in your mind: the universe as mandala, the self as mandala, or the universe as the self and vice versa. You can sit inside a mandala, such as a medicine wheel. You can walk the winding course of a mandala, as in a labyrinth, whether in Chartres Cathedral or on a painted canvas (see Chapter 14), symbolically traveling to the center of yourself. Or you can place or hang a picture of a mandala in front of you.

To use a mandala as a visual point of focus during meditation, make sure the mandala is easily viewed from your meditation position. Ideally, it should be four to six feet away from you at eye level. Points of focus for meditation should be eye level to put as little strain on the eye as possible, and for centering the body.

♦ Gaze at the mandala's center.

♦ Travel the winding paths (in labyrinth-types) with your eyes.

Using a pencil, trace the path of the Chartres Cathedral labyrinth.

♦ Look at the edges and let the mandala draw your eyes naturally toward the center.

♦ Look at the entire picture and contemplate how it represents you and your spiritual search.

♦ If you have created your own mandala with a *yantra*-like mantra or affirmation in the center, you can gaze at the center while repeating the words written there.

♦ Or simply contemplate the mandala's beauty and mindfully await impressions that might come to you.

Mindful Minute

A **yantra** is a figure similar to a mandala, and the two are often confused and, in some representations, even combined. However, a yantra is primarily linear in nature, consisting of straight lines forming a roughly circular shape (rather than curved lines). Yantras often have syllables or short written directions in the center, and unlike mandalas, which are often considered transitory constructions, yantras are often used repeatedly, sometimes as amulets or as diagrams to be buried in protection rituals, such as for the protection of a child, a loved one, someone on a journey, or a home.

However you choose to use mandalas, they can be a beautiful, symbolic, inspiring, and sacred addition to your meditation practice.

The Power of Imagery

Mandalas are just one way to meditate with a visual focus. Using imagery during meditation is an excellent way to help maintain a focus, induce relaxation, exercise the mind, and even transform reality!

Perhaps you're skeptical. "How," you ask yourself, "can imagining something actually change the nature of reality?" Well, first of all, we aren't saying that if you concentrate on that spoon in your hand it will suddenly bend in two or that you can make a chair slide across the floor simply by staring with all your might. But changing your life, improving your health, finding personal happiness and success, becoming your ideal self—these things are far more complex and affected by far more factors than a spoon or a chair. You need to concentrate on your body-mind well-being; your mind-body factors in here. If you get a cold, for example, you might say, "Oh, it's because my daughter brought it home from school," or "If that client hadn't sneezed in my face, I wouldn't have this cold!" Sure, cold germs might have been introduced into your system in one of these ways. But why wasn't your immune system able to fight it off? Your child's teacher isn't sick. Your business partner got sneezed on, too, but she's feeling great.

> **Bliss Byte**
>
> Start directing your thoughts and energies toward realizing your goals and dreams for the future. Doing something as simple as writing down a list or chart containing your goals for the week, the month, and/or the year will trigger amazing creative processes within yourself that will help you make your goals a reality. Don't be afraid to dream big dreams, either: As long as you're honest with yourself and realize that it will take work to reach your goals, the power of your mind can get you started on the right path.

Thinking in a positive way and visualizing in a positive, pleasant, and life-affirming manner might help you ward off complications of that cold (pneumonia, bronchitis, ear infection), speed your healing, and if nothing else, make your cold seem a whole lot more bearable.

Although it's true that many, many things are definitely beyond your control—including how other people act and what happens in the world—how you react to what happens to you *is always in your control.* Recent research indicates that the way you think and feel at any given moment has specific physical effects on your body and soul. Simply changing your thinking in favor of a positive outcome could dramatically increase your mind-body's healing power.

Please do remember, though, that *no one* is responsible for bringing on their own illnesses; we don't want you to feel you need to take the blame or responsibility for getting that cold. What we *do* want you to do is to use your mind's natural healing power to send beneficial thoughts and messages that will speed your body's return to health—and your mind-body's return to a state of balanced well-being.

> **Mindful Minute**
>
> An *affirmation* is a verbalized desire stated in positive terms. Affirmations are most effectively stated in terms of the present, such as "I open myself to the joy and happiness of life," or "Thank you patience, for teaching me your lesson." Repeating affirmations on a daily, even an hourly, basis can significantly influence your reality. If you change your mind, you change your life.

Welcome to the Imagi-Nation

Remember what an important part of your life imagination played when you were a child? Adults tend to underestimate the power of the imagination, and, thus, neglect to exercise their imaginations like they did as children. What a waste! Adult life sometimes leaves little time or space for indulging your more fanciful instincts, but your imagination is an amazing resource that can change your life for the better—including making it a lot more fun!

If you haven't visited the *imagi-nation* lately, however, you might find you're in unfamiliar territory. How long has it been since you've really flexed that imagination muscle?

Before you launch into *guided imagery* or *creative visualization*, get your imagination back in shape with a few simple exercises. Think like a kid again, and with some practice, you'll be ready for some serious visualization work.

> **From A to Om**
>
> Guided imagery is meditation facilitated by another person (or your own voice on a tape). **Creative visualization** is a one-person affair in which the meditator imagines that the conditions or things he or she desires are already manifest, which helps bring those conditions into being.

Try one of the following exercises every day for two weeks:

◆ Go outside on a clear day, spread a blanket on the lawn, lie on your back, and look at the clouds. What do you see? Animals? People? Monsters? Castles? Angels?

◆ Set aside 20 minutes for daydreaming. If you could be anybody in the world just for a day, who would you be? What would it be like?

◆ Did you ever have an imaginary friend? Invent one! We can all use another friend to talk to now and then, especially one who is such a good listener. Imagine your friend, then talk—pour out your heart!

◆ Suck on a piece of hard candy. Really concentrate on the candy, its taste, and its texture. Make it last as long as you can.

◆ Go to a local park and swing on the swings.

◆ Rake leaves and jump in the pile. Or shovel snow and jump in that pile. Make a snowman. Build a fort. Wear red mittens!

> **Mindful Minute**
>
> A recent study printed in *Alternative Therapy Journal* showed that relaxed attention to oneself via relaxation techniques, meditation, and imagery techniques enhanced connectivity between the brain and the body.

◆ Walk around (inside!) your house on your hands and knees. What different perspective do you get? Next, walk around your house looking down into a hand-held mirror pointed at the ceiling. Pretend you are walking on the ceiling. Or if you don't mind what the neighbors think, crawl around the yard. Who knows what you'll discover!

◆ Pretend you are your favorite animal. How would you move? What sound would you make? What would you do all day? Try moving like your favorite animal. (This is a great game to play with kids.)

◆ Take a walk and imagine you are hiking through a foreign land. Imagine everything familiar is something exotic and new. Or imagine you are a foreigner seeing your neighborhood for the first time.

◆ Play with kids. If you run out of ideas for imaginative games, they'll always be able to think of more.

Guided Imagery: A Self-Tour

Guided imagery allows you to get inside yourself. With the help of a voice that tells your mind where to go, you can explore your inner landscape like a pioneer. Your mind-body can reveal a lot of information if you are willing to listen. In fact, it might just be waiting for you to pay attention.

In the following guided imagery meditations, either have a trusted friend read the script for you (after which you can reciprocate the favor) or tape your own voice reading it. Read slowly in a soothing voice, pausing where it seems appropriate, or where you see an ellipsis (…) in the script.

Introduction to Yourself

This first guided imagery experience is a good introduction to guided imagery. Think of it as an "imagination warm-up."

Close your eyes and breathe deeply. Let your breath fill you with peace, and breathe out tension with every exhalation until you feel very relaxed …

Now, think of a place that is special to you, a place where you feel comfortable, secure, and loved. It can be a place you have been many times or a place that exists only in your imagination. Imagine yourself in that place. See the place in your mind. What do you see around you? What colors and shapes do you see? What textures can you feel? What aromas do you smell? Do you hear sounds? Let yourself observe the place with all your senses for a moment, feeling safe, secure, and comfortable …

Now, from that place, imagine yourself getting up and walking. Walk through your place until you see a large oak door. You can see white light glowing around the door. Walk up to the door and open it to reveal a beautiful, glowing light. Step into it and walk through it. As you step through the light, you see you are now on a white beach and the ocean is a brilliant sapphire blue. You are standing among some small dunes dotted with sea oats and white flowers. You walk through the dunes and onto the beach itself. The sand is soft and warm. The sun is warm on your skin, and a light breeze gently caresses you. You walk along the line of the surf, and friendly waves foam around your feet. The water is warm, too. You look out over the ocean, and the pale blue sky seems to merge with the bright blue sea so that you can hardly tell where they meet.

Far off in the sea, you see a school of dolphins jumping high into the air. A flock of bright white pelicans soars high above you. Look around. Feel the place with all your senses …

Then you see another door, this one set into a sand dune. Curious, you walk back up the beach and open the door. Again you see the white light. You walk into the light, and as you step out of it, you hear the rustle of leaves underfoot. You are in a beautiful forest of tall green trees. In front of you is a winding, leaf-covered path. You walk slowly down the path, looking around.

Sunlight filters through the leaves and dapples the path with light. Wind plays in the leaves, and their gentle rustle soothes you. Somewhere nearby you hear the sound of water. The path veers off to the right, and you follow it down to a brook filled with smooth, colored stones. Along the banks are bluebells, and a willow tree dangles its fronds into the water. Water splashes and tumbles over the stones. A few large stones protrude from the water. Using them as stepping-stones, you step easily across the brook.

The path continues up the opposite bank and then the forest opens into a bright green glade filled with yellow daffodils. You walk through the glade and sit in the middle of the flowers. The trees surrounding the glade are a silvery green in the light. You sit and take in the place using all your senses …

Then you see a little house on the other side of the glade. You get up, walk over to it, and open the door. You walk through the familiar white light and find yourself back in that place you love. You smile, happy to be home. You lie back, relax, close your eyes, and think about the beautiful places you have been today. Then slowly, when you are ready, open your eyes.

Bliss Byte

If visualizing is hard for you, perhaps one of your other senses might work better. For example, hold a flower, close your eyes, and stroke the petals. Stay with the feelings that come from this. Or smell the flower and let the fragrance linger silently in your mind, bringing forth whatever impressions it might. If you have a hard time visualizing in images, just allow yourself to feel the instructions in any way that makes sense to you. You don't have to "see" them.

The Happiness Trip

Guided imagery can help you to confront the emotional issues in your life that are keeping you from being happy. Try this guided imagery exercise when you feel low self-esteem, when you feel that your life has gone off-course, or when you are simply feeling low or down.

Close your eyes and breathe deeply. Let your breath fill you with peace, and breathe out tension with every exhalation until you feel very relaxed …

Now think of a place where you feel comfortable and secure. It can be a place you have been many times or one that exists only in your imagination. Imagine yourself in that place. See the place in your mind. What do you see around you? What colors and shapes do you see? What textures do you feel? What aromas do you smell? Do you hear sounds? Let yourself observe the place with all your senses for a moment, feeling safe, secure, and comfortable …

Imagine yourself standing up because you hear someone coming. You feel a sense of happy anticipation as you hear the small footsteps of a child coming toward you. Suddenly, a little child appears. You smile at the child, step forward, and it reaches its hands up for your embrace. You take the child into your arms and give it a long, loving hug …

Now you put the child down and together you walk, hand in hand, through your safe place. You show the child around and explain why the place is special to you. The child listens with interest, then the two of you sit together. Suddenly, the child begins to weep softly. "What's wrong?" you ask with concern, stroking the child's hair. The child crawls into your lap and, feeling ultimately safe, begins to tell you. Listen. What does the child say? …

Think about what the child has told you. Is it about a feeling? A health problem? An inner pain? Then take the child in your arms again, hold it close to you, and promise the child that everything will be okay. No matter what has happened, you are here now, and as an adult, you promise the child you will take care of it from now on and that nothing in the past can hurt it anymore. Promise it the love, safety, security, medical attention, and emotional attention it might not have gotten before. All that is over. You are in charge now. Promise the child. Promise yourself …

The child looks up at you with a smile, and you know everything will be fine. The child leans toward you and whispers in your ear: "It's me!" You look closely at the child's face, and you realize the child is you, as a child. You smile because it makes so much sense that this child is you. As the child stands, kisses you on the cheek, says thank you, and skips away, you know you will see this child again soon. Take a few moments to contemplate all you have learned, then open your eyes.

Mindful Minute

Not everyone is visually oriented. Joan has had many meditation students who find it incredibly difficult or impossible to actually "see" images with their eyes closed. However, guided imagery–based meditation can be a highly effective method for balancing the mind-body in people who find it difficult. Sometimes the things that are the hardest for us are the things that are most beneficial because in strengthening our weak spots, we approach inner equilibrium.

Creative Visualization: You Are What You See

Creative visualization is a lot like guided imagery, except you do it on your own, without the help of an outside voice to guide you. Creative visualization is a little like a full-color, three-dimensional daily affirmation. Instead of beginning each day by saying "Every day in every way I'm getting better and better," or whatever other daily affirmations you might have heard, creative visualization helps you see and experience yourself "better and better," with the help of your imagination.

> **Mindful Minute**
>
> "You may not be what you think you are, but what you think, you are."
>
> —Jim Clark, Big Sur poet

The purpose behind creative visualization is to change your thinking and, by changing your thinking, change your life. Use the following visualization exercises as springboards, and fill them in with your own hopes, goals, dreams, and aspirations—in other words, shape these exercises so they follow the path of your own personal evolution.

> **Bliss Byte**
>
> Daily affirmations can be like a "quickie" visualization. Try repeating any of the following 10 times each morning:
>
> ◆ I am becoming happier.
> ◆ The core of my being is at peace.
> ◆ Each experience I have is an opportunity for greater growth.
> ◆ There are no mistakes in life, only lessons.
> ◆ I forgive all who have hurt me.
> ◆ I forgive myself for all I have hurt.
> ◆ I go forth in love and peace.
> ◆ I embrace the universe.
> ◆ I send loving thoughts to all human beings and wish for their happiness and well-being.

Everything You Ever Wanted

What do you want? Health? Wealth? Love? Success? Happiness? Beauty? All of the above? Creative visualization can help you achieve everything you ever wanted. No, it won't magically cause you to win the lottery or reconstruct your flawed nose. But it can subtly change your thought processes, which will change your motivations and actions, which will change your energy, which will attract good fortune and repel bad fortune.

Every morning before you get out of bed and every night before you go to sleep, spend 10 to 20 minutes visualizing yourself with everything you ever wanted. Imagine yourself living in your dream house, maintaining your ideal weight, becoming an overnight business success, falling in love with the perfect mate, or being in perfect health. Imagine all the details. How do you look? How do your surroundings look? What do you do? What do you say? Don't waste time during these visualization sessions worrying about how impossible the vision is or how you couldn't possibly attain it. Expend your energy on nothing but the richly detailed visualization of you with your dreams fulfilled.

Interestingly, the more you practice creative visualization, the more you might find that what you really want is different than what you thought you wanted. For example, maybe you think you want great wealth. Money is certainly a handy thing to have, but the more you imagine having a lot of money—including all the details, implications, and effects—the more you might become bored. So you can buy whatever car you want—so what? What else is there?

Eventually, your visualizations might take on a more spiritual tone. You'll imagine yourself truly happy, truly content, truly interested in the world around you and humankind's spiritual quest. You'll be more concerned with achieving the dreams for the inner you rather than the outer you.

But you can achieve them all—the inner goals and the outer goals—as long as they are truly important to you. We aren't saying it is easy, but if you are committed enough to visualize every day, you will become committed enough to adjusting your life in ways that will make your dreams come true. Visualization helps you define your dreams, pinpoint your goals, and work out strategies for achievement—even without realizing it on a conscious level. Commit yourself to creative visualization, and watch your life transform. Before you know it, the only thing left to visualize will be reality!

The Least You Need to Know

- Mandalas come in many forms, from simple circles to highly intricate artwork.
- The circle is a symbol of life, eternity, and divinity in many cultures and can be considered an archetype, or common symbol, to all humankind.
- Cultivating the power of your imagination can help you make your dreams come true.
- Guided imagery uses a vocal guide to help you toward greater self-knowledge, healing, and happiness.
- Creative visualization helps you live the life you've always wanted—today!

Chapter 18

Achieving the Flow State: Meditation and Creativity

In This Chapter

♦ Achieving flow

♦ Automatic writing as meditation

♦ Automatic drawing as meditation

♦ Sports as meditation

We've said it before: Anything can be meditation. In fact, when you practice mindfulness during work and play, you might find your performance, not to mention your concentration, improves dramatically. Mindful sports, mindful art, mindful reading, mindful creativity—you might be surprised at the heights you can reach when you focus all your attention on what you are doing.

Perhaps you've heard of the concept of *flow*. Flow occurs when you immerse yourself in any task and become completely absorbed in it. Time and space seem to disappear. Only you and the task you are absorbed in—whether your tennis game or your drawing of a still life—exist to you in those moments. Flow is really just mindful meditation while *doing*. It is an amazing experience that can enrich your life and bring out talents, creativity, and skill you never knew you had.

Achieving Flow

Did you ever burn a hole in a piece of paper by focusing the sun's rays through a magnifying glass or a pair of eyeglasses? That's a little like flow. The sun itself can't burn paper, but when *concentrated* through a magnifying glass, it becomes much hotter and more intense. Your concentration can act like that magnifying glass, focusing your skills, attention, and abilities. You probably never thought you could burn holes in your work, your play, your daily activity—but you can! (Figuratively, anyway.)

Flow comes easily to kids. Have you ever watched small children engaged in a game of pretend? Coloring with crayons? Making animal shapes from Play-Doh? If you try to get their attention, it might take a minute or two. They're so absorbed in their work that they might not hear you at first. Kids haven't been exposed to the levels of stress and responsibilities familiar to adults, so they are less easily distracted. They know how to concentrate. We've lost this art of concentration as we've become consumed by the thousand details of daily living.

But achieving flow is a skill worth cultivating because being able to live in a state of flow is highly satisfying. It allows you to perform at full capacity. Regaining the ability to achieve flow isn't easy, but it can be done with practice. Basically, flow is more easily achieved when you have control over your mental state, and to gain control, you need to keep your mind in shape, just like you keep your body in shape. You need to devote yourself to those mental workouts. Just like bodily control, mental control comes through exercise.

The Optimal State of Peak Performance

Even if you can't control when it happens, you've probably experienced flow before. Have you ever …

◆ Been playing sports (from basketball to billiards) and suddenly could do no wrong, every move and every play executed with perfection?

◆ Been writing a report, a short story, or a diary entry and lost complete track of time because you were so focused on your writing?

◆ Been giving a speech or a presentation and suddenly, every word was perfect, your jokes were a big hit, and even when you ad-libbed, you were a sensation?

◆ Been playing or singing music when suddenly the sound seemed to change and you played or sang better and with greater skill than you ever thought you could?

◆ Been making repairs on your house or working in your garden with such absorption and single-mindedness that the whole day went by without any sense of time passing?

◆ Been painting, drawing, sculpting, or even doodling, when time seemed to stop and suddenly you looked at your creation and thought, "How could I have made such a beautiful thing?"

◆ Been reading a novel or a poem and been so completely transported into the story or imagery that you didn't notice distractions around you?

 Relax

If your flow seems as if it's flown the coop and you're continually frustrated by attempts to get it moving, perhaps you have a physiological upset that a regular check-up with your doctor can mend or therapy with a professional counselor can address. Through it all, keep that beautiful mind of yours open to new possibilities for inspiration. They are all around you!

We could go on and on. Examples are endless because flow can happen no matter what you are doing. When it happens, you know it. Afterward, you think, *Whew! That was amazing!* You find yourself with a feeling of *being* the project, speech, garden, painting, music, baseball, or whatever it is that you're experiencing so fully. In another way, you can view it as the subject of your absorption flowing through *you*, the garden, painting, or baseball moves through your experience of it while you maintain a sense of detachment. That's flow.

What if we could achieve flow whenever we wanted it? What if every moment of our lives could be similarly amazing? Such a state of being is the reward and result of cultivating mindfulness.

The Zen of Being in the Moment of Doing

We've talked about mindfulness before, of course, but it's worth repeating in terms of flow. To achieve flow during your everyday activities, one thing and one thing only is necessary:

Do for the sake of doing, not for the sake of the end result.

Sound familiar? This concept is integral to the Zen way of life, the Buddha preached it, and it is the ideal state for the practice of many different spiritual pursuits, from moving meditations, to daily seated meditation. The aim of flow and the aim of meditation isn't to *accomplish* things but to experience them. The idea sounds simple, but it's easier said than done. As soon as you begin to live mindfully in the moment, your mind-body resists. You fidget and grow restless; your thoughts wander into the future, back to the past, anywhere but now. But when your mind-body wanders, *you are missing the now*, and *now* is when *everything happens*. Don't miss your life. Live mindfully, and you'll step into the state of flow.

Lazy Brain Syndrome

But as we said before, learning to live in the moment and do for the sake of doing takes practice. It also takes an active brain, ready to engage in active pursuit.

Do you have a couch-potato brain? Lots of us do. How many of the following statements are true for you? (Check those that apply.)

❏ After a long, difficult day, I usually watch TV to relax.

❏ I'm uncomfortable with silence. If I'm alone in the house, I have to have the TV or radio on.

❏ I like to read magazines or the newspaper, but books take too much concentration.

❏ I don't even try to understand poetry.

❏ The last time I learned a new word was in school.

❏ Sometimes I do crossword puzzles, but I never finish them.

❏ Conversation is only for exchanging information.

❏ I get impatient listening to music.

❏ If people around me start talking about philosophical subjects, I tune out.

❏ Now that I'm not in school and have a good job, I don't need to learn things anymore, unless they are directly relevant to my job.

❏ I don't have any hobbies.

If you checked one or two boxes, your mind is respectably active. More than that, though, and you've got couch-potato mind. Make no mistake: We're not saying you're unintelligent. Being lazy has nothing to do with intelligence. It could simply be the result of unhealthy habits. Or it could be a side effect of overwork and not enough rest—common ailments in our fast-paced, information-packed society. Will changing take effort? Of course. Will you enjoy it? Not always. Will you be glad you did it? Yes!

Having a lazy mind might seem much easier than having an active, toned mind, just like it's deceptively easier to lie on the couch than to go on a brisk two-mile walk or take an aerobics class. But those people who do exercise—both body and mind—will tell you that once you get into the exercise habit, the lazy habits are far less desirable and far less tempting. And what seems "easy" can be more painful to your mind-body in the long run; not only does it make us feel less alive and connected to others and to ourselves, it opens the door to premature aging and greater susceptibility to illness.

 Relax

Too much exercise can be just as unhealthy as not enough! If you work in a stressful job all day, then go to the gym and run at top speed on the treadmill for an hour to blaring music and lights, you're gearing your body and mind up for sensory overload. A quiet run in the park, followed by 20 minutes of seated meditation, might be more suited to your overworked body and mind.

How do you break lazy habits? The key is to set up some guidelines for yourself and stick to them. Just knowing, in some vague way, that you need to be more mentally active won't be much help. If you've set up some hard-and-fast rules, however, you'll know exactly what you need to do. Changing your thinking patterns will be easier and finally within reach.

Rule 1: Not all activities are equally conducive to flow. Once every day, spend at least 30 minutes on stimulating, mind-stretching, creative activities that engage you and challenge you, such as writing, painting, drawing, playing sports, making music, dancing, or playing games such as chess or word puzzles.

Rule 2: Find pleasure in complex thought. The next time someone starts a conversation about some philosophical, hypothetical, or historical subject, join in. The next time you see an article or run across a book on a subject you don't know anything about but that strikes your fancy, read it—all of it. You might find the effort worthwhile.

Rule 3: Revive the lost art of conversation. Once each month, invite friends over just to talk. No television, no rented videos, just interesting, animated conversation. Have everyone come armed with three topics meant to spark discussion.

Rule 4: Revive the lost art of letter-writing. In the telecommunications age, it's easy to forget the pleasure of a written letter—e-mails and instant messaging, though efficient, often contribute to our sense of isolation and sound-byte communication instead of bringing us a feeling of shared intimacy. Put thought, care, and effort into your letters to faraway friends and relatives. You'll get just as much out of the writing as they will out of receiving your letters. Try to write a letter to someone once every week, or at least once a month.

Rule 5: Allot one hour every weekend purely to mind play. Do the Sunday crossword puzzle. Work a jigsaw puzzle. Play bridge. Solve some math problems just for fun! (Really! It can be fun if you don't *have* to do it.) Read poetry and make an effort to understand it.

Rule 6: Create no-TV zones. Choose a day or a daily period of time in which the TV absolutely cannot be turned on. Watching TV can be fun and educational, but it also tends to be a mind-numbing activity that many use to fill up silence so their minds don't have to engage. Have you ever found yourself watching TV and, although you aren't enjoying the program, find yourself unable to turn it off? Do your brain a favor. Turn it off. Just do it.

Rule 7: Create a silence zone. Spend one hour of every week in complete silence. No talking, no listening to television or radio, no communication with others. Ask the other members of your household to respect your hour of silence. Although you can't keep away every noise, don't focus on the noises you do hear. Make an effort to cultivate the stillness within. Get used to the silence of you.

> **Bliss Byte**
>
> French psychological anthropologist Roger Caillois divided pleasurable activities into four categories: *Agon* includes competitive games, including sports and other athletic events. *Alea* describes games of chance, such as bingo, blackjack, or fortune-telling. *Ilinx* refers to consciousness-altering games such as amusement park rides or high-risk activities such as skydiving. *Mimicry* describes imaginative games in which an alternate reality is created, such as acting in the theater, painting, writing, or other artistic endeavors. All these activities have the potential to induce flow.

Zen and the Art of Athletics

Sports are an art. Whether you prefer ballet or baseball, high jump or hackey-sack, mindfulness and complete absorption in your performance will bring out your highest skill and, more important, help you experience the true joy of the game.

But if you're an athlete (even just on Saturday afternoons), you know that you don't experience flow during every practice, every drill, and especially not during every game. If only you could! Flow in sports often seems like an elusive miracle. Sometimes you've got it; sometimes you don't. And when you see it happen—when you witness a teammate or watch a pro enter the flow state of mind-body excellence in sports— wow, what a wonderful sight!

You *can* have more control over when your athletic performance peaks and when it doesn't. Being healthy and in shape helps, of course. Practice helps, too. But the real key is mindfulness. When you're out there, on the court or the green or the field or the rink or the dance floor, you won't perform at your peak capacity unless you are completely absorbed in the *now* of your performance. When you do become one with your sport, your ability will leap higher than a ballerina, or a pole vaulter, or Michael Jordan! You'll make shots you never imagined you could make. You'll execute moves like a legend. You'll be "in the zone." And it will feel so good.

> **Mindful Minute**
>
> Home run slugger Mark McGwire has this to say about the art of flow of hitting homers:
>
> See the ball. Nice and easy. Get a pitch to hit.
>
> How's that for a baseball meditation mantra?

When you experience flow while playing sports, you have the opportunity to experience something rare: You'll *be* poetry in motion. You'll *remember* because you were paying attention. You were paying attention to such a degree that you became the game. And when you are the game, your ego dissolves, your worries about who is watching or how you are playing dissolve, even time and space dissolve. It's like one of those slo-mo moments in a movie, but it isn't a movie. It's real, it's life, and it's you. All that is left is *the game*, and the game is you, and suddenly, you know exactly how to play. It's easy. It's almost effortless.

To refine your powers of concentration and mindfulness during physical activity, try the following exercises, which are all forms of meditation in action:

> **Relax**
>
> Before you start any new fitness program, be sure to consult your doctor. If you've never considered yourself particularly athletic but are interested in getting "physical," you might want to try gentle moving meditations such as yoga. A daily practice of moving yoga meditation can be a great way to prepare for an athletic flow state.

- Dribble a basketball and see how many times you can dribble before your mind wanders. Keep practicing and watch your time increase.

- Play a game of catch with a friend, using a football, a baseball, or even a Nerf ball! Never take your eye off the ball, even for a second. See how long you can go before your eyes shift away.

♦ Go running and time your breath with your steps. For example, inhale for 5 steps, exhale for 10 steps. How far can you run before you lose track of the breath? (If you become short of breath, decrease the number of steps per breath rather than giving up the count.)

♦ Hold a prop from your sport during meditation. Whether a volleyball or a ballet slipper, focus on the object. Turn it around in your hands. Notice everything about it. Imagine it being used in your sport. Imagine using it yourself. Pour your energy into the object and try to discern its energy. Concentrate until you feel like you have become one with the object. (It might take more than one meditation session.)

♦ Spend 15 to 20 minutes every day sitting quietly and visualizing yourself performing your sport well. Watch how perfectly you execute the plays, the steps, the moves. See yourself totally absorbed in your performance. Feel how it feels. If you think it, you can do it!

Cultivating flow in your athletic performance might take a little time and concentration, but you'll be glad you did. You'll be a better athlete and a more awake and alive human being.

A Rose Is a Rose Is a Rose Is ...

Sports isn't the only activity in which you can cultivate flow. Ideally, you could live in flow, and the more you practice, the more it will happen to you. Two of the best activities for helping your mind achieve flow are automatic writing and automatic drawing. Whether you consider yourself a skilled writer or artist doesn't matter. The point of these automatic processes is to free the normal constraints on your thinking and let your subconscious mind peek through. It's a great way to engender creativity, get you out of creative ruts, and open new ways of perception.

Bliss Byte

If you find yourself in a creative rut, here are a few tips to help you get all four tires back on the road again: skip, run in the rain, take a shower and sing as loud as you can, face toward people in the elevator (as opposed to the door), smile at everything. When you return to your creative project, you'll have a fresh perspective and awareness to bring to your efforts. Hey, you could even take a 20-minute, mindful walking meditation break!

Automatic Writing: What's on Your Mind?

Gertrude Stein (1874–1946) was an eccentric and avant-garde American writer who lived in Paris and was most famous for her *stream-of-consciousness* writing. (She is the author of the phrase borrowed for the title of this section, "A rose is a rose is a rose is ….") According to Stein, writing should illuminate the present moment, and the present moment can only truly be described using fragmentation, repetition, and simplification. Stein wrote from her subconscious. Following is a sample of her automatic writing, from *Tender Buttons* (1914):

GLAZED GLITTER.

Nickel, what is nickel, it is originally rid of a cover.

The change in that is that red weakens an hour. The change has come. There is no search. But there is, there is that hope and that interpretation and sometime, surely any is unwelcome, sometime there is breath and there will be a sinecure and charming very charming is that clean and cleansing. Certainly glittering is handsome and convincing.

There is no gratitude in mercy and in medicine. There can be breakages in Japanese. That is no programme. That is no color chosen. It was chosen yesterday, that showed spitting and perhaps washing and polishing. It certainly showed no obligation and perhaps if borrowing is not natural there is some use in giving.

From A to Om

Stream of consciousness refers to an unchecked flow of thoughts, either spoken or written, as a literary technique designed to portray the preconscious impressions of the mind before they can be logically arranged. Therefore, stream-of-consciousness expression usually appears nonsensical, lacking cohesiveness and logical sequence. Famous writers to use the technique are Gertrude Stein, James Joyce, William Faulkner, and Virginia Woolf.

It doesn't make sense, you say? It doesn't have to make sense, and neither does your automatic writing. But it might make sense to you, and it might reveal you to yourself.

To practice automatic writing as meditation, start an automatic-writing journal. Every day for at least 15 minutes, sit down and write without stopping. Write anything that comes into your head. It can be clever; it can be silly; it can be nonsense; it can be the same word over and over. It can be *I don't know what to write I don't know what to write I don't know what to write* for three pages. Believe us—after a few days or perhaps weeks, you'll know what to write, at least some of the time. When you don't, write what you are feeling, thinking, seeing, hearing … whatever. Don't judge it, don't analyze, don't interpret. Just let the words flow from your soul. You don't even have to read it when you are done. But if you look back on it a few weeks, months, or years later, you'll see clues to who you are, and your journey toward greater self-knowledge will advance another step or two.

Primal Pictures

Writing isn't the only form of pen-to-paper meditation. Automatic drawing can also be an integral part of your meditation practice. During automatic drawing, ideally the "I" or ego expands to encompass what you are drawing so you become the drawing process. You are your subject, and your subject is you. You become one with the process. You are meditating—and creating at the same time.

Another unique advantage of automatic drawing is that it forces you to become articulate in another system of symbols of expression and communication—that is, you begin to think in images, not in words. This process helps free the mind of its usual baggage of thought clutter and become absorbed in a new way of understanding—a visual one.

Drawing meditation does more than help you lose yourself for a short time each day. It also teaches you how to see. As you draw what you see, and as it absorbs you and consumes you, you begin to see the extraordinary in the ordinary. As you go through life, you'll begin to see in terms of subjects for a drawing, and everything will look different, more beautiful, and more miraculous.

> **Bliss Byte**
>
> Before you set pencil to paper, trace the basic shape of your subject on your paper with your finger to help you focus on your task, set your mind in the right place in reference to the paper, and keep your drawing its intended size. Scared of that white space? Just dive in. Automatic drawing is about free expression, not about artistic talent. What you draw doesn't have to be representational at all (although it can be). Blob down colors or make shapes that appeal to you. Keep a special sketchbook for your automatic drawings. Or if you'd like to create your own illustrated book, combine your automatic writing diary and your sketchbook—nineteenth-century artist and poet William Blake is famous for his poems annotated with watercolor drawings.

Automatic Drawing: What Do You See?

To try automatic drawing, keep a drawing pad or journal, and each day, for at least 15 minutes, sit down, look around, and draw something you see. Don't worry about how good your drawing is. Don't worry about whether your subject is a good subject. Don't worry about what others might think of your drawing. Don't even worry about looking too closely at the paper. Just draw from within. See the object and let what you see travel into you so you become it and it flows from your pencil. Maybe your drawing will be awkward, and maybe it will barely resemble what you see—at first. But keep it up. Teach yourself how to see that vegetable or tree or child playing or daffodil or sleeping cat or blue pitcher. Draw, and lose yourself in your art so that you become the act of drawing.

Another way to stimulate creativity in automatic drawing is to try sketching with your nondominant hand. By using the hand you don't normally use for writing, you're further distancing yourself from that world of words, language, and control your hands are accustomed to. You might find you're better able to let go and let your subconscious thoughts and feelings surface in your automatic drawing. And you might also become less concerned about the quality of your drawing and more interested in the freedom of the experience. Each hand is operated by the opposite side of the brain, so if you normally use your right hand, using your left hand will give the right side of your brain a little extra stimulation, and that's good for your inner balance.

We asked our illustrator Wendy Frost to contribute an automatic drawing to our book. Always the professional artist, Wendy's first question was, "What do you want me to draw, and what style do you want it in?" "Anything," we answered. "Draw whatever you want, however you want to, for 15 minutes. Then stop." Wendy chose to draw her two cats, Earl Grey and Bob Cat, who make a habit of lying on her drawing table as she works.

Our illustrator Wendy Frost's automatic drawing of Earl Grey and Bob Cat.

We asked Wendy to comment on the drawing afterward. She chose to draw the cats, she said, because they make her feel happy and contented. We believe Wendy's feelings of joy and affection for the animals made the automatic-drawing exercise that much more pleasant for Wendy. She chose an artistic flow experience that promoted an inner sense of calm and happiness. What a nice meditation break! And what a wonderful picture of two comfortable cats.

The Least You Need to Know

- ◆ "Flow" is the state of total absorption in an activity.
- ◆ You can achieve flow more often and with more intention if you train your brain.
- ◆ Sports can become an art form when performed during flow.
- ◆ Automatic writing and automatic drawing are good ways to practice achieving a state of flow and mindfulness.

19

Meditations You Can Do from Around the Globe

In This Chapter

◆ The benefits of cross-cultural meditation

◆ Meditation rituals and techniques adapted from Mexico, South America, Africa, and Europe

◆ More meditations from Israel, the Middle East, India, and Asia

◆ Aboriginal meditations from Native America

Meditation in one form or another is practiced in every major world tradition. To discover a little variety, to open your mind to the practices of other cultures, to add new techniques to your meditation repertoire, and just to keep meditation ever interesting, you can adapt the great traditions for use in your own meditative practice.

Trying out meditation techniques doesn't mean you are "betraying" your own beliefs, religion, or philosophy—or that you need to accept the beliefs and traditions of the religion or culture that created those techniques. It only means you are open to learning, growing, and understanding all your fellow sentient beings and the greater, wider path of humankind's spiritual journey, as a whole, throughout time and into the future. It means you're open to getting in touch with your roots, your ancestry, or a culture you never knew anything about.

Around the World in Eighty Oms

Learning about the meditations of other cultures can be a rich and rewarding experience. When you practice a meditation from another culture, we hope you will do so with an open heart and with the greatest respect and reverence for spiritual traditions that might differ from your own. The world is a very large place, but it is also very small when you consider that it is full of humans who are all trying to explain the spirituality and divinity they perceive, both beyond and within.

Also, please note that the following meditations aren't replicas of any ancient traditions. Not only are the details of many ancient traditions lost to us, but these meditations are *adapted* from other cultures in a way we think makes sense and is workable for beginning meditators raised in the Western tradition. Use these meditations as a starting point, and let those traditions that interest you prompt you to learn more about that culture. Do research. Meet people from that place. Learn some of the language. Find information on the Internet. The more you know about the world, the more you see how much we all have in common.

Happy sampling!

South of the Border

First, let's head south to the land where the Aztecs, Incas, Mayas, Toltecs, and other ancient cultures arose. The climate in Mexico, Central America, and South America is hot and sunny. Not surprisingly, the sun was a spiritual point of focus for many of these cultures. Try this Mayan-inspired sun meditation. This meditation works best on a warm day:

- Set your alarm for 30 minutes prior to the next morning's sunrise.
- When you awake, get dressed in loose, comfortable clothing and remove your shoes.
- Go outside. Face east and sit on the earth in a comfortable position, either cross-legged, on your knees, or on a folded blanket.
- Breathe deeply and quietly. Focus on the sunrise. As the sun rises, observe mindfully how the world around you changes: the colors, the smells, the movements, the sounds.

◆ Feel the sun on your face. Imagine taking the solar light into your heart, letting it cleanse you of all your worries and bathe you in pure light. Release it back to the sun with a message of love.

◆ When the sun has risen all the way above the horizon, stretch your arms straight out toward the sun and receive the sun's blessing, returning thanks to the sun for the life and creative energy it gives to the earth and all its inhabitants.

◆ Rise, mindful of how you are rising from the ground just as the sun has risen. Begin your day solar-powered!

Building an African-Inspired Altar

Now it's time to head east across the North Atlantic to the great continent of Africa. *Altars* are an important part of the religious tradition in African tribal cultures, where they stood outdoors, constructed at places thought to be boundaries between the material and spirit worlds, such as at the edges of forests or the banks of rivers. Typically decorated with objects thought to be magical, sacred, or otherwise spiritually powerful, altars were a focal point and important ritual for many native African cultures.

You can design your own outdoor altar, at the base of a tree, at the foot of a large rock, on a mountaintop, along the boundary of a garden or a pond, or wherever in nature seems like a sacred place to you, even if that place is in your own backyard. Your altar can be as simple as a pile of stones or as complex as a constructed bench or small table covered with meaningful objects such as flowers, pinecones, rocks, or anything that comes from nature and speaks to you. You can even draw or paint a mandala or other symbol on your altar. The point is to draw something that has spiritual significance to you.

From A to Om

An **altar** is a natural or constructed platform or table used for sacred purposes, upon which sacred objects can be placed to aid in worship.

Dedicate your altar to one particular virtue, such as courage, health, or friendship. Ask your ancestors to bless your altar and endow it with spiritual power.

With your altar's virtue in mind, draw or paint a diamond on your forehead over the area of your third eye, between and just above your eyes. Now, sit or kneel in front of your altar, relax, breathe, and ask for a blessing from your ancestors. Meditate on the virtue to which you have dedicated your altar.

Let the spirits of your ancestors and/or the African gods speak to you through your intuition, revealing the best path to the virtue represented by your altar. How can you best have courage or compassion? How can you best embrace forgiveness or moderation? How can you best live in love or promote peace? Listen for the answer. Your mind already knows.

Meditation à la European Traditions

Time to head north to Europe, where the religious traditions have varied over centuries but where Catholicism and Protestantism both flourished for centuries. Even though Jesus Christ came from the Middle East, Europe has long been a stronghold of Christianity and the home to thousands of monks and nuns in more or less sequestered monasteries. Let's try a day of prayer, set up in the structured format of a classic Catholic monastery.

> **Mindful Minute**
>
> The Catholic rosary is a string of beads used to keep track of the prayer cycle. Praying the rosary is a sort of multi-stepped mantra that can give structure and grounding to a meditative practice. The rosary consists of groups of 10 beads with dividers and a section extending from the loop, usually with a crucifix or cross pendant. Catholics believe that saying the rosary will achieve specific benefits for the person performing the ritual and for the subject of the prayer's meditation. A *chaplet* is a complete cycle of prayers through the entire rosary, consisting of working through one group of five divine mysteries. A *decade* is a group of 10 beads on the rosary. Each bead represents one recitation of the appropriate prayer. As each prayer progresses, the prayer moves his or her fingers to the next bead so the act of saying the rosary becomes a verbal, mental, and physical meditative practice.

Christian monks and nuns typically pray during eight structured times of day to keep God foremost in their minds, and you can, too. During each of the following prayers, take a few quiet moments to focus your thoughts on the purpose of that prayer, and direct your thoughts, thanks, questions, and praise toward God. Sit, stand, kneel, or pray in whatever position is comfortable, but do so in a private room if possible. Consider yourself temporarily "cloistered."

To follow the basic pattern of Catholic monastery prayers with freedom to adapt themes according to your own beliefs, try the following:

◆ **Early morning matins.** Contemplate the day ahead and focus on what you want to accomplish today.

- **Sunrise lauds.** Meditate on the sun and offer thanks and praise for the energy and illumination it gives our lives and the way it signals the coming of a new day ahead. Let hope suffuse your meditation.

- **Mid-morning prime.** Stop in the middle of your morning for a five-minute break to consider the work you do and the ways it is important to you and to others.

- **Late-morning terce.** Take another five-minute break to consider how you feel and to give yourself room, time, and space to breathe and be quiet within.

- **Noontime sext.** Contemplate the first half of the day behind you and the second half of the day ahead of you.

- **Mid-afternoon none.** Spend a few quiet moments talking to a loved one and telling them how much they mean to you.

- **Early evening vespers.** Lie down and do a body scan. Concentrate on total relaxation of your muscles and joints. Feel yourself relaxing into the floor and releasing the tensions of the day.

- **Before-sleep compline.** Survey your day and give thanks for all you have.

Kabbalah's Tree of Life Meditation

From Europe, let's drift across the Mediterranean Sea to Israel, the home of Judaism. Kabbalah, that mystical sect of Judaism, is largely based around a symbol of the universe, the body, and the journey of meditation called the Tree of Life. This "tree" consists of a branched shape with seven circles on the bottom and three circles on the top. Much has been made about the meaning of these 10 circles, each of which contains a different name and power or energy:

- **The *Kether*, or Crown.** The top circle is the highest power, representative of divinity and divine understanding. This is the power that governs and balances all the others.

- **The *Binah*.** The intelligence circle.

- **The *Chokmah*.** The wisdom circle.

- **The *Geburah*.** The severity circle (the energy that hinders evil; also called the death star).

- **The *Chesed*.** The mercy circle (also called the star of life).

- **The *Tepereth*.** The unity circle, the mediator between creator and creation; this is the center circle of the tree.

- **The *Hod*.** The thought circle, in which mind conquers matter.

- **The *Netsah*.** The emotion circle, in which justice triumphs.

- **The *Jesod*.** The identity circle, which is the foundation of all belief and philosophy.

- **The *Malkuth*.** The circle at the base of the tree, this is the body circle, representing God's creation of both body and universe.

Many philosophies link the tree of life with the body's chakras (see Chapter 7), the body's form, and the hierarchy of the universe. The circles also represent the steps of meditation, wherein the meditator begins in the body, works up through increasingly higher stages of consciousness, and at last opens the third eye or crown of the tree and attains enlightened understanding.

To use the Tree of Life in meditation, you can gaze upon it as a whole (using it as a mandala), you can concentrate on each circle in succession, or you can simply contemplate the idea of the Tree of Life. But according to the teachings of Kabbalah, you must first light the tree by speaking one of the 25 names of God. You must pick the correct name for the process to work. To find the name that will work for you, slowly scan the following list and say each name to yourself, contemplating its meaning. Whichever one feels right, especially if it floods you with a positive feeling, is the one for you. (The most commonly used names are *Yod He Vav He* and *Ahavah*.)

Mindful Minute

According to the Bible's Old Testament, the Garden of Eden contained two trees, the Tree of the Knowledge of Good and Evil (from whence the infamous forbidden fruit came) and the Tree of Life. Although Genesis doesn't say much about the Tree of Life, it is thought that this tree is symbolized by the Kabbalah Tree of Life.

- *Abicha:* Our Father

- *Abir:* Mighty One

- *Adonoi:* Lord

- *Ahavah:* Love

- *Anochi:* I

- *Chaim:* Life

- *Ehyeh:* I Am

- *Elohi:* Great Living One

- *Eshda:* The Firey Law

- *Gabor:* Mighty

- *Gadol:* Great

- *Ha Tzur:* The Rock

- *Kabud:* Honor

- *Kodosh:* Holy One

- *Masika:* Messiah

- *Nora:* Full of Awe

- *Olam:* Everlasting Worlds

- *Ra 'a Ya:* Shepherd

- *Shalom:* Peace

- *Tamim:* Perfect

- *Tehom:* Great Deep

- *Torah:* Law

- *Tsaddik:* Saint

- *Yod He Vav He:* Brilliant Name of Fire

- *Zion:* Place of God

Mindful Minute

In Judaism, the name of God is considered sacred, and should never be written or spoken lightly or casually. Also, it may never be erased or defaced. For this reason, in many texts, from books to the Internet, you may see the word *G-d* or something similar. Leaving out a letter prohibits others from defacing the name.

Once you've chosen a name, sit quietly in meditation and repeat the name over and over like a mantra. When you begin to feel a warm glow inside, the Tree of Life is lit for you. You can then meditate on the tree. Use your chosen name for God for meditation any time, especially when you need to feel centered and calm.

If you still aren't sure which name to choose, want to know how to pronounce all the names, or want to learn more, classes in Kabbalah are popular and widely available in larger cities. And please remember that in adapting the traditions of any religion to your own meditative practice, it is proper to pay the appropriate respect to the source of that devout ritual. Upon completing your meditation session, offer thanks to that particular tradition for inspiring your meditation and creating a ritual to benefit the welfare of humankind.

A Middle-Eastern Fasting Meditation

Now that we're in the Middle East, we can continue eastward into the land where Islam first arose and where it remains a stronghold. The religion of Islam is another religion of structure. The five pillars of Islam are five practices or observances Muslims practice to encourage self-discipline, purity, and piety. These five pillars are faith, prayer, charitable giving, a pilgrimage to *Mecca* for those who are able, and the practice of fasting during certain holy holidays such as *Ramadan*.

When practiced correctly, fasting can be a physically as well as spiritually purifying practice. However, when misused, it can be both physically and spiritually harmful. Try a simple day of fasting in the Muslim tradition, and join thousands of other Muslims by devoting your fast to the furtherance of peace in the world.

From A to Om

Mecca is the birthplace, in Saudi Arabia, of Muhammed, the founder of the Islamic religion. **Ramadan** is the ninth month in the Islamic calendar during which Muslims fast every day from sunrise to sunset. The Islamic calendar is a lunar calendar, 10 days shorter than the standard Western calendar of 365 years. Over the course of 10 years, the month of Ramadan has moved 100 days and varies slightly in length according to the year.

Muslims fast every day from sunrise to sunset during the month-long holiday of Ramadan, unless they are unable to fast for a good reason such as illness or pregnancy. In a true Muslim fast, not even water is allowed during the daylight hours.

However, if you are trying a fast apart from your religious beliefs, we suggest drinking water to prevent dehydration, or even the inclusion of juice, tea, and broth. We also suggest doing this fast only once a week, rather than every day for a month, especially for those who aren't used to fasting.

If you like, have a light snack of fruit or whole-grain toast before sunrise. Or make dinner from the night before your last meal. Get up early to watch the sunrise, and meditate to set your focus on the day ahead. Think about how you will cleanse and purify your body and set your mind free from a focus on food.

Fasting can be tough, especially if you are new to the practice. The more you try *not* to think about food, the more you might be inclined to dwell on it. However, keep drinking water, and whenever you feel tempted to eat, sit down, relax, breathe, and meditate on the cleansing and purifying of your body and the exercise of self-discipline for your mind. Let your spirit have room to move around in the absence of all that pesky digestion.

When you do finally break your fast at sunset (or tomorrow morning), eat lightly, something plant-based such as fruit, a salad, or some whole-grain toast. Honor your body by easing back into consumption.

Passage to India

From the Middle East, it's just a short trip southeast to India, the ancient home of yoga and the Buddha. Hinduism is the dominant religion in India today. Hindus have certain holy rituals and observances, including prayer facilitated by a holy mala. A yogi's mala contains 108 beads, including a larger bead called the meru. The mala is held in the right hand, and the beads are rolled one by one between the third finger and the thumb as the mantra is recited, in a manner similar to the recitation of the rosary. When the meditator has come full circle to achieve the meru bead, the sequence is reversed. For yogis without malas, a sequence of finger movements to count through each of the 108 repetitions can be performed.

The yogi's mala is used in the recitation of mantras.

The use of the Catholic's rosary and the Yogi's mala in meditation reflects the joining of individual and collective prayers in a striving toward perfect enlightenment: the circle and the divine sound of the universe. *Om, Aum, Amen, Hum, Amin*—sacred words to Jews, Christians, Egyptians, Greeks, Romans, Tibetans, and Muslims—are each based on the all-encompassing sound.

Mantra meditation is integral to Indian meditation. To add a Hindu flavor to your meditative practice, try mantra meditation using a mala (you can find them in stores that carry meditation supplies, yoga supplies, or wares from India), and try a mantra more common to India than to America, such as an excerpt from one of Patanjali's *Yoga Sutras*. Here are a few to try (as translated in the book *The Heart of Yoga* by T.K.V. Desikachar, Inner Traditions International Ltd., 1999) for a mantra or focus of meditation and/or contemplation:

> **Mindful Minute**
>
> Kahlil Gibran wrote, "Your pain is the breaking of the shell that encloses your understanding." When meditation, prayer, visualization, guided imagery, or any other form of inner exploration turns up difficult memories or feelings, go slowly while considering that perhaps this difficulty will open your awareness to new levels and insights.

- The more intense the faith and the effort, the closer the goal.

- What decays is the external. What does not is deep within us.

- The result of contentment is total happiness.

- Anything can be understood. With each attempt, fresh and spontaneous understanding arises.

- Freedom is when the mind has complete identity with the Perceiver.

The Sanskrit representation of om.

The Far East: Buddhist Sutra Meditations

Moving all the way to the Far East, we arrive in the land of Buddhism. China, Japan, Korea, Vietnam, and Thailand have all developed their individual forms of Buddhism since a man named Bodhidharma traveled from India to bring Buddhism to China in the sixth century. One legend about Bodhidharma says he cut off his own eyelids to stay awake during meditation (no, we don't advise this!). Meditation remains central to every Buddhist culture's spiritual practice. If the techniques vary slightly, the overriding principles are the same.

We've already suggested many Far East–inspired meditation techniques in this book. Here, we'd like to quote from the Buddha to give you either a mantra or a thought for focus on your meditation. We'll follow that with a couple classic Zen koans, those puzzles designed for contemplation that, when at last comprehended, pop your mind out of its usual rut into a more enlightened and antilogical way of thought.

Words of the Buddha

Many sutras, phrases, aphorisms, and anecdotes are attributed to the Buddha. One of the most popular and the most lovely is the Sutra on Loving Kindness. It is translated in various ways. Here is our version:

Be able, upright, perfectly upright, gentle, and humble.

Be contented, with few duties. Live lightly with senses controlled. Be discreet and not greedily attached to the people you love.

Do not commit that which you know to be wrong. Be happy and secure with a wholesome mind. Whatever living beings you encounter—feeble or strong, tall or short, small or large, seen or unseen, close to you or far away—let them be happy.

Do not deceive others or be deceived by others, despise others, or cause others to despise you. Do not let anger control you or cause you to harm others, or cause you to wish to harm others.

Let your thoughts be concerned with boundless love pervading the whole world without obstruction, obliterating hatred and enmity.

Do not fall into error. Instead, be virtuous and endowed with insight, that you might give up your attachment to sensual desires and free yourself from the suffering that comes with such attachment.

Whether you stand, walk, sit, or lie down, as long as you are awake, be mindful. This is the highest conduct possible.

Zen Koans for Contemplation

Devote your meditation to the consideration of these logical puzzles. Here's a hint: Logic has nothing to do with it!

◆ What is the sound of one hand clapping?

◆ Where do you go from the top of a flagpole?

◆ How does a goose escape from a long-necked bottle?

◆ Can a dog attain enlightenment?

◆ If you are hanging by your teeth to a branch over a great precipice and someone comes along and asks you a question, do you answer them?

Aboriginal Meditations

Many aboriginal cultures, from southernmost Australia to northernmost Siberia to Native America, have used meditation as a spiritual practice. Let's look at some of the meditative traditions of Native Americans.

Native American Medicine Wheels

The medicine wheel, as we mentioned in Chapter 17, is a sort of life-size, interactive mandala. You can create your own medicine wheel mandala, outdoors or indoors, for use during meditation.

Go into your yard or another outdoor place where you can collect stones. Walk around and look for stones that feel or look special to you. Collect 4 large stones (not so large that you can't carry them) and between 4 and 16 smaller stones. You can also collect other natural materials—pinecones, beautiful leaves, feathers, bits of coral, seashells, fossils, wood, and flowers.

To make your circle perfectly round, use a makeshift compass. Plant a stake in the ground tied with a string of between three and six feet long, and use this to guide you along the circle's outer edge. Place one stone at the northernmost point of the circle, one at the southernmost point, another at the easternmost point, and another at the westernmost point. Fill in the rest of the circle's border with your other stones and natural items, using the string as a guide.

Now, enter your circle from the east and walk to the center of your circle. Ask a blessing from each of the four directions, facing each direction as you ask. Each direction is associated with an element, so you might say something like:

Spirit of the East, spirit of air, bless this circle that it might be sacred.

Spirit of the South, spirit of water, bless this circle that it might be healing.

Spirit of the West, spirit of fire, bless this circle that it might be purified.

Spirit of the North, spirit of earth, bless this circle that it might impart inner strength.

Now, sit in the center, facing whichever direction seems right for your needs at the moment (for example, if you need strength, face north; if you need healing, face south). Sit with mindful awareness, and allow nature to speak to you.

You can also make a small medicine wheel for the inside your house, which you can use as a point of focus during meditation, just as you would a mandala. On any flat, clean surface, place a circle of natural items (they might remain more stable if you first cover the surface with sand or moss). You can leave the center open or fill it with a crystal, beautiful shell, or some other meaningful object.

Use the medicine wheel in a way that feels right for you. Following your instincts is more important than exactly replicating a tradition from another culture. Focus on the sacred and eternal nature of the circle, and let the circle's wisdom guide you.

Native American Life Meditations

The Native American tradition views everything on earth as imbued with spirit. People, animals, plants, rocks, mountains, water, and even human-made items such as clothing, bowls, weapons, and jewelry have their own spirits. Above all is Great Spirit, a divine fusion of male and female energy (yin/yang balance once again!).

Some Native American tribes also believe that each person has a totem. A totem is usually an animal but can also be a plant, a rock, or other item from nature. Your totem has knowledge and inspiration to offer you and can help you through your life if you are open to its wisdom. One way to discover your totem is to go on a vision quest, which allows your totem to reveal itself to you. This is a solitary trip into nature—the forest, the mountains, the seaside—to symbolize a trip into the inner self. On this trip you spend time with yourself and nature and observe the natural world around you to learn what it has to teach you.

Totemism does not believe in standing apart from nature, but rather in preserving the natural order. To quote a story reflecting this from the book *The World's Religions* by Huston Smith (Harper San Francisco, 1992):

At one point, the art department at Arizona State University decided to offer a course on basketweaving and approached a neighboring Indian reservation for an instructor. The tribe proposed its master weaver, an old woman, for the position. The entire course turned out to consist of trips to the plants that provide the fibers for her baskets, where myths involving the plant were recounted and supplicating songs and prayers were memorized. There was no weaving.

Although a typical vision quest involves several days of fasting and sitting within a medicine wheel (see Chapter 17) in nature, you also can take a "mini vision quest." Set aside an hour or two during which you can go outside and find a place that feels comfortable and good to you. It can be in your own yard, in a park, or in any other natural setting. The fewer signs of civilization, the better.

Construct a medicine wheel out of rocks and other natural materials. Thank each of the four directions, then sit in the middle. Ask Great Spirit to reveal your totem. Remain mindful and wait. Soak in the natural surroundings, breathe deeply, and relax. Don't try to figure out what your totem might be. Just sit in mindfulness, open to anything.

Bliss Byte

One way to show your reverence for nature is to learn how to walk silently through nature and leave no trace that you were ever there. Make a habit of taking walks in the woods or other natural areas and practice walking without making a sound, so as not to disturb the natural order around you. Remember, however, to breathe deeply and relax your body and mind as you take in the beauty around you.

In many cases, an animal will appear. Sometimes it will remain shyly on the perimeter. In a few cases, animals have come into the medicine wheel to commune with the meditator. Or you might find your attention suddenly drawn to a certain plant, tree, stone, or other item. Wait, listen to the message from nature, and allow your totem to be revealed. If you can wait in mindful silence for two hours (rather than giving up after 20 or 30 minutes out of boredom), your patience will likely be rewarded.

You might see several animals while engaged in your quest, but the animal that is your totem will come closer to you or capture your attention more fully than the others. Or perhaps a certain tree, rock, or other being will become central to your consciousness. Don't just assume the first animal you see or tree you notice is your totem—although it might be. Wait out the time, and by the end, you'll probably know.

Once your totem has been revealed to you—whether squirrel, blackbird, deer, eagle, oak tree, or other being or object—spend some time contemplating your totem.

Imagine what it feels like to be your totem. Continue to meditate on your totem as often as possible. Eventually, you will feel a oneness with your totem, and you will be ready for its guiding wisdom, which will also come to you during meditation, dreams, or contemplation.

Respecting the Earth

Native Americans also hold the earth in the highest respect. The earth represents the female energy of Great Spirit, and it has much to teach us. It shares its bounty and takes little in return. To share in this respect for the earth, live your life in an earth-friendly way. Don't litter, pollute, or waste. Try to make as little of an impact on the natural world as possible. Live in it, commune with it, but don't destroy it. Your life will seem easier, simpler, purer, and more loving when you don't spend your energy on destruction and waste.

You can also meditate on the earth. For a twist on the normal meditation pose, go outside, lie down on your stomach on the ground, spread your arms out, and feel as if you are holding the earth. Imagine that she in turn is rocking you. Feel at one with Mother Earth and imagine her energy filling you and your energy filling her. Stay in the position for 20 minutes, breathing deeply, and allowing the earth to speak to you and heal you. Don't forget to offer your thanks for the earth's blessing after your meditation is over.

Honoring the Ancestors

Native Americans also honor their ancestors and believe that the ancestral spirits are always available to offer counsel, inspiration, and strength to their descendents. You, too, can call on the power of your ancestors, even if you don't know anything about them.

- Sit comfortably with your back straight and breathe deeply.

- Raise your hands into the air, palms up, and say, "I call upon you, my ancestors, to offer me your wisdom so that I may live my life well."

- Lower your hands and leave them palms-up on your knees in the spirit of openness.

- Breathe normally and sit in mindfulness, open to any impressions that might come to you. If you are facing a particular life challenge or dilemma, imagine you see it in front of you, encased in a bubble with a big question mark on it.

- Continue to wait, mindfully. Perhaps a face or figure will come into your mind. Perhaps it will speak to you. Maybe it is someone you remember, or maybe it is an ancestor from long ago. Even if it is only a figment of your imagination, be open to the suggestions from your subconscious that might or might not be influenced by the energies (and genetics) of your ancestors.

- Sometimes, rather than a figure coming into your mind, a voice or an idea will present itself as a solution to your problem or a direction to take. Listen, then spend time in contemplation of what has come to you or been given to you.

> **CAUTION**
>
> **Relax**
>
> If you find your mind flooded with images and impressions, continue to repeat your mantra, either verbally or silently. With persistence, your mind will gain focus.

Meditating on Other Cultures

Sampling the traditions and techniques of other cultures can be fun, illuminating, and even enlightening! Wisdom comes in all shapes, sizes, languages, and disguises. If you can stop yourself from rejecting something just because you aren't used to it, you'll be surprised at what you might learn. Open your mind and watch it grow big enough to hold whatever you pour into it.

The Least You Need to Know

- You can vary your meditation practice by adopting aspects of meditation from many cultures.

- Try an adaptation of a Mayan sun meditation, make an African-inspired outdoor altar, or set aside a day of prayer in the style of a medieval European Catholic monastery.

- Meditate on the Kabbalah's Tree of Life, try an Islamic fast from sunrise to sunset, use the words of Patanjali or the Buddha in mantra meditation, or contemplate a classic Zen khan.

- Make a Native American–inspired medicine wheel in your yard or inside your home, or try a totem meditation.

Part 6

Meditation for Your Life

Meditation doesn't have to remain a separate part of your life. You can design your life to enhance your meditation, and in turn, meditation will enhance your life. What you eat and how you eat it can directly affect your meditation efforts. We'll show you what foods and food attitudes will make meditation a breeze. We'll also describe how meditation can help ease you through the challenges of being a woman, a man, a family member, a kid, or a senior.

Meditation can help to enhance your health and address your health concerns. We'll offer some meditations to help your body heal, from your head to toe, heart to liver. And last, we'll offer our thoughts on how each of us can help respect, love, live in, and heal the world through meditation. Each of us is a member of a vast and precious community of sentient beings, all part of a unique and amazing planet. Meditation can bring us together in peace. What a wonderful future we all have in store—and what a fine time we'll have getting there, awake and alive with the help of meditation!

Chapter 20

Food for Thought: Fueling Your Body and Your Mind

In This Chapter

- ◆ Knowing what foods are healthful

- ◆ The pros and cons of meditation and being a vegetarian

- ◆ Foods that boost brain power

- ◆ All about supplements

- ◆ Fasting: good or bad?

According to René Descartes, you think, therefore you are. We would like to take that one step further: You eat, therefore you think. (Which would lead, logically, to the conclusion that you are what you eat!)

Everyone knows that too many calories and too much fat can increase the number on that bathroom scale as well as clog your arteries and lead to a variety of health problems, but what about your ability to think, remember, solve problems, react quickly—all that brain-related stuff? What about your ability to meditate?

Research clearly demonstrates that laboratory animals live longer when they consume fewer calories than the recommended daily allowances. Studies also show that people who consume a low-calorie meal can concentrate better than those who chow down, so your ability to finish that afternoon project might very well be related to what you had for lunch. The way food affects your ability to concentrate—and, thus, to meditate—is exactly what we explore in this chapter.

Brain Food: The Theory

Food plays a crucial role in your brain's ability to function both over the short term and the long term. The meal you ate just a few hours ago directly influences the way your brain is working right now. And over time, deficiencies in diet may lead to serious cognitive problems.

All this is directly relevant to meditation and also to cultivating a state of mindfulness and of flow in daily life (see Chapter 18). Why? Because if you've eaten the wrong thing for dinner, you might find it next to impossible to sit still or stay awake for your evening meditation. You might find mindfulness an incredible challenge after one kind of breakfast and a snap after another kind.

Could facilitating mindfulness and meditation really be as easy as making a few dietary adjustments? It sure can help. We'll explain how.

Another factor to consider is that the emotional and mental state of the food preparer goes right into the food. This is why it's a good idea to cook your own food as often as possible, putting positive energies into the food. Don't cook, let alone eat, when you're in a rotten mood! Also, blessing the food is most beneficial to neutralize any negative energy and put positive, healthy vibrations into the food you're about to eat.

Bliss Byte

While yoga philosophy advocates the consumption of a fresh, pure, vegetarian diet, it also insists that any food, when eaten with complete awareness and enjoyment, will nourish the body. Likewise, any food, no matter how healthy, will be unhealthy for the body if eaten in a rushed, tense, stressed, or angry manner. So maybe we shouldn't say "You are what you eat," but instead, "You are *how* you eat!" The next time you are preparing for a meal, make a conscious effort to relax and smile, then savor every bite.

Living Healthy in a Toxic World

Eating good food, breathing clean air, and drinking pure water used to be easy. You went out into your garden, your orchard, or the chicken coop, selected your dinner, scooped some water from the well, took a few deep breaths of air, picked some flowers for the table, and went on with your day, feeling refreshed and healthy. Back then, daily life also included quite a bit more exercise, most of it outside, than what we experience today. Sure, life was hard in many ways back then.

Indeed, the world looks a lot different today, as we all know. Food is shipped from thousands of miles away; coated with wax, dyes, preservatives, and pesticides; or injected with hormones, antibiotics, and chemicals. Food also comes packaged in boxes and preserved so it can last and last and last on the supermarket shelf. Even locally grown produce tends to be sprayed with pesticides, unless it is organic.

Our rivers, lakes, and oceans are filled with waste, our air is filled with smog, and in some cities, breathing can actually hurt as the polluted air oxidizes your lung tissue. Ouch!

Bliss Byte

Pollution exists on many levels. The lighting from our larger cities has drastically reduced the view of the stars. Since 1972, Tucson, Arizona, has fitted outdoor lights with shields that greatly reduce light pollution for the benefit of local observatories and the Tucson population in general. Tucson is one of the few cities where you can actually stargaze! When was the last time you saw stars for miles around you?

Never mind (for the moment) the disrespect for Mother Earth and future generations such antistewardship of the earth has wrought. What about us, right here, right now? What *on earth* are we stuffing into our bodies, and how does it impact our health, our mental state, and our spiritual selves?

Although it isn't as easy as it used to be, it is possible to live healthfully and eat well in a toxic world. An increasing number of consumers are demanding organic food, free-range meat and eggs, and locally grown produce. Because food with such high levels of preservatives, pesticides, and processing is a relatively recent occurrence, we have yet to fully witness the effects on the general population. Why take chances? Whenever you can, choose food closest to its natural state, organically grown, and with as little processing and packaging as possible. As you change your diet, you might notice that you are thinking more clearly and with more ease than you were on that diet of frozen dinners and diet soda.

Good Nutrition for Mind Power

Good nutrition and strategic nutrition are both crucial for optimum brain functioning. How much do you know about how food affects your brain? Take our true-false test to see.

True	False	Food for Thought
_____	_____	You'll probably think more clearly and more quickly if your breakfast consists of protein (peanut butter or turkey sandwich, an egg, a yogurt shake) than carbohydrates (bran muffin, cereal).
_____	_____	A cup of coffee in the morning ups your brain power.
_____	_____	A cup of coffee during a mid-afternoon break will pull you out of that slump and revive your brain power.
_____	_____	When you eat dinner, it's best for your brain power to eat the salad and bread first, then the main course protein source.
_____	_____	Everyone should start their day with breakfast as soon as they wake up to perform well during the day.
_____	_____	A candy bar or a chocolate-chip cookie is a good pick-me-up, offering a burst of energy.

Now, see how you did: The first three items are true, the second three are false. Really!

Starting the morning with protein rather than carbohydrates will definitely provide for better mental activity. Protein contains an amino acid called *tyrosine*, which leads to increased energy and alertness. Carbohydrates, on the other hand, lead to the production of *serotonin*, a neurotransmitter that has a calming effect. Also, beginning a meal with carbohydrates (as in that salad and bread) actually allows an amino acid called *tryptophan* to reach your brain first, blocking the tyrosine from having its energizing effect. In addition, tryptophan converts to serotonin in your brain, making you even drowsier and less able to concentrate.

From A to Om

Serotonin is a neurotransmitter, a chemical in your brain responsible for transmitting messages, which has a calming, relaxing effect and can cause drowsiness. **Tyrosine** and **tryptophan** are two amino acids that come from protein in the food we eat. If tryptophan gets to the brain first, you'll be more likely to become drowsy. If tyrosine gets there first, you'll be more likely to become more energized and alert.

The effect is even more extreme in people over age 40. One study performed at the Chicago Medical School measured concentration, memory, and performance on mental tasks of 184 adults after they had eaten a meal of either turkey (protein) or sherbet (carbohydrates). Those over age 40 had twice as much trouble with concentration, memory, and mental tasks when they ate the sherbet. The difference was less extreme in those younger than 40.

Several other studies also demonstrate the positive effects of protein versus the negative effects of carbohydrates on brain power. One study conducted at the Massachusetts Institute of Technology (MIT) involved providing a turkey lunch containing approximately 3 ounces of protein for 40 men between 18 and 28 years old. Then the men were given complex mental tasks. On a different day, the men were given a lunch containing 4 ounces of wheat starch, which is almost pure carbohydrates. They then performed the same mental tasks. According to the study, after the wheat starch lunch, performance was "significantly impaired" compared to the protein lunch.

We aren't saying carbohydrates are bad. Far from it! Your body needs carbohydrates, especially the complex kind (found in fruits, vegetables, and whole grains), for fiber, vitamins, and minerals. The trick, when it comes to revving up your brain for clearer thinking, is to eat the protein *first*. And whole-grain, high-fiber cereal is a good breakfast, as long as you top it off with protein-rich milk. (That bran muffin probably has a lot of fat. Go for the cereal instead.)

And what about that coffee? Coffee isn't for everyone, and caffeinated beverages with lots of sugar such as soda or coffee or tea loaded with sugar and cream aren't good for anyone. But a single cup of morning coffee actually has been shown to improve mental activity within minutes, and the effects might last as long as six hours, according to a MIT study. The caffeine is the responsible party and has a similar effect when consumed in the mid-afternoon, when many people begin to feel drowsy.

Of course, like the Buddha, we like to preach moderation in all things! Drinking coffee from dawn until dusk is overusing caffeine, which can wreak havoc on your nerves. If you like it and drink it already, one cup will do. Or if you don't like the idea of consuming any mind-altering chemicals (although technically, all the food we eat contains chemicals that influence the mind), stick with the high-protein breakfast and peanut butter and crackers for a mid-day snack. (Remember that consuming caffeine and sugar can lead to a physical dependence on these substances.)

> **Mindful Minute**
>
> For more on addressing your potentially destructive behaviors and breaking out of the old familiar patterns, read *The Complete Idiot's Guide to Breaking Bad Habits, Second Edition* (Alpha Books, 2001).

Breakfast, studies show, isn't actually the necessity we once believed. For children, breakfast is crucial and boosts school performance. But for adults, who are better able to maintain stable blood sugar levels overnight, breakfast is an option. If you aren't hungry first thing in the morning, don't eat anything. When you get hungry later in the morning, have breakfast. Eating when you aren't hungry is a nasty habit, anyway. Learn to listen to your body. (And if you think it's telling you it wants chocolate doughnuts for breakfast, remember that's your negative habit, probably combined with unstable insulin levels talking, not a call from your body that you require dough-nuts.) Very often our bodies send us messages that might not be reliable, based more on our bad dietary habits than on genuine, healthful needs. Often we need to retrain our bodies to desire healthful foods!

Do You Have to Be a Vegetarian?

If you've studied the traditions of other cultures, you've probably discovered that many practice and advocate a vegetarian diet. The yoga principle of nonviolence necessitates a vegetarian diet because eating animals involves killing them first, and whether you or someone else does the killing doesn't matter to a yogi. Violence was involved. Buddhists, too, typically practice a vegetarian diet. The first of the five Buddhist precepts says, "I will refrain from harming any living beings," and that includes, of course, the killing of animals for food.

> **Bliss Byte**
>
> You can still get plenty of protein if you are a vegetarian. Dairy products, milk, yogurt, cheese, and especially eggs are excellent protein sources. Some vegetarians refrain from all animal products, receiving their necessary protein from brown rice, legumes, whole grains, nuts, seitan, and nut butters. And don't forget soy, in its many manifestations—soy milk, tofu, miso, tempeh, edamame, dry-roasted soy-beans, soy flour, etc. Soy is not only protein-rich, but is now thought to be an excellent cancer fighter and might help regulate and maintain estrogen levels in the body before, during, and after menopause.

If you want to practice Zen meditation or yoga meditation, does that mean you have to be a vegetarian, too? Absolutely not. *But* (isn't there always a but?), you might find that the more you practice your meditation, the less appealing meat will become. The problem with your question, "Do I have to be a vegetarian?" is the "have to" part. If you feel that being a vegetarian is a "have to" kind of thing, an undesirable obligation or sacrifice (you'll know that's true if you find yourself wandering wistfully toward the meat counter whenever you are grocery shopping), then you aren't ready to be a vegetarian. Maybe you won't ever become one. But plenty of people who begin to meditate eventually decide to phase meat out of their lives.

In other words, vegetarianism is just one part of the yoga meditation journey, and maybe you won't decide to take that path. *But* (another but), just for a little incentive, studies do show that vegetarians are generally healthier, suffer from fewer minor illnesses, and live longer than their meat-eating counterparts.

Mindful Minute

Countries with high meat consumption typically have correspondingly high cancer mortality rates. Coincidence? You decide!

The Ten Best Foods for Meditation

So what exactly should you eat if you want to boost your brain power and have an easier time with meditation and mindfulness? We've compiled a list of the 10 best foods for the meditating mind. Try to incorporate all or most of them into your diet at least once every week or two, and you'll benefit from the brain-boosting power of these foods—plus you'll have less room for food that does your meditating brain a disservice. If you choose not to eat meat or any animal products at all, edit this list accordingly.

- **Eggs.** Eggs are an excellent, high-quality protein source, and egg yolks are a great source of lecithin, a fatty substance that provides choline to the brain, which is transformed into acetylcholine in the brain. Acetylcholine is responsible for the ability to learn and the ability to remember. Look for eggs from free-range chickens. They are better for you, and they taste better, too. Scramble some firm tofu into scrambled eggs for variety, sprinkled with turmeric (a spice) for color.

- **Oatmeal.** Oatmeal has protein (even more when topped with milk) and is another good source of choline. Steel-cut or whole oats (old-fashioned oats) are better than instant.

- **Brown rice.** Brown rice has both protein and choline plus a healthy dose of fiber and B vitamins. B vitamins are crucial for brain function because they are responsible for catalyzing many of the brain's chemical reactions. If you hate cooking rice, invest in a rice cooker to make the task easy.

- **Low-fat cottage cheese.** Chock full of protein, but with very little fat, cottage cheese is fast, easy, and a real brain booster. It might also help kill your craving for less-healthy foods like chips because it has a salty taste. Nevertheless, low-salt varieties are healthiest. Also try soy cheeses for a change.

◆ **Seitan.** Made of whole-wheat gluten, this is an excellent substitute for steaks! It can be prepared in the same manner as steak and looks very much like steak. We know how difficult it is to give up those steaks. By the way, cows are vegetarians, too.

◆ **Fish.** Fish is low in fat and carbohydrates and high in protein. It also contains the much-publicized omega-3 fatty acid thought to improve brain function, not to mention regulate your cholesterol level to a more favorable balance. Salmon, tuna, mackeral, and herring are good choices. Rich in omega-3, these cold-water fish are also less likely to be contaminated by environmental pollutants. By the way, if you eat fish, you are not, strictly speaking, a vegetarian.

◆ **Soybeans and other soy products (like soy milk and tofu).** Soy is rich in lecithin and high in protein, and soybean oil contains polyunsaturated fat. In one study, rats fed a diet of soybean oil learned 20 percent faster and remembered what they learned better than rats on a regular diet. Look for organically grown soybeans and products.

◆ **Spinach.** Spinach contains folate (a B vitamin), which the brain uses to make brain tissue and neurotransmitters. Spinach is also iron-rich, and iron helps your brain receive oxygen and make neurotransmitters. It also contains manganese and magnesium, which help your brain use energy from other nutrients. Look for organic spinach at your grocery store, health-food market, or local produce stand.

◆ **Lean meat.** Chicken and turkey are excellent sources of protein, zinc, and iron, and when you eat the white meat only, they are low-fat, too. Tyrosine-rich, lean meat means more energy and alertness. Zinc is a mineral that aids the brain in transmitting its electrical impulses. Free-range meat is best.

Relax

Watch your fat intake: High-fat foods take a lot more effort to digest than low-fat foods, diverting blood from your brain. Go for the low-fat meal, and you'll be in better shape to think, remember, concentrate, and react. When you choose fat, go for olive oil and canola oil, which might actually have a positive effect on your brain.

◆ **Peanuts, walnuts, almonds, and nut butters.** Peanuts, walnuts, and almonds have protein, lecithin, and B vitamins. They also have a host of phytochemicals thought to benefit the body in many ways. Nuts are high in fat, though, so don't overindulge. A handful of nuts or a couple tablespoons of peanut or almond butter on whole-wheat bread or a whole-rain bagel makes a delicious snack. Look for the natural nut butters without added sugar.

◆ **Dried fruit.** Raisins, dates, and prunes contain iron and boron, a mineral thought to be important for maintaining the brain's electrical activity. Look for dried fruit without added sulfites, available in health-food stores.

Of course, this list isn't inclusive. All healthy foods benefit your brain in one way or another, whether directly or by improving your general health. And remember, earth-friendly eating will help you to feel more in harmony with the planet. You might notice a gradual peace come over you as you change your eating habits. Mindful eating will come naturally. Your cravings for junk food will gently decline until they disappear completely. Your body will become leaner, stronger, and more energetic. And your brain—why, meditation will be as easy as eating a delicious stir-fry of fresh, crisp organic vegetables over nutty brown rice!

Herbs and Botanicals to Grow By

As you visit your local health-food market, or even your local supermarket, you might notice that a good deal of the store is dedicated not to food but to lots of little bottles, jars, and packets of *herbs* and botanicals. Herbal remedies are big business these days, and even mainstream markets are looking for a piece of the herbal pie. But should you spend your hard-earned cash on herbal supplements and remedies? That depends on who you talk to, but more and more people are saying yes—if you know what you are buying.

Because the sale of herbs as dietary supplements isn't yet regulated by the Food and Drug Administration (FDA), anyone can sell them and the products don't have to pass any standards. The only requirement is that labels on marketed herbs can't say they cure medical problems (even if they do sometimes bestow healthful benefits when taken properly in the correct amounts) unless they have gone through the rigorous, expensive, and time-consuming process of getting FDA approval. Of course, some make the claims anyway, hoping nobody will give them trouble about it.

> **From A to Om**
>
> **Herbs** are plant parts used for medicinal or therapeutic purposes (and also for cooking).

So an herb such as gingko biloba, which is thought to have amazing effects on brain circulation and is thought to be a possible remedy for the symptoms of Alzheimer's disease, can't legally say it improves the symptoms of Alzheimer's disease. In addition, a bottle of pills marked "gingko biloba" might or might not have an amount of gingko biloba equivalent to amounts used in scientific studies. A pill could have hardly any gingko biloba at all but still advertise itself as a gingko biloba supplement. In fact, many herbal supplements don't even list their ingredients on the bottle. Who knows what you're getting!

> **CAUTION Relax** _____
>
> Before beginning to take any herb or botanical in any form, consult your physician or a licensed natural medicine professional. Herbs and botanicals, though "natural," have effects on the body like any drug or chemical. Herbs, botanicals, and other supplements, such as vitamin supplements, might also interact with any drug treatments prescribed by your physician in potentially adverse ways. See your doctor first before you take anything!

In response to consumer protest, many companies are coming out with more explicit packaging, listing concentrations of the herbs in their products and making a good effort to prove that their products are of the highest quality, including the standardization of herbs equivalent to dosages used in medical studies or recommended by holistic health practitioners. Read the labels and research the companies (you might be surprised to find out who really makes those herbs with the attractive earthy packaging and quaint company name). In other words, buyer beware.

> **Bliss Byte** _____
>
> If you have a window in your kitchen, try growing a few of your favorite herbs. Most varieties require minimal space and can be grown in small pots. Grow from seeds or buy small plants from a local garden center or herbalist. Easy varieties to grow in kitchen gardens are basil, oregano, thyme, parsley, cilantro, sage, rosemary, peppermint, lavender, and feverfew. Also try growing garlic bulbs and aloe vera plants. Keep plants in a sunny location, keep soil moist, and grow in well-drained pots.

Which herbs and botanicals are supposed to improve brain function and which might prove helpful supports in a meditation practice? Although what works for you might be different than what works for other people, we'll tell you a little bit about the big three, the herbs most known for their brain-boosting power. The following herbs have all been the subjects of scientific studies providing evidence that they do indeed provide health benefits (although not all studies were equally rigorous or accepted by the mainstream community):

- **Gingko biloba.** The number-one-selling herb in the United States today, gingko biloba has been used as a prescription medicine in Europe for years and is one of the most well-studied herbal remedies. Made from the leaves of the Gingko tree, this herb is thought to improve brain function and alertness, promote blood flow and fights free radicals in the brain, and improve short-term memory, headache, depression, and other neurological disorders (as well as a host of functions in the rest of your body!). Gingko biloba has a blood-thinning effect; we urge you to consult your physician before taking this or any herb.

- **Ginseng.** Made from a root, ginseng may increase blood supply to the brain, lower blood sugar levels, increase energy, and increase the body's resistance to stress.

- **St. John's wort.** Sometimes called the "herbal Prozac," this herb, made from the plant's flowers and leaves, has been shown to have a significant effect on people suffering from clinical depression. It also relieves anxiety.

There are hundreds of other herbs and botanicals available in many forms, from pills to teas to those in homeopathic remedies. To be safe, do your homework on any herbal remedy you think might help you, and/or consult a reputable herbalist along with your medical doctor if you are taking medications (whether over the counter or prescription!).

Vitamins and Supplements: Are They Worth It?

As long as you're browsing the aisles for herbal remedies, why not pick up a few vitamin and mineral supplements? Are you wasting your money with these? Maybe, depending on what you buy. Your brain actually requires a wide range of nutrients, including many different vitamins and minerals, to keep it operating at its peak. You might not be able to get enough of everything every day, even with a healthy, varied diet. A complete vitamin and mineral supplement is a good insurance policy against deficiencies.

CAUTION

Relax _____

> If you are pregnant or nursing a baby, you must be extra careful about any herbs and excess vitamins and minerals you ingest. Levels of certain chemicals within herbs that would be safe for you might not be safe for a baby. Same goes for mega-doses of certain vitamins. Never take any herbs without the guidance of your physician or trained herbalist when you are pregnant, and don't drink herbal teas except those that contain only food-grade herbs, such as orange, lemon, cinnamon, peppermint, or ginger tea.

On the other hand, megadoses of vitamins and minerals might not do you any good and could even cause unpleasant—even dangerous—side effects. Most doctors and nutritionists who recommend supplements suggest taking a regular multivitamin and mineral supplement with doses at approximately 100 percent DV (daily value), unless you have a specific problem that might be addressed by higher dosages.

Is Fasting Good for Meditation?

Many cultures include fasting as a part of their religious traditions or rituals. Jesus supposedly fasted for 40 days in the desert, and many Protestants and Catholics fast during certain holidays or as a part of a personal retreat or sacrifice. Muslims fast from sunrise to sunset during the entire month of Ramadan. Native Americans fast during vision quests. Shamans and holy men in many indigenous cultures use fasting and meditation to sharpen awareness and sometimes to induce visions. For many Westerners, regular fasting (for example, one day every week or three or four days out of every month) has even become a way to cleanse and purify the body.

But does it help meditation? Many people who fast get what is known as a "fasting high" on the second or third day of a fast, during which they feel as if their minds have become exceptionally clear. This might well be an ideal time for meditation. However, fast with caution. If you aren't in good health, it can further compromise your system.

We like half-day and one-day fasts best. These give the digestive system a chance to rest and give the mind and spirit a little more room in the whole mind-body equation. These short fasts take plenty of discipline but because you know you will be eating again soon, they aren't impossible, which is helpful, especially for beginners.

We also recommend juice fasts as safer than water fasts. During a juice fast, you refrain from solid foods but consume fruit and vegetable juices and vegetable broth. To read more about fasting, check out *The Complete Idiot's Guide to Fasting*, by Eve Adamson and Linda Horning, R.D.

Fasting for short periods opens up a nice space for meditation. Try fasting for one day each week or each month, or a half-day once or twice a week. On your fasting day, avoid excessive exposure to good food sights and smells (no point in torturing yourself) and spend some quiet time alone in meditation to contemplate the kindness you are doing your body and your mind.

Here are some sample fasts for you to try:

♦ **Half-day fast.** On the day of your half-day fast, eat a light vegetarian lunch, then have a light snack of fruit at 3 P.M. After that, drink only fresh fruit juice, herbal tea, and vegetable broth for the rest of the day, only in small sips, and only when you feel hungry or thirsty. Include between 16 and 32 ounces of water. Spend 20 to 30 minutes in quiet evening meditation before bedtime, being mindful about how your body feels without judging. Break your fast the next morning with a breakfast of fresh fruit and a little juice. Eat slowly.

♦ **Sunrise-to-sunset fast.** Get up before sunrise and have a piece of fruit, such as an apple, a pear, or a handful of grapes. If possible, go outside. Meditate as you watch the sunrise. Throughout the day, drink only fresh fruit juice, herbal tea, and vegetable broth. Also drink 32 to 64 ounces of water throughout the day. Whenever you feel hungry, have something to drink. Once every two hours, spend 5 to 10 minutes in quiet meditation. Take it easy, perhaps taking a walk in the fresh air or doing some easy yoga. You will probably have a lot of energy, so let your mind and spirit soar. Take advantage of the mental acuity and heightened awareness. Break your fast after the sun sets with a light salad and some fresh fruit, then have a nice, restful sleep.

♦ **Thirty-six-hour fast.** Once a month or so, try a 36-hour fast. This fast is also a good one to do on each solstice and equinox, to "reset" your body at the beginning of each new season. The night before your fast, have a light vegetarian dinner. Go to bed early. Wake up early and meditate before starting your day, preferably while watching the sunrise. As with the sunrise-to-sunset fast, drink only fresh fruit juice, herbal tea, and vegetable broth throughout the day, plus at least 64 ounces of water (that's eight 8-ounce glasses). Walk, do yoga, and meditate whenever you can. Remember to spend the day in mindfulness to take full advantage of your fast. Go to bed when you are tired, and break your fast the next morning with a breakfast of fresh fruit and a little juice. Eat slowly.

> **Bliss Byte**
>
> By not eating at least four to five hours before sleep, you permit your body to fast naturally and cleanse itself while you sleep. When you awaken, don't shock your system with heavy foods. Start with a room-temperature or slightly warm glass of water (with a few drops of lemon juice if desired, to warm up the digestive process). Then, have some fresh fruit or whole grains.

Making dietary changes should be a slow, gradual process. Sudden changes usually don't stick. If you're committed to health and to helping yourself maintain the optimal mental state at all times, work on one area at a time. Even if it takes a couple years, you can change your diet for the better, and any change for the better will be well worth the journey.

The Least You Need to Know

- ◆ You can eat well even in a polluted world.

- ◆ You don't have to be a vegetarian to meditate, but meditation might make you want to become a vegetarian.

- ◆ Certain foods are particularly good for boosting brain power and facilitating your meditation practice.

- ◆ Herbal and vitamin/mineral supplements may provide good nutritional support to a well-balanced, varied diet of healthy, fresh foods.

- ◆ Fasting for short periods on occasion can cleanse your body, clear your mind, and balance your spirit, making meditation easier and more productive.

Chapter 21

Meditation for Women, Men, and the Whole Family

In This Chapter

- Meditation's special benefits for women
- Meditation's special benefits for men
- Meditating as a family
- Kids and seniors, too

Now we'd like to give you something special. We know you're someone special: a woman, a man, a parent, young or old, growing, aging, and seeking. Not every meditation fits every person, but we'd like to tailor some meditations for your situation. We know you are out there, so read on. This one's for you!

For Women Only

Although it hasn't always been fashionable to say so, women are different than men. Beyond the obvious anatomical differences, women have many subtle physical and mental differences as well. Your hormonal makeup is different. Your brains are different. The area connecting the two hemispheres of the brain is larger in women than in men, and when women concentrate, they use more areas in their brains than men, suggesting that women integrate both sides more effectively and might be able to multitask more efficiently. Women also tend to have better fine motor coordination.

One study showed that in a crowded room, men are able to carry on a conversation and completely tune out the conversations around them, while women tend to find this almost impossible and can't help hearing what others around them are saying. (You aren't eavesdropping—you can't help it! It's the nature of your brains!) Women tend to be more left-brain dominated, which is the realm of language, and women are typically more verbal, talk earlier, and are more dependent on verbal skills for communication. You like to talk things out. (We understand. We do, too. Let's talk about it!)

Because women tend to express themselves verbally and because you are so used to doing five things at once, meditation can be a real challenge. "What, sit there for 20 minutes without discussing it with anyone? Yikes! And can't I do the dishes while I'm meditating, or fold the laundry, or get some of that work I brought home done?" Girlfriends, you may be ultraefficient, but you are running those poor brains of yours ragged! Especially in this day and age, when women are often expected to do it all— have a great career, manage the money and pay the bills, keep a sparkling home, keep our men happy, manage a family, feed the dog, help with homework, stay in shape, engage in scintillating conversation about current events, and appear eternally young … yikes!—you can really use a daily meditation break or two.

Stress gets to you, but you don't like to admit it, or show it. You hold on and hold on, holding everything together, until suddenly you realize you've taken on too much and have to let go of everything at once. What a mess! (Ugh—more cleaning up to do!)

 Bliss Byte

The universe operates in a balanced way. The planets maintain a certain range of distance from the sun, and the moon remains a certain range of distance from the earth. In yoga, the sun/solar energy is viewed as male, and the moon/lunar energy is viewed as female. However, both principles—solar and lunar energy— exist within all people.

Let meditation become a part of your daily mental maintenance, and you'll be in much better shape to take it all on. You'll also realize which of those things you used to think you *had* to do aren't really all that important. Simplify your life and eliminate those aspects that weigh you down or don't matter in the scheme of things. Take time to relax, enjoy your life, and breathe. And when you are folding that laundry, do it mindfully. Fold it for the sake of folding the laundry. How much sweeter life can be! (Especially when you realize that the happy, well-fed man in the recliner can fold laundry just as easily as you can!)

Meditation and Your Cycle

Until they reach the end of childbearing years, just about all women have to face the challenge and gift of monthly menstruation. Our culture views menstruation as a painful, negative time, shrouded in the mysterious "premenstrual syndrome" (PMS), which can turn the most rational woman into an unpredictable emotional wreck riddled with the most uncomfortable physical symptoms.

But women don't have to view the monthly cycle as a negative thing. In fact, when viewed in a positive light (as other cultures have done before us), PMS symptoms might actually lessen. The next time you begin to feel the first discomfort related to your monthly cycle, try the following meditation:

1. Lie flat on your back on the floor as in shavasana (see Chapter 15). Place a small pillow under your lower back and another under your knees. Lace your fingers together and place your hands on your lower abdomen. Breathe deeply three times.

2. Visualize yourself standing on a beach at night. The sky is clear, the breeze is warm, and you can hear palm trees rustling behind you. The water is quiet and dark, and the waves lap rhythmically at your feet, spreading foam along the shoreline. Imagine a bright, white full moon is slowly rising above the horizon where the midnight-blue sky meets the ocean. Watch it rise slowly into the peaceful darkness until it is high in the sky. The dark, rhythmic ocean reflects the silvery light of the moon and the waves are painted with light.

3. Now, see the moon waning, gradually becoming eclipsed by darkness. Watch the bright area grow thinner and thinner until only a pale crescent remains in the sky. Feel the breeze blowing the salty air around you and breathe it in deeply. Feel the rhythm of the waves in your body. Now, imagine the moon waxing again, the dark area fading, and the brightness growing larger and larger until the moon is a full, bright disk again. Feel the moon's energy pulling on the waves and gently rolling them onto the shore.

> **Mindful Minute**
>
> The ocean tides are created by the gravitational pull of the moon. That moon (lunar energy) has a lot of clout here on earth!

Feel the moon's energy in you, moving your internal physical structure to its own rhythm, which is also your rhythm. Feel at one with the rhythm of the ocean and the moon. Let the movement move you. Go with it. Don't fight it. It is you.

4. Breathe deeply and feel the lunar rhythm for 10 minutes or more. Then slowly, open your eyes.

Meditation to Help Boost Fertility

For a woman suffering from infertility, it might seem that everyone around her is having children. Infertility can become consuming, making life a frustrating, heart-breaking, stressful battle. Fortunately, technology has come a long way in addressing infertility. Yet approximately 10 million American couples of childbearing age are infertile, and technology might not be able to help them all.

If you are a woman and have been diagnosed as infertile, the most important thing you can do is love yourself. Being infertile isn't some divine punishment for anything in your past. It isn't due to some hidden agenda of your subconscious mind. It doesn't mean you are somehow faulty. But it could be, in part, related to stress.

Two organs at the base of your brain are largely responsible for releasing stress hor-mones in your body: the pituitary gland and the hypothalamus. The hypothalamus also releases chemical signals that stimulate the pituitary gland to produce two hor-mones that stimulate ovulation. An overproduction of stress hormones can disrupt this process and may cause menstruation and ovulation to become irregular or, in extreme cases, stop.

Although women have conceived in the most stressful situations imaginable (even in concentration camps), if you have a physical problem that reduces your fertility, stress might be the factor inhibiting your infertility. Eliminating stress will only increase your chances of conception, and at worst, it will help you come to terms with who you are as a whole person, beyond the part of you who wants a baby.

> **Mindful Minute**
>
> Preliminary results suggest that stress-reduction techniques may indeed enhance fer-tility. In one informal study conducted by the Faulkner Centre for Reproductive Medicine in Boston, 54 women were taught a relaxation technique and were asked to practice for 20 minutes twice per day for 10 weeks. Within 6 months after the pro-gram, 34 percent of the women became pregnant, an average higher than typical for women being treated for infertility.

If you're struggling with infertility, being treated for infertility, grieving about your infertility, or simply attempting to conceive, meditation is an important ally. Try to meditate for at least 20 minutes each day. Here is a meditation to help you on your way:

Sit comfortably with your back straight and your eyes closed. Rest your hands on your knees, palms up, to signify your receptiveness. Breathe deeply and slowly. Now imagine a beautiful, glowing divine presence. Perhaps it is God, perhaps it is Mother Earth, perhaps an angel. Imagine the presence surrounding you, emanating love. With each deep inhalation, you breathe in this love, and it fills your body until you develop a beautiful halo of rose light around your entire self. Visualize the presence lifting, effortlessly bearing your weight and gently holding you. You've never felt such all-encompassing love and acceptance. You hear a voice whispering, "I love you. You are perfect. I love you. You are perfect," over and over. Say the words along with the voice and say them to yourself: *I love you. You are perfect.* Know that you are loved and that you are perfect. Continue to breathe and relax into this complete and unconditional love and acceptance for at least 15 minutes.

> **Bliss Byte**
>
> Shavasana (see Chapter 15) is a wonderful technique for pregnancy. Use plenty of pillows to make yourself comfortable. Don't lie flat on your back after your twentieth week of pregnancy, however. You can cut off circulation to your extremities. Instead, lie on your left side with pillows under your head and at least one pillow between your knees. Then meditate your stress away and focus on the love that lies within and all around you.

Meditation for Pregnancy and Childbirth

Under the best of circumstances, pregnancy and childbirth are stressful events. The stress is often good stress, but good stress is still stress. Meditation during pregnancy is a great way to relax, reduce your stress level, and bond with your not-yet-born baby. Pregnancy tends to magnify any stress you already have, so manage that stress:

1. Sit in a comfortable chair with your feet up on a stool, ottoman, or stack of pillows. Get really comfy, then place your hands on your belly. Breathe deeply and relax. With each inhalation, imagine love flowing into your lungs, into your blood, and into your baby. With each exhalation, imagine your baby's love flowing back out to you.

2. Gently rub your hands over your belly, and on the exhalation, make a soft, vibrating *mmm*. Feel the sound vibrating through your body and let it be a sound of love your baby can feel. Your baby can't understand language, but it

can feel this expression of your love. Continue to breathe, inhaling love into your baby, exhaling your baby's love into the air around you.

3. Perform this meditation every day.

During childbirth, meditation can be a great way to move through the pain of labor, but the most important thing for childbirth is mindfulness. Remaining completely aware and mindful through the experience will help you remember every precious moment (even the painful ones will someday seem precious). Mindful awareness and objective observation of labor pains might make them more bearable, but even if you choose to have some type of pain relief—many of us do, although some of us didn't intend it that way—be mindful of every feeling, every sensation, and that fantastic feeling when the pain stops. Also be mindful of your disappointment if your birth didn't go the way you planned, and ever thankful for the gift you receive at the end, no matter the method of getting there.

This squatting pose can help you to relax, open your hips, and prepare for labor. Stack pillows on the floor as high as you need for comfort. The squat is an active pose; don't strain your joints and muscles or push the pose to the point of pain or stress. After holding the pose comfortably for as long as you desire, relax down to a seated pose on the floor and continue your practice of relaxation and meditation.

When you first see that baby of yours, be there. Be awake and aware. Live that moment, and someday you can tell your child all about it because you'll *remember*.

Mindful Minute

Stress can make a pregnancy more difficult, but some studies suggest that attitude is an even more important factor. One study found that pregnant women who had to work despite their desire to stay home were at a much greater risk of preterm labor and giving birth to babies with low birth weight—probably not because of the work, but because of the extra stress working against their desires.

Meditation and Breastfeeding

If you watch a breastfeeding mother, you might think it looks like the most effortless and natural act imaginable. And it is—after the first few weeks. Those first few weeks can be tough ones for many women, and many give up trying to breastfeed before they get over this hump. Experts agree, however, that breastfeeding is the best way to feed your baby; no formula can duplicate breast milk, which is individually tailored for your baby's needs. Breastfed babies are typically healthier and suffer from fewer health problems, and studies also suggest that breastfed babies might have higher IQs when they reach school age.

But before you get the hang of it and before your baby has the hang of it, breastfeeding can be difficult, frustrating, and in those postpartum days, might sometimes reduce you (and baby) to tears. When you feel like you want to quit even though you know you don't *really* want to quit, you need to relax, regroup, and remember your original intention. Try this meditation:

Bliss Byte

Touch is crucial for babies, so bring your baby into your meditation practice. As your little one sleeps, rest its little hand upon your upturned hand and accept your baby's beautiful energy into your own energy. Send lots of loving energy back in return. Meditate on your baby's face, potential, and the bond between the two of you. When your baby gets a little older, let him or her continue to join you in your meditation practice. If baby sees you meditating each day and always feels a part of it, eventually your baby will make meditation a part of his or her own life as well. What a wonderful gift for a mother to bestow on her child!

Lie back on a big pile of pillows or in a comfortable chair with your feet up. Hold your baby in your arms when it isn't particularly hungry and isn't crying. Hold it against your heart. Close your eyes and breathe in deeply, then breathe out. Imagine you and your baby are surrounded by a warm yellow glow that encompasses you both as if you were one being. Feel your baby against you. Feel its breathing. Then, match your breathing to your baby's, at a rate of approximately four of your baby's breaths to one of your own (find a ratio that feels comfortable). Continue with this rhythm until it becomes as natural as breathing on your own and until you feel like you and your baby are as in harmony as you were when your baby was still inside you.

Mom Meditation

Once your kids get past the newborn stage, chaos sets in. It will probably last for the next, oh, 20 years or so. You can't eliminate chaos completely in a house with kids, so you're better off learning to manage it. Stressed-out moms can use a little mothering. Whenever you start to feel the chaos rising, stop what you're doing, breathe in deeply, feel the strength of the ground beneath your feet, and as you exhale, say (or think) the following five-element mantra:

> *Mother Earth, breathe peace into me.*
>
> *Mother Earth, let peace glow in me.*
>
> *Mother Earth, flood me with peace.*
>
> *Mother Earth, peace grows in me.*
>
> *Mother Earth, your peace ascends.*

Meditation to Ease Menopause

One segment of the arc of womanhood involves the winding down of the childbearing years. This time marks an important transition in the life of a woman. Symbolically, life's purpose can shift now. Even if your children have been on their own for a while or even if they aren't quite out of the nest yet, menopause marks that period of life when your life can at last become your own. It is a time to return to the world, a time when the capacity to love becomes greater, more galactic, and inclusive, as your focus broadens beyond your immediate family to include the community. Balance, as ever, is the key between care of the self and care of the world.

Women are brought up in our society to be giving. But there is a time for giving and a time for living. Sure, you can do them both at the same time, but sometimes it's nice to focus solely on the latter. Finding your own strength, your own individuality, your own desires, journeying out into the world or into the soul, or both, is the promise of life after childbearing. Make the most of yours! And if menopause is accompanied by discomfort or difficult symptoms, see your doctor, but also, keep meditating:

Sit comfortably with your back straight and your eyes closed. Breathe deeply and prepare to count very slowly to 20. As you count, say and visualize the following:

1. *I am a baby, playing, laughing, crawling, learning.*

2. *I am a small child, toddling, walking, loving, learning.*

3. *I am in school, making friends, living, learning.*

4. *I am in high school, making friends, exploring life, learning.*

5. *I am a young adult, finding a career, meeting people who will become important in my life* (you can name them), *learning.*

6. *I am in middle age, enjoying my friends, my family, still learning.*

7. *I am in my senior years, beautiful, wise, loving, beloved, and still learning.*

Now, relax and reflect upon how much you still have to learn, how much of life you have left, and how your life has really just begun.

For Men

Don't worry, guys. We haven't forgotten you. You are unique, too, biologically, hormonally, and emotionally. You tend to be right-brain dominated, better at thinking spatially, such as knowing where one object is in relation to others. That's why you never ask for directions—you can find your way on your own! Your brain is typically bigger than the female brain (no snide comments, please), and you might be more likely to depend on a single area of your brain to help you accomplish tasks, making it easier for you to focus your attention on one thing to the exclusion of distractions. That means meditation might be easier for you than it is for women.

Because you tend to be right-brained, you also tend to excel at reasoning and math problems, though verbal skills might take a little more practice. Of course, none of these biological factors hem you in. Maybe you're a fantastic speaker and/or writer. Maybe you're lousy at math or can't find where you're going without a map to save your life. We're all individuals, but we also have a lot in common, and one of those commonalties is the ability to benefit from meditation.

There's No Edge on a Circle

Men don't have it easy in the modern world, either. You guys are under a lot of pressure. You're supposed to earn a respectable living, but that's nothing new. In addition, however, you're now expected to be a caring, nurturing partner, be a loving and giving dad, help out with the housework, and look really good, too. At least, that's what we're all led to believe by television, movies, and the current literature. Yes, you're supposed to be Superman.

Of course, no one is really Superman, and chances are, like most men, you excel in a couple of these areas but other areas just aren't your forte. The result of trying to live up to such unrealistic expectations, however, is a lot of stress, and stress tends to set men on edge. Maybe you get angry, irritable, or depressed. In fact, a recent study showed a link between depression and aggression. And speaking of edge, you may hear a lot about having the competitive edge, being on the cutting edge, edging out the other guy—it's enough to send a man right over the edge!

> **Relax** ———
>
> Hey there guys! Meditation is not a competitive sport, so rein in your tendency to make meditation another aggressive activity. It is an inner process of growth and understanding. The practice of meditation, though, can improve one's abilities, whether in the boardroom, at the keyboard, or on the racquetball court, by increasing your focus and concentration.

When life gets to be too much, there's nothing wrong with putting on the brakes and stepping back from the edge. You can set limits for yourself, and you can practice stress management. These days, it's almost a necessity. Take, for your symbol of calm, the circle. Circles don't have edges, and if you follow them with your eyes, they don't have a beginning or an ending. No finish line, no goal, just a continuous and eternal path. That's a much healthier and more realistic representation of how life works.

Perhaps you find it frustrating to conceive of a journey without an end, without competition, without a *goal*. Step into that challenge and see where it takes you. Once you set aside the idea of a goal, you'll be far more able to practice mindfulness. With mindfulness, the joy and the experience is in the doing, not in the "getting to." Try this meditation to train your mind toward this different perspective:

Sit comfortably with your back straight and your eyes closed. Breathe deeply, then visualize a golden circle in front of you. The circle grows, flattens out, and becomes a circular path. Imagine yourself stepping onto this circular path. You begin walking, then you begin running. But what's this? You're going in circles! You're not getting anywhere! Imagine that you feel frustrated at first because you are running the same track again and again. What's the point? Then, quite suddenly, you stop in your tracks. You look around you. There is no "point." Yet you haven't even noticed where you are! You look around again, and the air around you transforms into a beautiful landscape of tall green trees, bright blue lakes, snow-topped mountains. Where did this come from, you wonder? The circle is still beneath your feet, but as you stand still, you recognize it has a spectacular view to offer. What more might there be to see?

Start walking very slowly, and with each step, a new and magnificent scene surrounds you. A rocky cliff overlooking a dramatic seascape. Rolling hills blanketed with snow and trees encased in ice crystals. A brilliant red and purple sunset over a desert canyon. A sensational waterfall tumbling into a blue-green grotto. And then something wonderful happens. The golden circle seems to come apart, falling, and as you look down, you see it has transformed into a spiral, still circular, yet universes have opened up below you, and you see you are just beginning an amazing journey. And the journey is in the journeying.

Walk along the spiral and live each step fully and completely for as long as you like, at least 10 minutes. When you've seen enough for today, take a few more deep, slow breaths and say the words, "Live for this moment. And this moment. And this moment." Open your eyes and start living!

Meditation for Your Prostate (and the Rest of You!)

Your prostate certainly is not the only area of concern when it comes to men's health. It's just the area that gets the most press! Other men's health issues include heart disease, colon cancer, impotence, the quest for longevity, and worries about looking good. Are you losing your hair? Gaining weight? Losing muscle?

You might wonder if meditation can keep you healthier, help you to live longer, and maybe even make you more virile? Meditation can certainly facilitate your body's healing efforts, and perhaps even more important, it can change your mind about your body. That's half the battle.

Each morning, begin your day with 20 minutes of seated meditation. Sit in mindfulness. Listen and feel your breath moving in and out of your body. When you are comfortable and feel calm, chant the following mantra: Say "Health in," then inhale deeply, from the lower abdomen (don't lift those shoulders or chest). Then say "Tension out," and exhale fully. Then say "Strength in," and inhale deeply, "Hesitation out," then exhale fully. Then say (and this part is important, so don't skip it!) "Love in," inhaling deeply, and "Anger out," exhaling fully. Repeat the sequence again and again until your

> **Mindful Minute**
>
> The Taoists have a good way of thinking about negative energy: They suggest that the negative vibes released are transformed by the earth, just as the garbage and scraps you put into your backyard compost are transformed.

> **CAUTION Relax**
>
> Rein in your anger, which some experts define as "depression turned outward." Anger can motivate us to make necessary changes, and it can also destroy us. Find ways to use anger constructively. A professional therapist might be able to help in this healing journey.

20 minutes is up. Feel the words, and visualize health and strength and love flowing into you and tension and hesitation and anger flowing out of you. Let the words and the breath merge and become you.

This meditation is also great for anger management, impatience, and ebbing self-esteem—something men often experience but are far less likely to admit. Whenever you are feeling depressed, unworthy, unable, or insecure, take a few minutes to breathe and say the mantra: "Health in, tension released. Strength in, hesitation released. Love in, anger released." You can be who you want to be, and you can have a wonderful, satisfying, fulfilling life.

For the Whole Family

Meditation doesn't have to be a solitary pursuit. It can also be a family affair! This is great news for parents who rarely have a moment to themselves. Peace and tranquility with the kids in tow? Could it be possible?

Meditation with kids isn't the same as meditation on your own or even meditation with another adult partner. But it can still be fulfilling and relaxing. It also provides your family with one more activity to do together, and the relaxing and spiritual nature of meditation will help bond you together. Let meditation serve as a common ground and family priority, and your family will grow stronger. Meditation is also a great way to teach children the techniques of stress reduction, contemplation, conflict management, and spiritual reflection. The sooner they learn these skills, the better they'll be able to navigate adult life. Try this meditation with the whole family:

Have everyone sit in a circle, legs crossed, knees touching. For younger kids (say, under five years) who can't be expected to sit still, allow them to sit or lie in the middle of the circle. (If they squirm or roll around, that's okay. You're setting an example, and they'll catch on eventually.)

Next, have each person in the circle place their hands, palms up, on their knees, joining each thumb and first finger and touching knuckles or fingers of the person on either side. Now, the family is connected in a physical circle and an energy circle.

Each member seated in the family circle makes the om mudra.

Now, lead your family in the following mantra pattern. Begin by saying each word, then have each family member repeat it, one at a time, around the circle. When the mantra reaches you again, change to the next word. Go through the cycle three times and have the whole family say the sequence of mantras in unison three more times:

- *Love*

- *Peace*

- *Happiness*

- *Serenity*

- *Family*

- *One*

Bliss Byte

Teaching kids to be mindful will do more than help them in school. It will also teach them to be more attentive, better listeners, more empathetic, more loving, and more joyful and appreciative of the beautiful and fascinating world around them. Children can also use mindfulness and quiet reflection as tools to help them through difficult times, whether peer rejection, an excruciating test, or even a family tragedy. The best way to teach kids mindfulness is by your own example.

As You Age

As you pass midlife and head into your golden years, meditation can be more than a stress-reduction technique. It can also be a center of peace in your life, a way to manage health problems, a method of health maintenance, and a great way to boost and maintain your self-esteem.

Aging doesn't have to be accompanied by health problems, but it often is. It doesn't have to be accompanied by depression, but it often is. It doesn't have to be accompanied by a loss of joy, ambition, and purpose, but it often is. If you start now to combat all these negative conditions, you'll enjoy your golden years more.

Mindful Minute

Gerontologists from Tufts University put a group of frail nursing-home residents ages 87 to 96 on a weight-training program and found that within 8 weeks, the residents experienced a 300 percent increase in muscle tone. So seniors, try some gentle movement meditation, walking meditation, or yoga. Keep using that mind-body! Be sure to consult your physician before beginning any exercise program, though.

Even if you do have to deal with some of the conditions associated with aging, you'll be better equipped to handle them.

As menopause is a major transition for women, retirement is a huge one for men and, increasingly, for women, too. Because men have traditionally been the "breadwinners," however, and have associated their lives so closely with their professions, they might experience feelings of no longer having value or a purpose, whereas women might tend to have other sources of self-worth. Joseph Campbell (1904–1987), an American author specializing in comparative mythology, once said that men and women often change roles as they age: Women become stronger, more assertive, and more involved in the outside world. Men become more nurturing, more interested in staying at home, and more interested in pursuits of the home, including gardening and cooking. Campbell also once said that as his own body aged, it was a great reminder to him that it was time to move more into spiritual pursuits.

These could be the best years of your life. Make the most of the wisdom, experience, and perspective you've earned and live life for all its worth. Show those young'uns how it's done!

Any of the meditations in this book are appropriate for you, but you can also try this one:

- Sit on the floor or in a comfortable chair with your back straight and your eyes closed. Breathe deeply a few times. Scan your body for spots of tension, and breathe into those areas.

- When you feel fairly relaxed, visualize yourself walking easily down a winding stone path. The sun is warm and mild. On either side of you are beautiful trees with bright green leaves and white blossoms. Petals flutter onto the path as a gentle, cool spring breeze rustles the trees. You feel happy and energetic. You've got a spring in your step and happiness in your heart. Look all around you and notice every detail of this lovely spring day.

- Soon, the path turns a bend and the trees grow thicker, taller, and more lush. You smell the scent of freshly mown grass, and the air is decorated with birdsong. The sun is higher in the sky and warmer, but still comfortable and comforting. The stone path is lined with bright lilies and wild roses, like a garden gone slightly wild. The breeze is warm and smells vaguely of the ocean. You feel calm and content. Look all around you and notice every detail of this languid summer day.

- Now, the path turns another bend and the trees begin to blush. The breeze is fresh and cool, and it rustles the leaves on the trees as they slowly change into scarlet, bright orange, yellow, and many shades of red. Leaves float down through the cool air and decorate the path with their bright colors. You breathe deeply, and your heart fills with joy. What a beautiful place to be! You notice a wooden bench on the side of the path and decide to sit for a while. You sit, and the bench is surprisingly comfortable. The trees are on fire with color, and the cool air is bracing and energizing. Breathe it in and relish the smell of autumn. You feel such a surge of energy that you rise from the bench and return to the path, walking with a renewed sense of purpose and direction.

♦ As you move through the lovely autumn day, gratitude and thanksgiving overflow in your heart, and you find yourself joyfully chanting the words "Love, love, love!" because you know this is your life, and it is the most beautiful phase of life you've yet experienced. You can hardly wait to see what comes next! Continue to breathe, and when you are ready, open your eyes and embrace the day.

Meditation, mindfulness, visualization, and attention to the breath are right for any gender, any age, and any inclination. Embrace meditation and make it your own, then watch your life burst into bloom.

The Least You Need to Know

♦ Meditation can help women cope with the discomfort of menstruation, infertility stress, pregnancy, breastfeeding, motherhood, and menopause.

♦ Meditation can help men learn to view life in new ways, boost their physical and mental health, and mend self-esteem.

♦ Meditation is a great family activity and can help kids grow into adults who can handle stress and enjoy life.

♦ Meditation can help seniors make the most of the best years of their lives: the golden years!

22

Rx: Meditation

In This Chapter

◆ Achieving a balance

◆ Healing and the mind-body

◆ Meditation, health, and your well-being

◆ Reiki, acupuncture, biofeedback, and therapeutic touch

◆ Meditation for what ails you

Meditation itself doesn't exactly heal. Chanting a mantra won't slay bacteria, and mindfulness won't mend a broken bone. In fact, we want to make it clear right from the start that no matter how in-tune your mind-body connection is, you should seek medical care when you're sick or injured. Meditation, however, can be a remarkably helpful adjunct: It can remove some of the obstacles that might be keeping your body from healing itself. In this chapter, we'll help you explore the role meditation can play in your own health and healing.

Ayurveda Equals Homeostasis

Different cultures have all developed their own systems of health and medicine. The history of medicine around the world would make a fascinating and lengthy book. But one of the oldest systems of health, and one of the most holistic (which means it looks at and treats all aspects of the mind-body) is the Indian system of *Ayurveda*.

Ayurveda has literally been translated as "science of life," and it is just that: an all-encompassing approach to living. According to Ayurveda, humans have the capacity to live far longer life spans than we currently do. The only reason our lives are cut short is because we don't optimize our mind-body systems. Ayurveda helps keep the body in balance so it can operate the way it was meant to and remain healthy far into old age.

> **From A to Om**
>
> **Ayurveda** is the oldest organized system of health care. Literally "science of living" or "art of life," Ayurveda involves a combination of customized diet, yoga exercises, meditation, hygiene rituals, massage, and a structured routine into a philosophical system of energy balancing. Ayurveda has recently become popular in the West largely due to the writings and influence of Deepak Chopra, M.D.

A Western word for this balance is *homeostasis*. Homeostasis is the tendency of a body (or even an entire ecosystem) to remain in a balanced state. For example, even when it's really hot outside, your body makes adjustments so its internal temperature remains at approximately 98.6°F. Few bodies operate in true homeostasis in a world full of toxins, addictions, pollutants, stress, and negative habits, but for a truly healthy mind-body, finding and maintaining balance is crucial. Your body is trying continually to find that balance, so help it along. Remove those roadblocks (such as negativity, eating junk food, being sedentary, and letting stress get to you)!

Ayurveda utilizes many methods to maintain mind-body homeostasis, including aromatherapy, massage, a diet tailored to your individual tendencies, herbal medicine, special hygiene practices, and the diagnosis of imbalances through the learned reading of the pulse. One of the most important aspects of Ayurveda is meditation.

> **From A to Om**
>
> **Homeostasis** is the tendency of a system (such as a body, a group, or an ecosystem) to maintain an equilibrium or balanced state.

The point of meditation as part of Ayurveda is to cleanse the mind by refining thought to subtler and subtler levels until it finally stills, giving the mind complete peace, rest, and renewal. Now your body can heal itself a little bit more easily.

Using Your Body Knowledge to Heal

You know yourself better than you might think. You know what it means to have a vague sense that something isn't "right," that you're "coming down with something," or that you're "under the weather." You might not be able to produce the technical term for what's wrong, but you know. And your body knows, too.

> **Mindful Minute** _____
>
> According to an article published by the BBC in 2002, two studies carried out at the Department of Complementary Medicine at the University of Exeter followed people with moderate to severe asthma who were previously unresponsive to asthma medication. Patients were divided into two groups. One practiced a yoga-based form of meditation while the other practiced either simple relaxation techniques or visualization techniques. After four months, the patients practicing yoga meditation responded better to asthma medication than the groups practicing simple relaxation or visualization techniques. To find out more about this study, see news.bbc.co.uk/2/hi/health/1787548.stm.

You can use this body knowledge to your healing advantage, and meditation is the connection, the translator, and the conduit for healing energy your mind sends to your body. Visualizations can help your body send you a message. And don't forget good old-fashioned intuition. Don't ignore that "sixth sense."

Natural Medicine Goes with the Flow

It's great to learn how to direct your own energy, but maybe you have a true gift for healing and could help heal the energy of others. Many are doing just that, practicing different forms of healing and bodywork to help re-align and replenish life-force energy in others, as well as teaching others to replenish and manage their own energy. Techniques abound, but here are a few of the most popular.

Reiki

Pronounced *ray-kee*, Reiki is a type of bodywork that emphasizes the manipulation of life-force energy through the chakras. The Reiki practitioner places his or her hands on the receiver over the chakras, working along the front and the back of the body. Each touch is held for several minutes, allowing universal life-force energy to flow through the practitioner into the receiver (the energy comes from the universe, not from the Reiki practitioner, who serves as a channel, not as an energy source).

The theory is that chakras are special places on the body where energy can enter, and placing hands over them allows them to open and receive energy. The more energy in the body, the better it can heal, align, and balance itself.

There are several levels of Reiki accomplishment, culminating in the title of Reiki Master. Training involves a process that unblocks the practitioner's own chakras so they can serve as ideal energy channelers.

Although you can't learn Reiki from a book alone, try the following Reiki meditation. The area you are holding is your point of concentration. Remember those chakras? Work through each one, holding your hands over the area for about three minutes each. As you hold your hands over your chakras, imagine tapping life-force energy from the universe and feel it flowing into your chakras, suffusing your body and soul with vitality:

1. Sit or stand comfortably with your back straight. Place the fingers of both hands along your eyebrows with your little fingers resting on the bridge of your nose. Your palms should be cupping your cheeks. Press very gently with your fingers around the eyes. Hold.

2. Place your palms on either side of your head so your fingers barely touch across the crown of your head. Hold.

3. Reach around to the back of your head and, fingers barely touching, cradle the back of your skull. Hold.

4. Next, place your right hand gently on your throat and your left hand across the top of your sternum so the fingers of your left hand rest beneath the wrist of your right hand. Hold.

5. Now place your palms on your lower chest near the bottom ribs. Hold.

6. Place your palms over your stomach so your fingers touch over your navel. Hold.

7. Place your palms over your lower abdomen with your fingers pointing diagonally downward and touching just over your pubic bone. Hold.

8. Place your hands over your shoulders behind you and press your palms against your upper back, fingers pointed down. Hold.

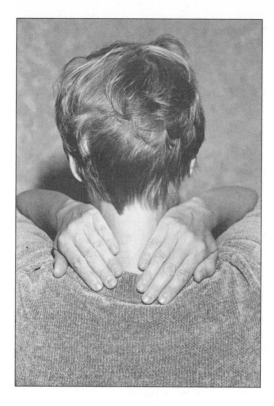

Joan performs step eight in this self-Reiki meditation.

9. Bend your left arm behind you and rest your hand over your right shoulder blade. Hold. Repeat on the other side. Hold.

10. Place both hands around your lower rib cage on your back, just above your waist. Hold.

11. Place both hands over the tops of your hip bones on your back, just above your buttocks. Hold.

12. Now, bring your hands back to the front and cup your right hand in your left hand. Breathe in and out naturally for another three minutes, feeling the life-force energy moving through your body, flushing away negativity and replacing it with healing and joy.

Acupuncture

Acupuncture is a centuries-old technique that originated in China. Hair-thin needles are inserted into pressure points for pain relief and healing. The theory is that by stimulating pressure points, acupuncture releases blocked areas and equalizes life-force energy, allowing the body to solve its own pain and heal itself. Some people meditate during their acupuncture treatments to facilitate the process.

Many insurance companies in the United States now cover acupuncture treatments, and although many mainstream physicians admit they don't know why it works, they also admit that it *does* work. Before receiving treatment, make sure you find an acupuncturist who is properly trained and licensed.

Biofeedback

Biofeedback is a type of therapy that teaches individuals to gain control over the parts of the nervous system that regulate bodily functions such as skin temperature, heart rate, brain waves, and blood flow. By watching or listening to representations of bodily functions via a monitor, individuals learn how different states "feel" and gradually can learn to alter those feelings, thereby altering the function itself.

Although biofeedback techniques can be used to teach people to control a wide range of body functions, some of the most common are breathing, heart rate, muscle tension, skin temperature, electrodermal activity (subtle changes in sweat activity), pulse, and brain wave activity. Biofeedback can be a great partner for meditation. The techniques it teaches promote body control and mental focus, both of which make meditation more effective.

Bliss Byte

Proponents of energy therapies often quote physicist Albert Einstein because his theories (to drastically simplify them) postulate that all objects are surrounded by electromagnetic fields of energy about to become matter. His famous equation, $E = mc^2$, theorizes that energy and matter can each be transformed into the other, back and forth. Einstein once said, "Up to the twentieth century, reality was everything humans could touch, smell, see, and hear. Since the initial publication of the chart of the electromagnetic spectrum, humans have learned that what they can touch, smell, see, and hear is less than one-millionth of reality."

Therapeutic Touch

Therapeutic Touch (TT) is a controversial technique in which patients are treated by practitioners who never touch them. The theory behind TT is similar to the theory behind Reiki: life-force energy can become imbalanced, and the TT therapist acts as a channel for life-force energy to flow into the receiver. However, in TT, the practitioner's hands usually stay about four to six inches above the skin of the receiver, touching only the body's energy field. Some practitioners even incorporate guided visualizations, transforming the session into a sort of mind-body meditation.

How to Talk to Your Doctor About Holistic Health

Just a few years ago, few medical doctors gave serious credence to natural medicine. Now, however, an increasing number of M.D.s recognize both the popularity and the legitimacy of the holistic health approach, although many are still skeptical of treatments and therapies that haven't been validated by a host of scientific studies, and most recommend a complementary approach, using holistic medicine for some conditions and conventional medicine for others.

Mindful Minute

One reason natural medicine is gaining in popularity in the West so quickly is because people are losing faith in conventional health care. Among the top 10 reasons for hospitalization in the United States are adverse reactions and side effects from medications. Overmedication and adverse affects from drug interactions are a common problem, especially in the elderly. Plus, meditation today is cheaper than surgery tomorrow!

You should be cautious about who is responsible for your health and what therapy he or she uses to treat you. You don't want to throw your health into the hands of someone who doesn't know what he is doing or who is using substances and techniques that might prove harmful. But many holistic health therapies have been well tested, and if your doctor is doing his or her homework, you should be able to work together to provide a safe, effective, and more natural health plan for you.

Relax

When choosing any health-care practitioner, whether of traditional medicine or alternative natural medicine, be sure he or she is a licensed professional (if that particular field uses licensing) or he or she has been in practice for a while and has good references. Any new treatment regimen you begin should coordinate with your primary care physician's plan for you. A coordinated treatment plan, created by a health-care team composed of *all* your health-care providers, is the best way to ensure your maximum health and well-being and to guard against any dangerous drug/herb interactions or therapies working against each other.

Make an appointment for a checkup with your primary care physician, then explain that you are interested in combining natural medicine with your regular health-care routine. Whether you're seeking help for some chronic condition or are hoping to head off disease by practicing preventive medicine, your doctor might be able to tell you which therapies can prove helpful to you. He or she might also be able to warn you away from therapies that might be dangerous, or at best, a waste of money.

Health Is Balance

To holistic health practitioners, health means balanced life-force energy. It tends to be much more focused on maintaining health and preventing disease than on treatment.

Conventional Western medicine, also called *allopathic medicine*, works in just the opposite way. It tends to focus on treating diseases once they occur rather than on helping the body and mind maintain health in the most natural ways possible.

Many holistic healing methods, such as Ayurveda, homeopathy, herbalism, aromatherapy, traditional Chinese medicine, and folk medicine, use the concept of balancing the whole system in one way or another. One way to balance the body is to first balance the mind. A balanced mind encourages a balanced body by making symptoms of imbalance more clear to the mind-body, rather than masking them with emotional or psychological symptoms.

Types of Natural Medicine Popular in the West

Type	Description
Aromatherapy	The treatment of imbalances through the inhalation or application to the skin of essential oils
Ayurveda	The Indian "science of life"
Folk medicine	A return to traditional healing methods originating in different countries at a very local level, which might include use of herbs and food-based remedies
Herbalism	The treatment of disease with herbs
Homeopathy	A subtle medical therapy based on the idea that "like cures like"—remedies that would cause certain symptoms are given in extremely diluted doses to cure those symptoms
Traditional Chinese medicine (TCM)	The ancient Chinese system of acupuncture and herbal medicine

Creating a Health-Care Team

Assembling your own health-care team starts with selecting a primary care physician who has a similar view about health issues as you do. If you like to get in and out of the doctor's office with as little fuss as possible, like to be told what to do without asking questions, and have no problem putting your whole trust in your doctor, then you'll be happier with a doctor who doesn't dilly-dally, gets down to business, tells you what you need to do without long, detailed explanations, then leaves you alone.

> **Bliss Byte**
>
> Depending on where you live and what your health-care options are, you might not be able to find a primary care physician who supports or knows a lot about natural medicine. That doesn't mean you can't make some changes in the way you take care of yourself, however. Take a cue from holistic medicine and practice preventive medicine by eating fresh, organic, unprocessed food, exercising regularly, and meditating.

If, on the other hand, you want to know exactly what the doctor is doing at all times, why he or she is prescribing certain medications or treatments, and what you can do in your life to improve your health, you'll want a doctor who is willing to spend time talking with you. You won't want an impatient doctor or a doctor who has no interest whatsoever in alternative treatments. Shop around. These days, some insurance plans are making it easier to switch doctors if your doctor isn't living up to your expectations. When choosing your insurance company or HMO (if your employer gives you a choice), be sure to find out about its policies on choosing and changing health-care providers. Of course, doctors aren't miracle-workers, but you should feel confident that your doctor makes your health and welfare a priority and is willing to engage in the level of communication you desire and that is reasonable.

> **Relax**
>
> Taking responsibility for your life and health is an important step in your own health care. Avoid blaming others, and don't be afraid to ask for help. Ask questions of the professionals on your health-care team and request their advice and counsel. Be proactive about your own well-being and participate in the care you receive.

Next, consider what other health-care practitioners you might use. Again, your doctor might be of some help here. Could you benefit from acupuncture? From massage therapy? From a chiropractor? Would any herbal remedies support your efforts toward creating a healthy lifestyle and maintaining internal balance? What about homeopathy? Does your doctor recommend any home remedies for minor conditions such as colds and coughs?

Choose the other members of your health-care team with care. Ask questions, make sure they have proper training and certification, and make sure you feel comfortable with them. If you and your qualified herbalist click, you'll be more able to put certain aspects of your health care in his or her hands. But if that massage therapist rubs you the wrong way (so to speak), you should keep looking for someone more suitable to your own personal needs and personality.

How the Mind Contributes to Healing

The research is still controversial, but the scientific community is becoming increasingly willing to admit that the mind does indeed contribute to healing.

Mindful Minute

Mindfulness-based stress reduction (MBSR) is a program developed from Jon Kabat-Zinn's successful Stress Reduction Clinic in Massachusetts. The program is designed to help people with chronic illness or psychological distress to improve their well-being and general health status. In following patients through one such MBSR program in Connecticut, researchers documented that those patients showed a significant decrease in chronic care and medical care doctor visits. Look for an MBSR program in your area; check with local hospitals or your local health agency.

Relaxation techniques actually lower levels of stress hormones in the body, slow heart and breathing rates, reduce blood pressure, and lessen the perception of pain in people who suffer from chronic pain.

People with positive attitudes tend to live longer, get sick less often, and heal faster. Mind and body are inextricable.

If you're facing surgery, you have a unique opportunity to use the power of your mind through meditation in a way that can dramatically reduce your presurgical anxiety and postsurgical pain. Studies have shown that patients facing surgery fared much better when they were given clear and complete instructions about what to expect and how to reduce postsurgical pain, when they were confident the surgery was necessary, when they understood what would happen during the surgery, and when they listened to music via headphones during surgery.

If you aren't given this information, just ask. Explain to your doctor that you want to know everything possible about what to expect. Ask about ways to reduce postsurgical pain. Get a second opinion about whether your surgery is necessary. Read about the surgery. Make sure your surgeon has performed the particular surgery many times before. And ask about whether you can bring a cassette player and headphones into surgery with you. Even under general anesthesia, evidence suggests you still perceive the music at some level, and so music that invokes a positive response might help your body deal with the surgery.

Some institutions are good about handling the patient's anxiety and informing the patient about ways in which he or she can take an active approach to preparation and recovery. Others aren't so good, especially where the staff is trained only in the procedures themselves and not in mollifying the patient. But don't accept the brush-off. You deserve to know everything you can about what will make surgery easier on your mind and body.

Bliss Byte

Many kinds of medical treatments can be enhanced using creative visualization techniques. For example, patients undergoing radiation treatments for cancer can imagine the radioactive particles as a healing army infusing the body with restorative warmth and flushing out the invading cancer cells (or an advancing tide flowing to shore to flush and remove the impurities as it retreats again). Patients who ask their health-care providers to explain how a specific treatment works inside their bodies can use this knowledge to develop creative visualization exercises that are based on the treatment process. The experience of the treatment is transformed, through the patient's imagination, into a healing ritual that is specifically nurturing to the mind-body of the person receiving treatment.

Meditations to Heal By

Although a book of meditations to fit every illness and injury would be hefty indeed, we'd like to give you a few suggestions for using meditation to heal some common health problems. In each of the following meditations, sit or lie comfortably and remember to breathe deeply, infusing your body with healing oxygen.

For the Heart

If you suffer from cardiovascular disease, you aren't alone. One million people die every year from cardiovascular disease, and it is the number-one killer in the United

States. One source estimates that 50 million Americans have cardiovascular disease and don't know it.

Perhaps your heart problem isn't so extreme. Whether you suffer from heart palpitations or serious angina (chest pain), heart-centered meditation can be therapeutic and can ease the anxiety that might exacerbate a heart condition.

Begin meditating by following your breath. When you feel relaxed, bring your attention to your Venus or heart chakra, the energy center behind your heart. Now, imagine your breath is shifting so you are breathing from your heart chakra. Feel your breath flowing around and past your heart, flooding it with healing energy. Imagine the arteries around your heart muscle opening and flowing with nutrients. Feel the rhythm of your heart. If you can't actually feel it beating, imagine a slow, strong beat and breath in rhythm with it, 5 beats per inhalation, 10 beats per exhalation. You can even put your hand over your heart and rub gently. Visualize your heart strong, pulsing with health, exuding compassionate energy. Stay with your heart for 10 or 15 minutes, then let your breathing return to normal.

> **Bliss Byte**
>
> Lie on your back with your knees bent. Bring your arms out so they make a T with your body. Let your knees fall to the left and your head to the right. Keep your shoulders against the floor. Relax. Open your heart. Breathe. After a comfortable time, bring your knees to the right and your head to the left. Breathe, relax, open. After a comfortable time, come back to center. Feel better?

Whenever you are feeling anxious or have a twinge of chest pain, relive the feeling of this heart meditation, visualizing the arteries opening and the sound of the slow, healthy, strong heartbeat. Many people also believe there is a connection between the occurrence of heart disease and issues having to do with love and emotional support. Form a support network to support all aspects of your heart, physically and symbolically.

For the Lungs

Whether it's asthma, pneumonia, tuberculosis, bronchitis, emphysema, or pleurisy, lung disorders can be scary. Few things induce a feeling of panic like not being able to take a deep breath or to breathe well enough to nourish the body with sufficient oxygen.

Asthma is particularly prevalent in the United States, and prevalence of asthma in all age groups rose 59 percent from 1982 to 1996. The American Lung Association estimated that in 2000, more than 7 percent of the adults in America suffer from asthma, and the incidence of hospitalization due to asthma in children is up 500 percent in the last 30 years! Yet many studies including several National Institutes of

Health–sponsored studies published in 2002 showed that meditation and other muscle-relaxation techniques may help to mitigate the symptoms of asthma.

More than two million people contract pneumonia each year in the United States, and between 40,000 and 70,000 die from it. According to the American Lung Association, 169,400 people will contract lung cancer in the United States in 2002. Lung cancer is the leading fatal cancer in the world, and each year, more women die from lung cancer than from breast cancer and ovarian cancer combined.

> **Mindful Minute**
>
> Researchers estimate that if Americans stopped all smoking today, lung cancer deaths would be dramatically reduced within 20 years. Eighty-five percent of lung cancers can be directly linked to smoking.

If you have a lung disease or condition, meditation can help ease anxiety, which in turn can help ease bronchial constriction. Also, because stress increases your respiration rate, forcing your lungs to work harder, stress management is important for lung problems. Try the following meditation:

Sit comfortably with your back straight to allow your rib cage (and, thus, your lungs) plenty of room to expand. Now, concentrate all your attention on your breath and attempt to breathe very slowly. Inhaling through your nose, see how high you can count without straining (at the rate of about one count per second). Then, exhaling through your nose or mouth (whichever is more comfortable and feels more natural), see if you can increase the count. Repeat, trying to increase the count each time. No speeding up your rate of counting! And no straining. Imagine prana, or life-force energy, filling your body and revitalizing your lungs with each inhalation.

If you feel your focus wandering away from the breath, gently bring it back. Once you've reached your maximum count, stay with it for a few more breaths, then breathe normally again, close your eyes, and feel the calm. According to Chinese medicine, lung problems might be related to issues of grief and sadness. With each exhalation, imagine releasing your grief, letting it go, and replacing it with life.

For the Digestive System

If the number of TV commercials for antacids and acid controllers is any indication, digestive problems are rampant in the United States. Whether you suffer from simple indigestion or a peptic ulcer, gastroenteritis or constipation, you know that digestive problems can make you miserable. What to do? Calm that pesky digestion with some targeted meditation.

Sit comfortably and place your hands on your stomach, lower abdomen, or wherever the discomfort lies. Breathe deeply for several breaths. Then, as you breathe, imagine you are breathing in the color blue. It is clear, soothing, cool blue energy. Feel it moving into you and imagine it flowing down your esophagus, into your stomach, and into your intestines, coating your entire digestive system in calming blue energy (see Chapter 7 for information on blue auras). Feel your muscles relax, including the muscles around your digestive system. Keep inhaling the soothing and refreshing blue energy until your stomach feels calm. (If you're experiencing stomach pain or nausea that makes you feel cold and clammy, imagine the color is a warm pink rather than a cool blue.)

> **Bliss Byte**
>
> If your stomach is upset, rub your abdomen slowly in a clockwise direction. As you rub, repeat the phrase, "With loving energy my digestion heals." Continue this affirmation as you slowly circle your stomach with healing energy.

For the Liver

Your liver, the second largest organ in your body (your skin is the largest), is actually a gland below your diaphragm in your abdominal cavity. Its function is to process carbohydrates, fats, and proteins; make bile; and filter out toxic products from the blood. Disorders of your liver might include hepatitis, cirrhosis of the liver (which might be caused by hepatitis or long-term alcohol abuse), and liver cancer. For liver disorders, try the following meditation:

Sit up very straight; slouching cramps your abdominal cavity. Imagine your liver sitting just below your diaphragm. Breathe in very deeply from the abdomen and imagine your bowl-shaped diaphragm compressing your liver as it expands downward to make room for your lungs. Continue to breathe very deeply and visualize that with every inhalation, all the toxins and impurities are gently pressed from your liver, and with every exhalation, the impurities flow out of you with your breath, transformed into life-affirming joy. Imagine your liver becoming cleaner, refreshed, and renewed. Continue for about 10 minutes, then sit quietly for a few more minutes and contemplate the feeling of inner purity.

In Chinese medicine, the liver is connected with anger issues. If you have liver problems, make an effort to resolve and heal any anger in your life.

For the Immune System

Lots of things can depress our immune systems, and stress is one of the most obvious. Whether you suffer from allergies, develop frequent colds, or suffer from full-blown immune system disorders like Hodgkin's disease or AIDS, you know how important it is to have a strong immune system. To help strengthen yours, lessen the stress in your life by meditating once or twice every day, come hell or high water. Try this one:

Lie flat on your back on the ground, as in shavasana (see Chapter 15). Close your eyes and breathe deeply several times, relaxing your muscles and feeling all impurities and toxins leaving your system with each exhalation. Now, bring your attention to your Mars chakra, the seat of action energy behind your navel. Visualize the chakra as a wheel slowly beginning to spin. As it spins, it begins to let out tiny sparks as it generates power. Imagine this spinning, sparking wheel is your immune system, gearing up to protect you. Slowly, the circle begins to expand as it grows in energy. It extends outward and spins until it encompasses your entire body in a transparent spinning shield of protective energy. Now the spinning slows and the shield begins to strengthen. Feel the shield seal itself around you so no germs, allergens, or impurities can reach you. Slowly open your eyes and attempt to retain this feeling of the spiritual barrier against negative energy you have created. Carry it with you throughout the day.

Bliss Byte

For a quick reduction in stress, increase the length of your exhalation to your inhalation. For example, inhale for four counts and exhale for eight counts.

For Chronic Pain, Especially Back Pain

If you live with chronic pain, you know how it can color every aspect of your life, even your thoughts. You experience stress that is seemingly unending. You might suffer from depression, a feeling of hopelessness, or a constant state of heightened emotion. Whether your pain is a headache, backache, joint pain, or something else, we understand how hard life can be for you. So do others, and pain clinics have sprung up around the country to help people manage chronic pain. One technique used for pain management is mindfulness. Try the following:

Lie comfortably on your back as if in shavasana (see Chapter 15) or in another position that minimizes your pain. Close your eyes, take several deep breaths, then breathe normally. Now open your awareness to your body. Rather than ignoring your pain, acknowledge it. Imagine you are an outside observer watching your pain. Give it a shape. Does the shape move? What color is it? If the pain changes, imagine the shape corresponding to the change. Watch your pain. Now, imagine it floats out of you and hangs in front of you where you can see it more easily. Watch it with interest. Try not to let your mind become engaged with the pain. Don't enter it. Stand back, but continue to watch its every move. Get to know it.

After you've spent several days on this meditation, you can try to consciously change the shape, color, and movement of your visualized pain (see Chapter 7 for more on aura colors). Is it bright red? Imagine painting it blue. Does it have a jerking motion? Imagine setting it on a lake and watching it bob gently on top of the water. Imagine changing its shape to a circle, then watching how it reacts.

Relax _____

Don't let chronic pain lead you toward feelings of hopelessness. Learning to live with chronic pain is a real challenge, but meditation can help you to enter the pain and see it in a different way, not as something that defines you but as something that is just one more part of your multi-faceted life, something to see and observe but not to let control you.

Eventually, you might be able to gain some degree of control over your pain, but don't rush this step. Just watching it as an observer and without entering it is often enough to make pain manageable. You might even find that you form a relationship with your pain. Why not? If you have to live together, for whatever length of time, it makes sense to get along.

We recognize that we have omitted many illnesses and conditions that could respond well to meditation, and only space alone limits the scope of this chapter, but we hope the meditations provided will give you inspiration to craft your meditation practice to meet your own individual health needs. When part of the mind-body falters, the _whole_ you can play a big part in the process of renewal.

The Least You Need to Know

♦ Ayurveda is a whole-life system of health that includes meditation in its efforts to balance the body for greater vitality and longevity.

♦ You can work in conjunction with your primary care doctor to form a health-care team that uses both conventional and natural medicine to best care for and maintain your health.

♦ Your mind can be a powerful ally in the healing and recovery process.

♦ Meditation can be a tonic for the heart, lungs, digestive system, liver, immune system, chronic pain (especially back pain), or whatever else might ail you.

Chapter 23

Healing the World with Meditation

In This Chapter

- ◆ The big picture: planet us
- ◆ Meditations for world peace
- ◆ Meditations to heal planet earth
- ◆ The world's most spiritual places

You've heard the expression "Mother Earth." You might or might not have heard any of the thousands of other names people throughout history have given the earth, such as *Gaia*, a name for the Greek earth goddess. Why have so many cultures across the earth come up with the same idea, of earth as some sort of female deity or entity to which we all belong? Because the earth is our mother, of course. Our *metaphorical* mother, right?

Actually, according to certain theories, the expression goes beyond the metaphorical. What if the earth actually has a consciousness of some sort? Or what if the collective unconsciousness of all the humans who live on the earth form a kind of planetary energy? We can't prove it, of course. At least, not yet. However, as telecommunication continues to evolve, the world looks smaller and smaller. You can have a real-time instant-message conversation with someone on the other side of the planet via your computer. You can correspond as easily with a friend in India or Russia or Bora Bora as you can with a friend living in the same state.

We know more about the world than ever before. Cultures merge. Languages combine. Cuisines, fashions, slang, and attitudes are becoming increasingly international. It's an exciting time—and a bit daunting for some, too. Yet the better we know our brothers and sisters around the world, the greater our vision for the future of the earth can become.

How can we use meditation to help the world community unite in a positive way? How can we use meditation to reverse the damage we have done to the planet? How can we use meditation to spread love into the universe?

We meditate. We live mindfully. Meditation will help us evolve.

The Earth as Body

In his books *Gaia: A New Look at Life on Earth* and *Healing Gaia: Practical Medicine for the Planet*, biologist James E. Lovelock proposes that earth is, indeed, a living entity and that all its parts, from its core of molten lava to its plant and animal life, are something like "body parts" making up the whole. Just as each of us is made of cells, which are made of molecules, which are made of atoms, perhaps we make up a smaller part of the earth itself.

> **From A to Om**
>
> **Gaia** is the Greek name for the earth goddess who produced all life. In the twenty-first century, *Gaia* is synonymous with biologist James E. Lovelock's theory of the self-regulating nature of planet earth, as its internal "homeostasis" responds to changes from internal and external stimuli.

An interesting theory, we think. What if humankind is the equivalent of a nervous system for the planet earth? Could the evolving consciousness of humankind mean that the planet is slowly developing consciousness as well? Is earth becoming self-aware?

Many ancient theories propose humans as manifestations of universal consciousness. If we are part of the awakening earth—its brain, perhaps—then we *are* the earth, just as a wave is the ocean but not the whole ocean (a common Zen analogy), or our brains are us but not the *whole* us. And if we are merely the "organs" of a larger consciousness, does that diminish us in any way? Do we die out the way our own cells die, sloughed off with a brush of the hand? Are we gone as fast as a wave disappears back into the ocean, no longer physically the same but ever-present in substance?

> **Bliss Byte**
>
> Devote an entire meditation session (or more) to expanding the limits of what you believe to be "you." First, visualize the spinning atoms that make up your body. Breathe as a collection of atoms. Then, slowly expand your consciousness to encompass the molecules, the cells, and the organs. Breathe as each of these. Expand into your astral layers and breathe through them. Expand into your family, your community, your country, your continent, and at last, the planet. Breathe as each of these in succession. Breathe through the bliss of your causal body, and feel the interpenetration of awareness through each body—physical, astral, and causal—as it achieves oneness with the earth and the universe. Imagine there is no dividing line separating your atoms from the planet, or even from the universe as a whole.

We think it makes sense that we hold the consciousness of the earth within our bodies. We are all evolving together, earth and all its parts. And we are all responsible for each other—for our fellow sentient beings, for the energy on the planet, and for the care and stewardship of the land and water that sustain us.

We're not just simply body, or simply mind, or simply individuals. We are mind-body; we are mind-body-spirit; we are mind-body-spirit-community-planet, ever interconnected.

What does meditation have to do with all this? Plenty. When we meditate, we not only benefit our own mind-bodies, but the earth's as well. Meditation, after all, is a conscious method of uniting mind, body, spirit, humankind, sentient beings, planet, and universe.

Our Earth, Our Responsibility

Seeing yourself as part of a living earth brings with it certain compelling responsibilities. Awesome responsibilities. Suddenly, the boundaries of "you" are much, much bigger. Taking care of yourself means more than eating right, exercising, and meditating once a day. It also means taking care of the planet.

Perhaps you eat well and avoid junk food, but occasionally toss that veggie burger wrapper on

> **Relax**
>
> Environmental destruction goes beyond a symbolic representation of the destruction of our own bodies. Pollution of the planet actually compromises the health of all those who inhabit it. Air pollution damages our lung tissue. Water pollution poisons our systems. And the sights of degradation and destruction depress us and increase our stress.

the ground when you can't find a convenient trash receptacle. Do you shun smoking, but drive your car every day—even when you could easily carpool, bike, or walk? Do you meditate but rarely spend time outside? Recognizing yourself as part of the entity that is the planet earth means that if you don't put junk food in you, you also don't subject the planet to it. That planet is you and you are that planet.

If you wouldn't pollute your own lungs with cigarette smoke, why would you pollute the air around you? If you work on your own mental health, why would you live in isolation from nature?

And don't we owe our Earth Mother respect and protection? She has taken care of us since the beginning of our habitation on the planet, providing us with food, water, air, and warmth; the means to build shelter; and unlimited opportunities. We haven't always been grateful children. We've taken and taken and taken. We've depleted her resources and covered her with pollution. Are we finally recognizing our errors? Perhaps slowly we are coming to understand how we should treat our mother. Or if you see humankind as truly a part of earth, maybe earth is at last recognizing, by means of the evolution of human consciousness, how to take care of herself.

> **Mindful Minute**
>
> Immanuel Kant (1724–1804) was a German philosopher whom many consider the most influential thinker of modern times. Kant believed that reason would always lead the individual to right action and that every individual should be given freedom of self-government because this freedom would allow individuals to act according to universal laws, which could be realized through reason.

> **Mindful Minute**
>
> Both research studies and anecdotal evidence suggest that animals change their behavior in response to impending events, from earthquakes to epileptic seizures in their owners. Animals seem to be more in-tune with the earth's natural rhythms and vibrations.

World Community

German philosopher Immanuel Kant believed that each individual, when given the freedom to create his own ethics and rules, would consciously obey the laws of the universe. He believed the world was evolving toward an ideal society ruled by reason, which would "bind every law giver to make his laws in such a way that they could have sprung from the united will of an entire people, and to regard every subject, in so far as he wishes to be a citizen, on the basis of whether he has conformed to that will."

But where does this universal law, this "united will of an entire people" come from? Why does it exist at all? Kant theorized that it did exist and that this collective unconscious force contained certain true principles. Moral laws were universal, Kant believed, whether or not a Supreme Being existed, and through reason, these laws would become apparent. We didn't make our laws randomly, Kant philosophized. The principles were out there in the ether somewhere, in the unconscious universal energy field. We like the idea of universal truths, whether they come from a higher power, the earth itself, or the collective unconsciousness of all sentient beings. These truths are something to contemplate during meditation. What are they? How can we further them?

Do We Think Together?

Have you ever felt so in-synch with someone that you could finish each other's sentences? Have you ever known, on an intuitive level, what someone was thinking?

If we are part of some greater, more complex, more spectacular whole, even if that whole consciousness—that earth consciousness—hasn't yet developed its awareness fully, perhaps the potential awareness of that whole is far beyond our individual potentials. Every step we make in our individual spiritual journeys might be combining to move humanity ever forward to some far greater understanding than we could ever reach on our own. Whether you believe that earth has a consciousness or that humankind has a collective unconscious or that God-consciousness directs humans who are listening, you can still progress in your spiritual journey with more than just yourself in mind.

In Buddhism, a *boddhisattva* is someone who is seeking enlightenment purely for the benefit of others, and that includes humankind as a whole. You can be a boddhisattva by serving your fellow sentient beings in whatever capacity best suits you and by making a connection with your fellow humans. Where would your brain be if your neurons didn't make connections with each other? Those connections are what give you intelligence and awareness. Be a neuron in the world community!

> **Bliss Byte**
>
> Consider the people in your life. What do they all have in common? What traits draw you to them and connect you to them? Do most of your loved ones share common traits? What does this say about who you are? Make a list of adjectives that describe the qualities you admire most in your family and friends. Take a look at the list. Use each word as a subject for meditation.

> **From A to Om**
>
> A **boddhisattva** is a follower of Buddhism and someone who serves not only humankind, but all sentient beings. Helping others is this person's spiritual quest, because he or she is already enlightened and awake. The boddhisattva chooses to remain of this world, delaying nirvana for the purpose of using compassion to ease the pain and suffering of others.

The World's Most Sacred Places

As we embrace the earth, the life on its surface, and the consciousness that ripples over the surface like a network of rivers and seas, some of us get filled with wanderlust. The more we know about the wide, wide world, the more we learn how much we all have in common. Yet some places have been seats of spiritual activity for millennia.

For anyone who cares to go exploring (as an armchair traveler, a virtual traveler on the Internet, or—for the intrepid—as a real traveler), the world is full of sacred places. You can learn all about these places and use that information to enrich and nourish your consciousness. We've presented several of the most spectacular spiritual hotspots around planet earth for your perusal in the following sections. Dream, imagine, do some research, and be inspired.

Adapting meditative poses, such as the one seen here in this Greek fertility statue, can be a profound way to incorporate your spiritual travels and discoveries into your daily meditation practice.

(Of course, if you really want to plan a trip abroad, do your research carefully and for the sake of safety, be sure to contact the U.S. Embassy for any country you are considering visiting before planning and attempting your travel. Some countries are politically volatile and might not be safe for travel at any given time.)

◆ **Yangon (Rangoon)** in southern Myanmar (formerly Burma, the country south of China and just northwest of Thailand) on the Yangon River is the home of the spectacular gold-plated Shwedagon Paya (pagoda), which stands high above the city on a hill. According to legend, the shrine was built to house eight of the Buddha's hairs. It is a beautiful place surrounded by statues, temples, shrines, images, and pavilions.

◆ **Dharamsala, India,** is the current home of the exiled Dalai Lama and a community of exiled Tibetan Buddhists. It has a Tibetan monastery and a school of Tibetan studies.

◆ The **T'aj Mahal** in Agra, India, has been described as the most extravagant monument ever built for love. When people think of India, they often think of the T'aj Mahal, which was built by Emperor Shah Jahan in honor of his second wife, who died in childbirth in 1631. The Emperor was so heartbroken by her death that it is said his hair turned gray overnight. Although not a place of worship (the T'aj Mahal has several false mosques and one true mosque, but it can't be used for worship because it faces the wrong way), its grandeur and spectacular beauty is inspirational.

◆ **Sukhothai-Si Satchanalai** is a magnificent abandoned ancient city in Thailand containing many Buddhist temples. *Sukhothai* literally means "dawn of happiness."

◆ The **Temple Gardens of Kyoto** in Japan are monuments to the concept of the Japanese garden. Kyoto is filled with sacred sites. The Higashiyama district offers the opportunity for quiet walks around its temples. The **Sanjusangen-do Temple** holds 1,001 statues of the Buddhist goddess of mercy. Northwest Kyoto has many beautiful Zen temples, including the **Kinkaku-ji Temple,** built in the twelfth century and burned to the ground in 1950, then rebuilt and completely covered in gold foil.

◆ Moving back west, **Jerusalem** contains the tombs of many of the Biblical patriarchs and lies at the foot of **Haram-ash Sharif/Temple Mount,** where Mohammed ascended to heaven and where God instructed Abraham to sacrifice his son. The **Dome of the Rock** mosque, Al-Aqsa Mosque, and Islamic Museum are on the Mount. The **Western Wall,** at the base, is the remains of the Jews' most holy shrine, the First Temple, now an open-air synagogue. Christians might also want to visit the **Church of the Holy Sepulchre,** built over the site where Jesus was supposedly crucified, buried, and resurrected. This church is the culmination of a walk down the **Via Dolorosa,** the route Jesus walked to crucifixion.

♦ **Luxor** is a city in Egypt built on the site of the ancient city of Thebes. **Luxor Temple,** built by Pharaoh Amenophis III, and the **Temples of Karnak** are on the site. The latter made up a primary place of worship in Thebian times.

> **CAUTION**
>
> **Relax** _____
>
> It is interesting that many holy cities, such as Luxor, are places of great spiritual insight—and also the sites of significant social unrest. This is perhaps an interesting subject for meditation on the powerful nature of spiritual places.

♦ Most people who visit Saudi Arabia are there for one reason: to make a pilgrimage to **Mecca,** the holy city of Islam. Mohammed was born in Mecca in the sixth century, and all Muslims are supposed to make a pilgrimage to Mecca once during their lifetimes—and that makes for a big crowd! The catch is, you can't visit Mecca unless you are a Muslim. **Taif,** located in the mountains above Mecca, can be visited by anyone.

♦ **Chartres Cathedral** in Paris, France, is the home of the Chartres labyrinth (see Chapter 14) through which seekers can walk, symbolically journeying into their own souls then back out again with new insights.

♦ **Vatican City** has its own head of state (who else but the pope?), its own postal service, its own money, media, train station, army, and tourist office. **St. Peter's Church** is there, as is the site of the original church built in 326 C.E. to honor the site of St. Peter's martyrdom and burial (the church was demolished in the early sixteenth century). The current church took 150 years to build and houses the spectacular Bernini altar and the work of Michelangelo, Raphael, and Bramante, among others. If your spiritual inspiration is art, don't miss the **Vatican Museums.**

♦ **Stonehenge,** that famous 5,000-year-old structure in rural England, consists of a ring of huge stones in a pattern set into the ground. The mystery of Stonehenge is how the 50-ton stones got to where they are from South Wales. For a less-touristy and jam-packed experience, check out the stones at **Avebury,** which are more accessible than Stonehenge and, according to some, even more impressive. Avebury's stones are dated from 2600 B.C.E. and include a stone dubbed the "Barber Surgeon Stone." Supposedly, a skeleton of a medieval traveling barber was found buried beneath the stone, which probably fell on him. Avebury (also the name of the village) is 30 miles east of Bath and just over 8 miles north of Stonehenge.

♦ Moving on to Central America, **Tikal** is a spectacular Mayan ruin in Guatemala, right in the middle of the jungle. The ruins include towering pyramids, plazas, an acropolis, temples, and a museum surrounded by real rain forest.

- **Palenque** is a Mayan ruin in Mexico. Palenque is also surrounded by jungle, and only 34 of the 500 Mayan buildings believed to be 1,500 years old have been excavated. All were built without metal tools, pack animals, or the wheel.

- **Mexico's Yucatán Peninsula** is considered by many to be the realm of the Maya, who live there today, in the same site as their ancestors. Mayan ruins can be found near Mérida at **Uxmal** and **Chichén Itzá.** Mayan ruins can also be found at Oaxaca, including Albán, Mitla, Yagul, and Cuilapan.

- In Lima, Peru (in South America), visit **Machu Picchu,** the "Lost City of the Incas," *the* must-see spiritual site on the continent, built by the Incas at the apex of their empire. On the Andes eastern slope, Machu Picchu rises 2,400 meters above a magnificent tropical forest. The pilgrimage to this site is filled with the splendor of ancient wonder and natural beauty.

- Arizona and New Mexico are filled with spiritual places of note. **Chaco Canyon,** an Anasazi (an-cient Native American) center of culture between 900 and 1130 C.E., contains approximately 30 ancient buildings of masonry, each containing hundreds of rooms. **Canyon de Chelly** and **Canyon del Muerto** are two spectacular can-yons in the heart of the Navajo nation that have provided shelter for Native Americans for 2,000 years. A trail runs to the bottom of Canyon de Chelly leading to the White House Ruins.

- **Mesa Verde** (Spanish for "green table") in Colorado is the first cultural park set aside by the U.S. National Park System in June 1906. Cliff dwellings and villages on the top of the mesa were built by ancestral Pueblo people between 600 and 1300 C.E. Mesa Verde National Park was also designated as a World Cultural Heritage Site in 1978.

Bliss Byte

One great way to keep a marriage or partnership strong and fueled with love is to remember at least once every day how the two of you are spiritually bonded. Let your mind transcend the mortgage, the kids, the daily routines, and all the other mundane things that bind you together. Get in touch with your deeper spiritual commitment, and you'll be better able to keep life, love, and expectations in perspective.

Meditations for Two or More

The strange and wonderful earth is full of strange and wonderful people, and, just like you, lots of them like to meditate. Although meditation seems like a solitary pursuit

CAUTION

Relax

Never underestimate the power of human touch. Holding hands without talking while walking together through nature is another great way to meditate together.

and is most effective when practiced alone, sometimes meditating with others will help keep you grounded and can also contribute to the fortification of a spiritual community. Group meditation might even help heal humanity by exponentially increasing the energy of love and peace in the world.

Try meditating with your life partner, your friend, your child, or a group containing a combination of friends and family. Here are a couple meditations to try.

Connecting the chakras through meditation with a partner.

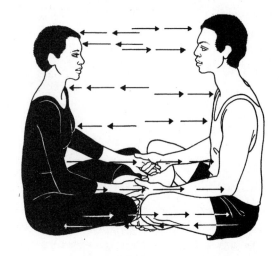

Bliss Byte

Sit next to your partner. Both of you close your eyes. Whisper into your partner's ear, "Who are you?" Let your partner respond. Continue asking softly these three simple words, "Who are you?" Wait patiently for responses. Continue asking. Continue discovering.

Put Your Heads Together

Practice shavasana (see Chapter 15) with a partner. Lie head-to-head so the crowns of your heads (your Thousand Petalled Lotuses) are touching. Don't speak. Simply lie in relaxed awareness for a pre-agreed period of time. Allow your energy to flow back and forth as it will, and allow yourself to feel the connection with your partner.

This exercise can also be practiced by more than two. Simply lie with heads touching, like spokes on a wheel. The wheel of life, perhaps? *Ommmmmmmm ...*

Breath of Peace Meditation

With a partner or in a group, sit facing each other or in a circle. Have everyone close his or her eyes and focus on the breath. As each person inhales, imagine inhaling the energy of the people in the room. Hold the breath in for several seconds, letting it combine with your own energy of love, compassion, and kindness, exhale this energy into the center of the circle. With your next inhale, imagine inhaling the living energy of everyone in your city. Combine it with your own energy of love, compassion, and kindness, exhale to center of room. Next, inhale the energy of everyone living in your state. Continue on, widening your circle—the country, the continent, the hemisphere, the world, the universe. With each breath, take in the energy of sentient beings in a wider and wider circle, combining it with your own energy of love, compassion, and kindness, and releasing it, unified, back into the universe. Finish with five minutes of contemplation on the power of a unified humanity bolstering each other toward evolution into a healed, more peaceful, intelligent, and spiritually enlightened planet.

The Healer Is You

Another way to expand the power and energy of your meditations beyond yourself is simply to keep humankind, societies across the globe, and the planet itself in mind during your meditation. When you meditate, spend some time consciously visualizing yourself sending positive healing energy out into the world so it showers over humankind like a healing rain. Send loving energy to the international community so that all countries and people might learn to coexist in harmony. Let your love, your optimism, and your positive energy influence the world, because it can. Expand your consciousness beyond the boundaries of yourself, and the evolving world and the evolving you will become one and the same.

Peace on the Journey

What a challenge and what a joy it is to be human and to be alive and conscious on the face of the planet this very moment. As we all journey through the labyrinth that is life on earth, moving toward and away from and back toward our own inner lights, we wish you a peaceful journey toward your own personal enlightenment. Your mind can change your own reality and quite possibly the reality of those around you. It can heal,

Bliss Byte

For a truly peaceful meditation, sit alone or with a partner or group and chant the mantra, "Om, shanti, shanti, shanti." *Shanti* means "peace," and *om* is, of course, that mantra-of-all-mantras meant to reflect the primal sound of the universe. The mantra can be interpreted as "Universal peace." (You could even say that, instead, if it makes you feel more comfortable.)

it can strengthen, it can energize, it can create, and it calm. Most of all, it can wake up and live.

We hope you will use meditation for all these reasons, to release the tension and stress of your life and to open the floodgates for the love and joy the universe has to offer you to come rushing in. Let meditation heal your pain, nurture your joy, and inspire you to serve your fellow human beings and your Mother Earth in the best way you can. Let meditation open that little window into your soul that wouldn't open until your mind grew quiet. Let meditation show you how to live, then do it: Live, live, live! We don't want you to waste one more minute of this precious life on this precious earth. Wake up with us. Let's change the world together. Let's meditate.

The Least You Need to Know

- Some people believe the earth is actually a living entity and that humans are one component of this entity. Others believe a collective unconscious governs our actions and imbues us with our internal morality.

- Being a working part of a conscious earth means we have the responsibility of caring for the earth as it cares for us and supporting all sentient beings who are part of the earth.

- Meditating with others could be a way to increase the energy of the collective unconscious.

- The world is filled with spiritual places we can learn about and experience, even if we never actually visit them.

- Your energy in meditation can heal and transform the world.

From A to Om: Glossary

acupressure   A technique originating in China that involves the stimulation of pressure points by pressing on them with fingers, elbows, palms, etc. for pain relief and healing. It works on the same theory as acupuncture but is less invasive.

acupuncture   A centuries-old technique that originated in China. Hair-thin needles are inserted into pressure points for pain relief and healing. The theory goes that by stimulating pressure points, acupuncture releases blocked areas and equalizes life-force energy, allowing the body to relieve its own pain and heal itself.

adrenal glands   Located at the top of each kidney, these glands produce special hormones in response to stress, such as adrenaline (also called epinephrine) and cortisol (also called hydrocortisone).

adrenaline   Also called epinephrine, adrenaline is a hormone released in the body in response to stress that prepares the body to react to a crisis by facilitating quicker response time, among other things.

affirmation   A verbalized desire stated in positive terms.

ahimsa   The yoga abstinence of nonviolence.

ajna chakra   *See* urna.

allopathic medicine   The conventional, mainstream Western approach to health care, based on treating symptoms and isolating a specific disorder rather than treating the whole person.

alpha waves   Brain waves that cycle up and down on an EEG about 8 to 12 times per second and usually correspond with a drowsy state or, in meditation, a very relaxed yet alert state.

altar   A natural or constructed platform or table used for sacred purposes, upon which sacred objects can be placed to aid in worship.

Anapanasati Sutta   *See Sutra on the Full Awareness of Breathing.*

angina   Chest pain or discomfort due to some degree of obstruction in the coronary arteries, sometimes caused by any condition in which the heart has to work harder, such as physical or emotional stress, strain, or exertion.

aparigraha   The yoga abstinence against greed.

archetypes   Symbols and concepts common to all human experience that arise separately in different cultures and times. Some common archetypes of human experience are the Anima and Animus (female and male spirits, respectively), the Wise Old Man, the Earth Mother, Darkness, and the Trickster.

aromatherapy   The therapeutic use of essential oils, either applied to the skin or inhaled, for healing and mood alteration. Essential oils are aromatic oils distilled from plant sources such as flowers, leaves, and bark. Pure essential oils are produced by steam distillation.

arteriosclerosis   A condition in which the arteries become hardened and/or lose elasticity, sometimes resulting in small cracks in artery walls.

artherosclerosis   A condition in which fatty deposits accumulate inside artery walls. These deposits often collect in the cracks caused by arteriosclerosis. When arteries become blocked by deposits or blood clots, heart attacks or strokes might result.

asanas   The postures or exercises of yoga designed to help the yogi master control of the body.

asteya   The yoga abstinence against stealing.

astral body   The realm of mind and emotions, extending slightly beyond the physical body.

aum   *See* om.

aura   The colored halolike visual result of the vibrations that surround every material object, including people, plants, animals, trees, and inanimate objects.

auric sight   The ability to see auras.

autonomic nervous system   The part of the nervous system responsible for bodily functions such as heartbeat, blood pressure, and digestion.

Ayurveda   From the Sanskrit roots *ayus*, meaning "life" and *veda*, meaning "knowledge" or "science," Ayurveda is an ancient system of health with the purpose of maximizing human potential and defying sickness and aging through specific healing techniques including the prescription of certain foods, herbs, exercises, massages, and meditations.

bandhas   Literally "to bind" or "to lock," these muscular locks are used during yoga postures and breathing exercises to intensify the energy of prana in the body. The three primary bandhas are mula bandha (at the perineum), uddiyani bandha (at the navel), and jalandhara bandha (behind the chin).

bardo   The intermediate state between death and rebirth into the next life, according to reincarnation philosophy.

Bardo Thödol   An instruction manual for death meant to be read to someone as they die and move into the bardo so they know what to do. According to this book, which gives a detailed explanation of what happens after death, the soul moves through several stages in the bardo, then back through the same stages toward rebirth. Also called the *Tibetan Book of the Dead*.

beta waves   Brain waves that cycle between 13 and about 30 cycles per second, sometimes associated with deep meditative states.

Bhakti Yoga   *See* yoga.

bija   The essence of the mantra that gives the mantra its energy.

biofeedback   A technique through which a person learns to control various internal processes, such as brain waves or blood pressure, by seeing them displayed on a monitor.

bliss sheath   The mind-body layer consisting of divine energy that houses our potential for inner peace and happiness. It is part of the causal body.

boddhisattva   Someone who is seeking enlightenment purely for the benefit of others. Boddhisattvas devote their lives to the service of humankind, and sometimes even defer their own personal spiritual quest to better serve humankind as a whole.

botanicals   Formulas made from plant sources, which include herbs, herbal combinations, and substances made from various parts of plants.

brahmacharya   The yoga abstinence involving the control of desire and lust.

Buddha   Literally "enlightened one," the term refers to anyone who has achieved enlightenment. However, most people think of a man named Siddhartha Gautama who lived in India in the sixth century B.C.E. Siddhartha Gautama was a prince who renounced his privileged life in search of truth and attained enlightenment at age 35. He spent the next 50 years teaching and traveling throughout India.

Buddhism   The religion based on the teachings of Siddhartha Gautama, Buddhism comes in many forms, but Zen Buddhism is probably the most well known in the West. Known as Ch'an Buddhism in China before reaching Japan in the second century, Zen Buddhism's aim is to achieve enlightenment through meditation, also called zazen (other forms of Buddhism advocate reaching enlightenment in other ways, such as service to mankind or study of sacred texts).

causal body   The realm of the spirit, extending slightly beyond the astral body.

Ch'an Buddhism   The Chinese form of Zen Buddhism.

chakras Psychospiritual energy centers in the body. The seven major chakras are called different things by different people; in this book, we refer to them as the Saturn chakra, the Jupiter chakra, the Mars chakra, the Venus chakra, the Mercury chakra, the Sun chakra, and the Thousand Petalled Lotus chakra.

chi (also *c'hi* or *Qi*) The Chinese word for "life-force energy."

chi kung *See* QiGong.

Chinese medicine Also called traditional Chinese medicine or TCM, Chinese medicine is a complex subject with many aspects, including the balance of forces within the body. The branches of Chinese medicine are meditation, astrology and geomancy, martial arts, diet, massage, acupuncture, moxibustion (burning herbs on the surface of the skin to stimulate healing), and herbal medicine.

clairvoyance The psychic ability to perceive things that can't be seen physically.

collective unconscious A concept developed by Carl Jung, one of Sigmund Freud's earliest colleagues and the founder of the school of analytical psychology. According to Jung, everyone has a personal unconscious containing the results of the individual's life experiences and also a collective unconscious, which contains experiences of the entire human race. The collective unconscious contains archetypes or basic ideas common to all people throughout time, and these archetypes can affect our behavior as intuition. It can also be viewed as an unconscious connection between all people of all times.

cortisol Also called hydrocortisone, this hormone is released in the body in response to stress and prepares the body to react in a crisis by providing improved healing action, among other things.

creative visualization A meditative technique in which the meditator imagines that the conditions or things he or she desires are already manifest, helping bring those conditions into being.

Dalai Lama Believed by Tibetan Buddhists to be a reincarnation of the Buddha; when a Dalai Lama dies, his soul is thought to enter a new life, who, after being identified by traditional tests, will become the next Dalai Lama.

delta waves Brain waves that cycle between one half to two times per second, and usually correspond with deep sleep.

Descartes, René (1596–1650) A French philosopher and mathematician who is sometimes called the father of modern philosophy. Descartes attempted to apply rational, inductive reasoning to philosophy using principles inherent in science and math.

devata The individual aspect of God associated with the mantra.

dharana The technique of orienting the mind toward a single point in order to cultivate concentration.

dharma A universal force or movement toward the good. It is sometimes translated as "duty" or "ethics," but is a force that exists apart from humans, as opposed to a moral code humans devised.

dhyana   The Sanskrit word for "meditation," referring to the process of quieting the mind to free it from preconceptions, illusions, and attachments.

dikenga   A symbol of the Congo religion consisting of a circle with a cross in the middle.

distance intentionality   A concept that refers to directing an intention toward something at a distance. Prayer is one example.

Eightfold Path   A system of standards and guidelines for living (and eventually, for attaining enlightenment) developed by the Indian sage Patanjali in his written text, the *Yoga Sutras*.

enlightenment   Also known as samadhi in Hinduism and nirvana or satori in Buddhism, enlightenment is that perfect state of supreme bliss in which the self is completely absorbed into a sense of oneness with the universe.

feng shui   The ancient Chinese art of placement. It involves arranging interior spaces and placing houses and buildings within a landscape to best facilitate the flow of energy and ensure health, prosperity, wisdom, and other positive qualities to the inhabitants.

fight-or-flight reaction   The body's response to extreme stress, allowing it to react more quickly and with greater strength and speed so it can fight or flee from a perceived threat.

five sheaths of existence   The sublayers of the subtle body, including the physical sheath, vital sheath, mind sheath, intellect sheath, and bliss sheath.

flow   A state of total concentration leading to complete absorption in an activity, whether sports, creative pursuits, work, or even working a crossword puzzle.

folk medicine   A return to true traditional healing methods originating in different countries at a local level, including the use of herbs and foods in various forms as medicine.

Freud, Sigmund (1856–1939)   An Austrian physician, neurologist, and the founder of psychoanalysis, a technique of talk therapy for investigating unconscious mental processes and treating psychological disorders and illnesses.

Gaia   The Greek name for the earth goddess who produced all life.

gamma waves   Brain waves that cycle faster than 30 cycles per second and are sometimes associated with advanced stages of meditation.

gassho   A Buddhist hand position in which the hands are held together in front of the chest as if in prayer.

Gautama, Siddhartha   *See* Buddha.

Goddess   The feminine principle in the universe, sometimes referred to as Mother Earth or represented by the great goddesses of mythology such as Athena, Artemis, or Persephone.

guided imagery   A meditation facilitated by another person (or your own voice on a tape).

guru   A personal spiritual advisor who assists in the attainment of enlightenment. The Sanskrit word literally means "dispeller of darkness."

Hahn, Thich Nhat   An exiled Vietnamese monk and peace activist who is one of the foremost contemporary proponents of mindfulness.

harmonics   Also called overtones, harmonics are a phenomenon connected with sound, in which faint higher tones, which are mathematical ratios of the base tone, can be heard when a tone is sounded.

Hatha Yoga   One form of yoga that emphasizes physical postures or positions, called asanas, for increased health and awareness.

hemoglobin   A molecule in red blood cells responsible for carrying oxygen from the lungs to the tissues and carbon dioxide from the tissues back to the lungs.

herbalism   The treatment of disease with herbs.

herbs   Plants used for medicinal or therapeutic purposes (and also for cooking).

holistic medicine   Sometimes called alternative medicine or natural medicine, this type of health care involves a whole mind-body approach to health, emphasizing preventive medicine and often effective at relieving chronic conditions such as recurrent colds, headaches, arthritis, and even cancer.

holotropic breathwork   A psychospiritual bodywork technique developed by Stanislav Grof, M.D., and his wife, Christina, in 1976. It combines rapid breathing with loud music and is meant to invoke an alternate state of consciousness that loosens psychological barriers and frees repressed memories and emotions.

homeopathy   A subtle medical therapy based on the idea that "like cures like"— remedies that would cause certain symptoms are given to cure those symptoms.

homeostasis   The tendency of a system (such as a body, a group, or an ecosystem) to maintain an equilibrium or balanced state.

hyperventilation   "Overbreathing," or breathing too rapidly and shallowly. It is characterized by a feeling of not being able to get enough air, as well as dizziness, racing heart, fainting, and muscle cramps.

hypnogogic state   The transitional state between waking and sleeping when the mind is particularly open to suggestions or images from the unconscious, and the individual might have strange visual, aural, or tactile "experiences" or hallucinations.

hypnopompic state   The transitional state between sleeping and waking when the mind is particularly open to suggestions or images from the unconscious, and the individual might have strange visual, aural, or tactile "experiences" or hallucinations.

insight meditation   *See* Vipassana meditation.

intellect sheath   The mind-body layer consisting of higher understanding and unclouded thought, extending slightly beyond the mind sheath. It is part of the causal body.

ishvara-pranidhana   The yoga observance of devotion.

jalandhara bandha   A yogic muscular lock behind the chin, used to intensify the energy of prana.

Jnana Yoga   *See* yoga.

Jung, Carl (1875–1961)   A Swiss psychiatrist who founded the analytical school of psychology. Jung coined many common psychological terms used today, such as "complexes" (as in "inferiority complex") and the notion of extroverts and introverts. He believed dreams were attempts to work toward wholeness by integrating the different levels of the unconscious.

Jupiter chakra   Psychospiritual energy center behind the lower abdomen, the source of creative energy.

Kant, Immanuel (1724–1804)   A German philosopher whom many consider the most influential thinker of modern times. Kant believed that reason would always lead the individual to right action, and that every individual should be given freedom of self-government because this freedom would allow individuals to act according to universal laws, which could be realized through reason.

karma   A Sanskrit word referring to the law of cause and effect, or universal balance. Everything you do, say, or think has an immediate effect on the universe that will reverberate back to you in some way.

Karma Yoga   *See* yoga.

ensho   Also called insight-wisdom, kensho is a sudden-understanding experience of seeing into the essence of things. It is considered a step toward true enlightenment.

ki   The Japanese word for life-force energy.

kilaka   The force required by the yogi to persist in working with the mantra.

Kirlian photography   A type of photography that allows energy fields or auras to be seen on film. During the 1940s, a Russian photographer named Kirlian developed the technique, which proved to many the existence of auras.

koan   A short question, riddle, or verbal illustration meant to demonstrate a Zen realization. Because words are contrary to Zen realizations, however, koans don't make sense on the surface. The point is to move your mind into a different, enlightened way of seeing.

kundalini   Literally meaning "she who is coiled," kundalini refers to an energy force in the body that lies inactive at the base of the spine but can be awakened. Often compared to a sleeping snake, when awakened it is said to travel up through the chakras to the crown of the head, where it can effect spiritual changes such as enlightenment and even, according to some, physical changes in the body, such as the ability to control previously involuntary bodily functions. It is the energy of self-actualization.

Kundalini Yoga   A mystical form of yoga centered around awakening and employing kundalini energy.

laughing meditation   A form of meditation in which the meditator laughs. In India, large groups of people gather together in the streets, make funny faces, and laugh together. Some advocate waking up each morning and laughing for five minutes before the day begins. The laughter may be forced at first but will soon become genuine as you realize how wonderfully funny life can be.

life-force energy   Energy that animates the body and the universe, and which, when unblocked and properly directed, can help the body to heal itself. Also called *chi*, *ch'i*, *Qi*, *ki*, *prana*, *pneuma*, and *rlun*.

lucid dreaming   The conscious awareness that you are dreaming.

Maharishi Mahesh Yogi   An Indian swami who came to the United States in 1955 after graduating from Allahabad University with a degree in physics, studying for 13 years with Swami Brahmananda Saraswati (a world-famous teacher) and spending two years in the Himalayas in silence. In the 1960s, the Maharishi had many celebrities as students, including The Beatles and The Beach Boys.

mala   Beads used to keep track of recited mantras. Malas contain 108 beads, including a larger bead called the meru.

mandala   A beautiful, usually circular geometric design that draws the eye to its center and can be used as a point of focus in meditation.

mantra   From the root *man*, meaning "to think," and *trai*, meaning "to protect or free from the bondage of the phenomenal world." It is a sacred sound or combination of sounds chanted during meditation that resonate in the body and is meant to evoke certain energies.

Mars chakra   Psychospiritual energy center behind the navel, the source of action energy.

meditation   From the Indian Sanskrit word *medha*, which can be translated as "doing the wisdom," and from the Latin root *meditari*, which means "to muse or ponder," meditation can refer to many different techniques meant to tone and/or relax the mind.

Mercury chakra   Psychospiritual energy center in the throat, the source of communication energy.

meru   *See* mala.

mind sheath   The mind-body layer consisting of emotions and thoughts, extending slightly beyond the vital sheath. It is part of the astral body.

mind-body, also **mindbody**   The whole self. The term carries with it the connotation that mind and body are inextricably linked and what affects, benefits, changes, or hurts one does the same for the other.

mindfulness   A form of meditation that was originally developed in the Buddhist traditions of Asia but is practiced today by many, from meditators in monasteries to physicians in stress-reduction clinics. Mindfulness can be defined as awareness of each moment as it occurs and a purposeful attention.

moxibustion   Burning herbs on the surface of the skin to stimulate healing.

mudra   A hand position that redirects energy emitted from the fingertips back into the mind-body by connecting the fingers and hands to each other in different ways.

mula bandha   A yogic muscular lock at the perineum, used to intensify the energy of prana.

mysticism   The belief in direct experience of God, universal consciousness, or intuitive truth.

Nada Yoga   The yoga of sound and sound vibrations.

nadis   Internal channels or pathways prana uses to flow through the body and through the chakras.

neurons   Nerve cells.

neurotransmitters   The chemicals produced in nerve cells that travel from one nerve cell to another, delivering marching orders from the brain to the rest of the body.

nirvana   The Buddhist term for the state of absolute bliss attained upon recognition that the self is an illusion and nonexistent.

niyamas   Five yoga observances or personal disciplines: (1) *shauca* means "purity," or "inner and outer cleanliness"; (2) *santosha* means "contentment"; (3) *tapas* means "self-discipline"; (4) *svadhyaya* means "self-study"; and (5) *ishvara-pranidhana* means "devotion."

om   Sometimes spelled aum, this Sanskrit word is the sound of the vibration of the universe according to yogic thought, and it is said that the entire world is manifested from this one sound. It is often used in meditation to help center and clear the mind so the mind-body can become more conscious.

overtones   *See* harmonics.

paradoxical sleep   *See* REM sleep.

parapsychologist   Someone who studies psychic phenomena.

Patanjali   Probably born between 200 B.C.E. and 400 C.E., Patanjali was an Indian sage and the author of the *Yoga Sutras*, a collection of succinct aphorisms in Sanskrit that have largely defined the modern practice of yoga.

physical body   The gross body we can see and touch.

physical sheath   The mind-body layer consisting of the physical body.

pilgrimage   A journey to a holy place.

placebo effect   The idea that if someone believes something, such as a pill, will work to cure a condition, the condition will seem to be cured even if the "cure" couldn't have had any direct affect.

pneuma   The ancient Greek word for "life-force energy."

prana   The Sanskrit word for the life-force energy that animates all physical matter, including the human body, and is taken into the body through the breath.

pranayama   The practice of breathing exercises designed to help master control of the breath and to infuse the body with prana.

pratyahara   The practice of withdrawing the senses and focusing inward.

pressure points   Points along the energy channels in the body where energy tends to pool or get blocked. Pressing, massaging, or otherwise manipulating these points can help to rejuvenate energy flows through the body, facilitating the body's ability to balance and heal itself.

psi   Psychic phenomena.

psychic   To be sensitive to forces beyond the physical world. Psychic phenomena is also sometimes called psi.

QiGong   Also called chi kung, QiGong means "energy skill" and is sometimes translated as "empowerment." It is a 5,000-year-old system of health and life-force energy maintenance and also a healing art. It is the forerunner of tai chi and the other martial arts systems from China. QiGong typically exists in three forms: martial, medical, and spiritual.

raga   The main melody line of a mantra, which should be imitated exactly to preserve the specific vibration of the mantra.

Raja Yoga   *See* yoga.

rajasic   A quality characterized by anxiety and agitation, according to yogic thought.

Reiki   A type of bodywork that emphasizes the manipulation of life-force energy through the chakras. The Reiki practitioner places his or her hands on the receiver over the chakras, working along the front and the back of the body.

reincarnation   The belief that the soul is reborn over and over in different bodies as it struggles to reach enlightenment. Once enlightenment, or true understanding, is achieved, the soul is released from the cycle of rebirth.

REM sleep   Sometimes called paradoxical sleep, REM sleep (or rapid eye movement sleep) is the stage of sleep in which dreams occur. During this stage, brain waves resemble waking brain waves, yet muscles are completely relaxed, producing a paralyzing effect (called atonia).

Rinzai Zen   A sect of Zen Buddhism that employs the use of koans during zazen.

Rishi   The ancient seer to whom the concept of the mantra was originally revealed thousands of years ago.

rlun   The Tibetan word for life-force energy.

rosary   A string of beads divided into different groups, with different short prayers, such as the Hail Mary, the Lord's Prayer, and the Fatima prayer, corresponding with each group, in the Catholic faith. Also, the prayers associated with these beads.

sakti   The dynamic creation energy released in the yogi through repetition of the mantra.

samadhi   *See* enlightenment.

santosha   The yoga observance of contentment.

satori   *See* enlightenment.

sattvic   A quality characterized by vitality, strength, and peace of mind, according to yogic thought.

Saturn chakra   Psychospiritual energy center at the base of the spine, the source of dormant, potential, or kundalini energy.

satya   The yoga abstinence involving truthfulness.

Saucha   The yoga niyama (observance) of purity.

sentient beings   All life forms who share the characteristic of consciousness and the ability to perceive.

serotonin   A neurotransmitter, a chemical in your brain responsible for transmitting messages, that has a calming, relaxing effect and can cause drowsiness.

shavasana   Literally "corpse pose," is a yoga pose designed to bring the body into total, conscious relaxation.

smudge stick   A bundle of dried herbs (sage is one of the most common) tied together and burned for the purpose of purification.

smudging   A burning and purification process of the Native American tradition involving the burning of smudge sticks.

Soto Zen   A sect of Zen Buddhism that employs a "just sitting" method in zazen, based on the idea that sitting like the Buddha when he attained enlightenment will eventually bring about enlightenment.

stream of consciousness   The unchecked flow of thoughts, either spoken or written, as a literary technique designed to portray the preconscious impressions of the mind before they can be logically arranged. Therefore, stream-of-consciousness expression usually appears nonsensical, lacking cohesiveness and logical sequence.

subtle body   The whole self, including all its various layers and energy fields, which extends slightly beyond the physical body.

Sun chakra   Psychospiritual energy center behind the forehead, the source of intuitive energy. *See also* urna.

sutra A Sanskrit term translated as "simple truth," "thread," or "bare bones." In yoga philosophy, a sutra is a precept or maxim, or a collection of these, such as Patajali's *Yoga Sutras*. Sutras use the fewest words to convey the teaching. In Buddhism, a sutra is a scriptural narrative, usually a discourse of the Buddha, such as in the *Sutra on the Full Awareness of Breathing*, where a disciple recounts a sermon of the Buddha.

Sutra on the Full Awareness of Breathing An ancient Buddhist text, also called the *Anapanasati Sutta*, considered by many to be among the most important meditation texts in existence. In this sutra, a disciple of the Buddha tells the story of the Buddha instructing his disciples on the importance of breathing in full awareness, which will eventually "lead to the perfect accomplishment of true understanding and complete liberation."

svadhyaya The yoga observance of self-study.

swami A title of respect for a spiritual person who has attained a certain level of understanding and wisdom.

tai chi Meaning "way of the fist," tai chi is a martial arts system and fitness method developed from QiGong. Today, tai chi has evolved from its martial arts origins into a practice of movement meditation for peaceful purposes.

tamasic A quality characterized by lethargy and inactivity, according to yogic thought.

Taoism Both a religion and a philosophy in China that advocates following the Tao, or the way of nature (although the word *Tao* is translated in many different ways, including "Way of the Cosmos," "Way of Heaven," "Way," "One," or "Path"). Simplicity, unity of all things, and becoming one with the Tao are all concepts of Taoism.

tapas The yoga observance of self-discipline.

TCM (traditional Chinese medicine) *See* Chinese medicine.

10 fetters According to Zen Buddhism, 10 fetters exist that keep us from true freedom and enlightenment: (1) the illusion of ego, (2) skepticism, (3) attachment to ritual, (4) the delusion of the senses, (5) ill will, (6) materialism, (7) desire for an immaterial life, (8) arrogance, (9) restlessness, and (10) ignorance of the true nature of reality. To be free of these 10 fetters leads to satori, or enlightenment.

10 perfections According to Zen Buddhism, 10 perfections exist that are qualities of an enlightened person and also are goals for the enlightened-to-be: (1) generosity, (2) morality, (3) renunciation, (4) wisdom, (5) energy, (6) patience, (7) truthfulness, (8) resolution, (9) lovingkindness, and (10) a calm mind.

Tenzin Gyatso The current and fourteenth Dalai Lama, who was forced into exile in India on March 16, 1959, by the Communist Chinese government occupying Tibet. In 1989, he received the Nobel Peace Price for leading nonviolent opposition to Chinese rule of Tibet.

Teresa of Avila, Saint (1515–1582)   A Carmelite nun and Christian mystic from Spain who founded the religious order of the Discalced (also called Barefoot) Carmelite nuns, who enforced strict observance of the original, severe Carmelite rules at the convent. Teresa's writings, all published posthumously, are still read today. Teresa was canonized in 1622; she was proclaimed a Doctor of the Church (the first woman to receive this honor) in 1970.

therapeutic touch (TT)   A controversial technique in which patients are treated by practitioners who never touch them. In TT, the practitioner's hands usually stay about four to six inches above the skin of the receiver, touching and manipulating the energy field, though not the body itself.

theta waves   Brain waves that cycle between three to seven times per second and usually correspond with light sleep or deep meditation.

Thousand Petalled Lotus chakra   Psychospiritual energy center at the crown of the head, the source of enlightenment energy.

Tibetan Book of the Dead   *See Bardo Thödol.*

TM (Transcendental Meditation)   *See* Transcendental Meditation.

traditional Chinese medicine (TCM)   *See* Chinese medicine.

Transcendental Meditation (TM)   Transcendental Meditation is a mantra-based form of meditation introduced to the West by the Maharishi Mahesh Yogi. Today, TM is the most studied form of meditation. More than 4,000 pages in more than 100 scientific journals have appeared describing scientific studies on the effects of TM.

trataka   A yogic eye exercise/meditation involving gazing at a candle or flame and designed to strengthen the inner vision.

tryptophan   An amino acid that comes from protein from the food we eat.

tyrosine   An amino acid that comes from protein from the food we eat.

uddiyani bandha   A yogic muscular lock at the navel, used to intensify the energy of prana.

unconscious mind   The thoughts, feelings, desires, and impulses of which the individual is unaware but that influence behavior.

urna   The third eye, or area of the forehead between and about an inch or two above the eyes within your head, thought to be an energy source and the source of unclouded perception. In Sanskrit, the spot is called the ajna chakra. In yoga, it is also sometimes called the Sun chakra.

Venus chakra   Psychospiritual energy center behind the heart, the source of compassionate energy.

vinyasa   A steady flow of connected yoga postures linked with breathing exercises in a continuous movement.

vipassana meditation   Also called insight meditation, *vipassana* means "insight," and the technique is considered a meditation method Buddha himself taught. It is simple and requires only mindful awareness and labeling of thoughts, feelings, and emotions as they are observed.

vital sheath   The mindbody layer consisting of life-force energy surrounding and flowing through and from the body. It is part of the astral body.

yamas   Five yoga abstinences or forms of discipline that purify the body and mind: (1) *ahimsa* means "nonviolence"; (2) *satya* means "truthfulness"; (3) *asteya* means "not stealing"; (4) *brahmacharya* means "chastity" or "nonlust"; and (5) *aparigraha* means "nongreed."

yang   *See* yin/yang.

yantra   A linear symbol similar to a mandala, often with a symbol or written words in the center.

yin   *See* yin/yang.

yin/yang   Two interconnected forces inherent in all things. Some things are more yin, such as the moon, the body, and the female nature. Some things are more yang, such as the sun, the mind, and the male nature. Yin and yang work together to keep the universe balanced.

yoga   From the Sanskrit root *yuj*, meaning "to yoke or join together," yoga is a 5,000-year-old method of mind-body health with the goal of enlightenment. It has many "paths" or methods, including Karma Yoga, which emphasizes action and service to others; Bhakti Yoga, which emphasizes love of God; Jnana Yoga, which emphasizes intellectual striving; and Raja Yoga, sometimes called the "King of Yogas," which emphasizes techniques for controlling both mind and body. These techniques include exercises, breathing and relaxation techniques, and meditation.

yogi   Someone who practices yoga.

zabuton   A thick meditation mat or small futon placed under the zafu. These items make meditation more comfortable and help put the body into a three-point or tripod position for greater stability.

zafu   A small pillow for sitting during zazen.

zazen   The Japanese word for the Zen Buddhist technique of seated meditation.

Zen Buddhism   A form of Buddhism emphasizing meditation as a way to achieve enlightenment.

zendo   A Zen meditation hall.

In Search of Nirvana: Suggested Reading

Adamson, Eve, and Linda Horning, R.D. *The Complete Idiot's Guide to Fasting*. Indianapolis: Alpha Books, 2002.

Andrews, Ted. *How to Uncover Your Past Lives*. St. Paul: Llewellyn Publications, 1997.

Artress, Lauren. *Walking a Sacred Path: Rediscovering the Labyrinth as a Spiritual Tool*. New York: Riverhead Books, 1995.

Austin, James, M.D. *Zen and the Brain*. Cambridge: MIT Press, 1998.

Ballentine, Rudolph, M.D. *Radical Healing*. New York: Three Rivers Press, 1999.

Benson, Herbert, M.D. *The Relaxation Response*. New York: Avon Books, 1975.

Brauen, Martin. *The Mandala: Sacred Circle in Tibetan Buddhism*. Boston: Shambhala, 1997.

Budilovsky, Joan, and Eve Adamson. *The Complete Idiot's Guide to Massage*. Indiana-polis: Alpha Books, 1998.

———. *The Complete Idiot's Guide to Yoga Illustrated, Third Edition*. Indianapolis: Alpha Books, 2003.

Cameron, Julia. *The Vein of Gold: A Journey to Your Creative Heart*. New York: Jeremy P. Tarcher/Putnam, 1996.

———. *The Artist's Way: A Spiritual Path to Higher Creativity*. New York: Jeremy P. Tarcher/Putnam, 1992.

Carradine, David, and David Nakahara. *David Carradine's Introduction to Chi Kung.* New York: Henry Holt and Company, 1997.

Chearney, Lee Ann. *Visits: Caring for an Aging Parent: Reflections and Advice.* New York: Three Rivers Press, 1998.

Chih-I, Thomas Cleary, trans. *Stopping and Seeing.* Boston: Shambhala, 1997.

Chopra, Deepak, M.D. *Ageless Body Timeless Mind.* New York: Harmony Books, 1993.

———. *Creating Health, Revised Edition.* Boston: Houghton Mifflin Co., 1991.

———. *Perfect Health.* New York: Harmony Books, 1991.

Cloutier, Marissa, M.S., R.D., Deborah S. Romaine, and Eve Adamson. *Beef Busters: Less Beef, Better Health!* Avon, MA: Adams Media Corporation, 2002.

Cortis, Bruno, M.D. *Heart and Soul.* New York: Pocket Books, 1995.

Crompton, Paul. *Tai Chi: A Practical Introduction.* Boston: Element Books, 1998.

Csikszentmihalyi, Mihaly. *Flow: The Psychology of Optimal Experience.* New York: HarperCollins, 1990.

Dalai Lama of Tibet. *Awakening the Mind, Lightening the Heart.* San Francisco: Harper San Francisco, 1995.

Dalai Lama of Tibet, *The Good Heart.* Boston: Wisdom Publications, 1998.

Dalai Lama of Tibet, and Howard C. Cutler, M.D. *The Art of Happiness: A Handbook for Living.* New York: Riverhead Books, 1998.

Davich, Victor N. *The Best Guide to Meditation.* Los Angeles: Renaissance Books, 1998.

DeMello, Anthony. *Awakenings: Conversations with the Master, Revised Edition.* Chicago: Loyola Press, 1998.

———. *Taking Flight: A Book of Story Meditations.* New York: Image Books, 1986.

———. *Wellspring: A Book of Spiritual Exercises.* New York: Image Books, 1990.

Epstein, Mark, M.D. *Going to Pieces Without Falling Apart: A Buddhist Perspective on Wholeness.* New York: Broadway Books, 1998.

Farhi, Donna. *The Breathing Book.* New York: Henry Holt and Company, 1996.

Feldman, Gail, Ph.D., and Katherine A. Gleason. *Releasing the Goddess Within.* Indianapolis: Alpha Books, 2003.

Franck, Frederick. *Zen Seeing, Zen Drawing.* New York: Bantam Books, 1993.

Fromm, Erich. *The Art of Loving.* New York: Harper and Row, 1956.

Gandhi, Mahatma. *All Men Are Brothers.* India: Navajivan Publishing, 1960.

Goddard, Dwight, ed. *A Buddhist Bible.* Boston: Beacon Press, 1938, 1966, 1970.

Goldman, Jonathan. *Healing Sounds: The Power of Harmonics.* Rockport, MA: Element Books Limited, 1997.

Goleman, Daniel. *Emotional Intelligence.* New York: Bantam Books, 1995.

Goleman, Daniel, and Joel Gurin, eds. *Mind Body Medicine.* Yonkers, NY: Consumer Reports Books, 1993.

Gore, Belinda. *Ecstatic Body Postures.* Santa Fe: Bear and Company, 1995.

Greeson, Janet, Ph.D. *It's Not What You're Eating, It's What's Eating You.* New York: Pocket Books, 1990.

Hanh, Thich Nhat. *Anger: Wisdom for Cooling the Flames.* New York: Riverhead Books, 2001.

———. *Breathe! You Are Alive.* Berkeley, CA: Parallax Press, 1996.

———. *The Miracle of Mindfulness.* Boston: Beacon Press, 1987.

———. *Peace Is Every Step.* New York: Bantam, 1991.

Herrigal, Eugen. *Zen in the Art of Archery.* New York: Vintage Books, 1953, 1981.

Iyengar, BKS. *Yoga: The Path to Holistic Health.* New York: DK Publishing, 2001.

Kabat-Zinn, Jon, Ph.D. *Full Catastrophe Living.* New York: Dell Publishing, 1990.

Kübler-Ross, Elisabeth, M.D. *On Death and Dying.* New York: Touchstone, 1997.

Langer, Ellen J. *Mind-Fulness.* Reading, MA: Addison-Wesley, 1989.

Levine, Stephen. *Guided Meditations, Explorations and Healings.* New York: Anchor Books, 1991.

Lewis, J. R. *The Dream Encyclopedia.* Washington, D.C.: Visible Ink Press, 1995.

Linn, Denise. *Quest: A Guide for Creating Your Own Vision Quest.* New York: Ballantine Books, 1997.

———. *Sacred Space: Clearing and Enhancing the Energy of Your Home.* New York: Ballantine Books, 1995.

Luk, Charles. *The Secrets of Chinese Meditation.* York Beach, ME: Samuel Weiser, Inc., 1994.

Maharishi Mahesh Yogi. *Science of Being and Art of Living: Transcendental Meditation.* New York: Meridian, 1995.

McClain, Gary, Ph.D., and Eve Adamson. *The Complete Idiot's Guide to Zen Living.* Indianapolis: Alpha Books, 2001.

Moore, Thomas. *Care of the Soul.* New York: HarperCollins, 1992.

Moyers, Bill. *Healing and the Mind.* New York: Doubleday, 1993.

Osho. *Meditation: The First and Last Freedom.* New York: St. Martin's Griffin, 1996.

Pliskin, Marci, and Shari L. Just. *The Complete Idiot's Guide to Interpreting Your Dreams.* Indianapolis: Alpha Books, 1998.

Reid, Daniel. *Traditional Chinese Medicine.* Boston: Shambhala, 1996.

Rama, Swami, Ballentine, Rudolph, M.D., and Ajaya Swami, Ph.D. *Yoga and Psychotherapy The Evolution of Consciousness.* Pennsylvania: Himalayan Institute, 1976.

Reps, Paul, and Nyogen Senzaki, compilers. *Zen Flesh, Zen Bones: A Collection of Zen and Pre-Zen Writings.* Boston: Tuttle Publishing, 1957, 1985, 1998.

Rinpoche, Sogyal. *The Tibetan Book of Living and Dying.* San Francisco: HarperCollins, 1992.

Roberts, Elizabeth, and Elias Amidon, eds. *Life Prayers.* San Francisco: HarperCollins, 1996.

Robinson, Lynn, and Lavonne Carlson-Finnerty. *The Complete Idiot's Guide to Being Psychic.* Indianapolis: Alpha Books, 1998.

Rothfeld, Glenn, M.D., and Suzanne LeVert. *Ginkgo Biloba.* New York: Dell, 1998.

Samuels, Michael, and Mary Rockwood Lane. *Creative Healing.* San Francisco: Harper San Francisco, 1998.

Schubert, William H. *CURRICULUM Perspective, Paradigm, and Possibility.* New Jersey: Prentice Hall, 1987.

Schulz, Mona Lisa, M.D., Ph.D. *Awakening Intuition.* New York: Harmony Books, 1998.

Serure, Pamela. *The 3-Day Energy Fast.* New York: HarperCollins, 1997.

Siegel, Bernie, M.D. *Love, Medicine and Miracles.* New York: Harper Perennial Library, 1990.

———. *Prescriptions for Living.* New York: HarperCollins, 1998.

Smith, Jean. *The Beginner's Guide to Zen Buddhism.* New York: Bell Tower, 2000.

Swami Sivananda Radha. *Mantras: Words of Power.* Spokane: Timeless Books, 1994.

Teresa of Avila, and E. Allison Peers, trans. and ed. *Interior Castle.* New York: Image Books, 1972.

Trungpa, Chögyam. *Meditation in Action.* Boston: Shambhala, 1996.

Van de Castle, Robert L., Ph.D. *Our Dreaming Mind.* New York: Ballantine Books, 1994.

Varela, Francisco J., Ph.D., ed. *Sleeping, Dreaming, and Dying: An Exploration of Consciousness with the Dalai Lama.* Boston: Wisdom Publications, 1997.

Weil, Andrew, M.D. *Spontaneous Healing.* New York: Ballantine Books, 1995.

Weiss, Brian L., M.D. *Through Time into Healing.* New York: Simon & Schuster, 1992.

Wise, Anna. *The High-Performance Mind.* New York: Tarcher/Putnam, 1995.

Yogananda, Paramahansa. *Autobiography of a Yogi.* Self Realization Fellowship, 1993.

Index

Quality CDs, Tapes, and Books by Joan Budilovsky

Special offer for readers of *The Complete Idiot's Guide to Meditation, Second Edition*

Meditation CD

Body and Soul Meditation   Within this CD, your practice is given the foundation for a true body and soul experience. Joan will guide you into learning how to meditate through the chanting of mantras, the enchantment of the harp, and the charm of your own special voice.   **Only $10.00**

Yoga CD

Beginning Yoga with Joan   An hour of relaxing yet invigorating postures and breathwork.   **$12.00**

Yoga Audio Cassettes

Total Relaxation with Shavasana   Shavasana is the total relaxation pose of yoga. Let this pose help you begin the day, get through the day, end your day, and deepen your meditation practice.   **$10.00**

Breathworks!   Thirty minutes of yoga deep-breathing exercises.   **$10.00**

Sun-Salutations! with Joan   A dynamic series of yoga postures with a 20-minute bell meditation exercise.   **$10.00**

Yoga at the Beach   Yoga fun in the sun with Joan.   **$10.00**

Massage Video

My Swedish Massage with Joan   Spirited and instructional video on many of the massage strokes featured in *The Complete Idiot's Guide to Massage*.   **$19.50**

Massage Audio Cassettes

The Art of Massage Made Simple   Joan guides you in giving a full-body, one-hour massage.   **$10.50**

Foot Massage for Body, Mind, and Sole   Relax your feet. Relax your whole body.   **$10.00**

And More Yoga Books

The Little Yogi Water Book   Splish, splash, and learn water yoga with Joan.   **$8.00**

The Little Yogi Energy Book   Energize yourself with these terrific yoga postures.   **$8.00**

Yoga for a New Day   The first little book Joan wrote on the yoga *yamas*, *niyamas*, and simple postures to pose by.   **$10.00**

Yo Joan!   Thoughtful responses to your yoga questions from the popular "Yoyoga!" website.   **$10.00**

Come visit Joan at her "Yoyoga!" website: www.yoyoga.com

Order form on NEXT PAGE

YES, send me my copies of Joan's wonderful CDs, tapes, and books.

Special CD Offer

❏ *Body and Soul Meditation* — $10.00

Yoga CD

❏ *Beginning Yoga with Joan* — $12.00

Yoga Audio Cassettes

❏ *Total Relaxation with Shavasana* — $10.00
❏ *Breathworks!* — $10.00
❏ *Sun-Salutations! with Joan* — $10.00
❏ *Yoga at the Beach* — $10.00

Massage Video

❏ *My Swedish Massage with Joan* — $19.50

Massage Audio Cassettes

❏ *The Art of Massage Made Simple* — $10.50
❏ *Foot Massage for Body, Mind, and Sole* — $10.00

Yoga Books

❏ *The Little Yogi Water Book* — $8.00
❏ *The Little Yogi Energy Book* — $8.00
❏ *Yoga for a New Day* — $10.00
❏ *Yo Joan!* — $10.00

Shipping/handling charges:
Audio/book Add $2.50 for one or two items; add $.50 for each additional item. _____
Video Add $4.50 for first video tape; add $1.00 for each additional video tape. _____

Subtotal	_____
Illinois residents add 6.75% sales tax	_____
Outside United States add $5.00 additional shipping and handling	_____
TOTAL	_____

Payment to be made in U.S. funds. Prices and availability are subject to change without notice.

❏ Check or money order enclosed.
❏ I would like to charge to: ❏ MasterCard   ❏ Visa

Acct. #: _____

Exp. Date: _____

Signature: _____

Send this order form with your check, money order, or charge information to:

Yoyoga, Inc.
PO Box 5013
Oak Brook, IL 60522
Fax: 630-963-4001

Allow four to six weeks for delivery.

Ship to:

Name: _____

Address: _____

City, State, Zip: _____

Telephone: _____

Check Out These
Best-Selling
COMPLETE IDIOT'S GUIDES®

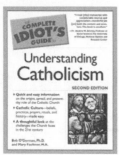

Understanding Catholicism
SECOND EDITION

1-59257-085-2
$18.95

Learning Spanish
THIRD EDITION

0-02-864451-4
$18.95

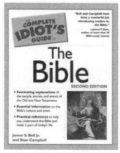

The Bible
SECOND EDITION

0-02-864382-8
$18.95

Being a Groom
SECOND EDITION

0-02-864456-5
$9.95

Grammar and Style
SECOND EDITION

1-59257-115-8
$16.95

Playing the Guitar

0-02-864244-9
$21.95 w/CD

Personal Finance in Your 20s & 30s
SECOND EDITION

0-02-864374-7
$19.95

Knitting and Crocheting
SECOND EDITION
Illustrated

1-59257-089-5
$16.95

The Perfect Resume
THIRD EDITION

0-02-864440-9
$14.95

Buying and Selling a Home
FOURTH EDITION

1-59257-120-4
$18.95

Low-Carb Meals

1-59257-180-8
$18.95

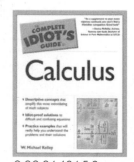

Calculus

0-02-864365-8
$18.95

More than *450 titles* in *30 different categories*
Available at booksellers everywhere

ALPHA